THE RHETORIC OF
SEXUALITY AND
THE LITERATURE OF
THE FRENCH
RENAISSANCE

This book investigates the relationship between psychoanalytic theory and the literature of the French Renaissance by exploring the issues of gender, the body, and the dynamics of repression in key literary figures of the period: Pernette du Guillet, Scève, Rabelais, Marot, Marguerite de Navarre, Ronsard, and Montaigne. In detailed readings of individual texts, Lawrence Kritzman examines how sexuality functions as a rhetorical trope through which desire is represented. The strategy of reading underlying his study focuses on the issue of object relations as the generative force behind the fiction-making process.

Professor Kritzman's book concentrates on three major objectives: the representation of gender identity and sexual difference in French Renaissance texts; the question of how the body is portrayed in the *blasons*, love poetry, and prose of the period; and the ways in which figural language depicts the libidinal, political, and social tensions at work in texts. It is the first wide-ranging theoretical study which provides reading models to investigate the taboo subject of sexuality underlying literary production in the French Renaissance.

THE RHETORIC OF SEXUALITY AND THE LITERATURE OF THE FRENCH RENAISSANCE

LAWRENCE D. KRITZMAN

PROFESSOR OF FRENCH AND COMPARATIVE LITERATURE,
DARTMOUTH COLLEGE, NEW HAMPSHIRE

COLUMBIA UNIVERSITY PRESS

NEW YORK

Columbia University Press Morningside Edition
Columbia University Press
New York   Oxford

Copyright © 1991 Cambridge University Press

Library of Congress Cataloging-in-Publication Data
Kritzman, Lawrence D.
The rhetoric of sexuality and the literature of the French Renaissance/
Lawrence D. Kritzman.
p.   cm.
Includes bibliographical references and index.
ISBN 0-231-08269-X : $16.95
1. French literature – 16th century – History and criticism.
2. Psychoanalysis and literature.   3. Renaissance – France.
4. Rhetoric – 1500–1800.   5. Sex in literature.   I. Title.
PQ239.K75   1993
840.9'353 – dc20   93-3676 CIP

∞

Casebound editions of Columbia University Press books are
printed on permanent and durable acid-free paper.

Printed in the United States of America

p 10 9 8 7 6 5 4 3 2 1

CONTENTS

ABBREVIATIONS

Ch.   Chanson
D.   Dizain
Epig. Epigram

To Daisy

ACKNOWLEDGMENTS

I am grateful to a number of institutions who, by inviting me to lecture, forced me to come to terms with my work in progress and clarify some of my ideas. I would like to acknowledge my gratitude to Brown, Columbia, Dartmouth, Duke, the Graduate Center of the City University of New York, the Université de Haute Bretagne, the New York University Institute for the Humanities, Oxford, Queens College, U.C.L.A., the University of Southern California, Vanderbilt, Wesleyan, and the University of Western Ontario.

I cannot mention here all those who have helped in different ways, but I am grateful for specific suggestions from Jules Brody, Michel de Certeau, Françoise Charpentier, Natalie Davis, Dr. D. Dilldock, Floyd Gray, Philippe Hamon, Alice Y. Kaplan, Vivian Kogan, Raymond C. La Charité, Gisèle Mathieu-Castellani, Ian D. McFarlane, Edouard Morot-Sir, Stephen G. Nichols, Michael Riffaterre, Michel Simonin, and Domna Stanton.

Elizabeth Ladenson helped with a first version translation of chapter 6 from the original French.

Malcolm Bowie and Kate Brett have been exceptional editors. I owe a special debt of gratitude to them for their continued advice and encouragement.

I would like especially to acknowledge the friendship and support of Marcel Tetel whose belief in my work both in times of despair and triumph has sustained me throughout this project. He asked me more questions than I could possibly answer and taught me more than I could ever record. Without his encouragement and advice I would never have completed this study.

ix

Acknowledgments

A number of essays included in this volume have appeared in an earlier form, in some cases with a slightly different title. For permission to reprint these pieces in revised form I wish to thank the respective editors: chapter 4, the Duke University Press and *The Journal of Medieval and Renaissance Studies* 15; chapter 8, *The Journal of Medieval and Renaissance Studies* 13; chapter 10, the University of Wisconsin Press and *Substance* 28; Raymond C. La Charité, *Rabelais's Incomparable Book. Essays on His Art* (Lexington: French Forum, 1986), pp. 141–54; and the *Romanic Review* 75 and the Trustees of Columbia University in the City of New York.

INTRODUCTION

The essays in this book have been written over a number of years in the wake of the revolution in French critical theory and its transatlantic exportation. They mark the trajectory of my intellectual development from an interest in literary formalism and the "literariness" of the text to post-structuralist concerns, particularly the powerful convergence of psychoanalysis, gender theory, and a cultural semiotics conditioned by various intertextual traditions. I have chosen to discuss the question of the rhetoric of sexuality in its many formulations in the works of sixteenth-century French writers, ranging from Rabelais and Montaigne to Marot, Marguerite de Navarre, Pernette du Guillet, Scève, and Ronsard. By focusing on the issue of rhetoric, I have been led to examine the enigmas that haunt literary texts and the ways in which the *topoi* of sexuality reveal a work's underlying self-conscious preoccupations. Implicit in my readings of these early modern texts is the conviction I share with Perry Meisel – who warns against the dangers inherent in Freud's literary speculations as psychosexual reductions – that the mechanisms of a psychoanalytic reading of literary work are already inscribed in the mechanisms of its language.[1]

Recent criticism has amply demonstrated how the laws of unconscious desire are played out in a text's representational modes.[2] In departing from the theoretical presuppositions of classical applied psychoanalytic criticism, relating a somewhat positivistic rapport between author and text, I too have been concerned with mapping the strategies deployed to figure the libido of the writing subject. To be sure, subjectivity, as I con-

1

ceive of it in this study, is a rhetorical effect; it is a phenomenon that is enacted through psychic tropes, staged fictions of the self, structured like a language and mediated by the conflict between narcissistic fantasy and the imaginary desire of the other. Within this context the notion of what is sexual cannot be regarded simply in terms of biological drives alone, but is meant to include fantasy production manifested as shifts of desire in language beyond what the text actively articulates. What I wish to suggest here is that the hermeneutic operation involved in analytic discourse is not that of uncovering the "truth" of sexuality *per se*, but rather of describing its rhetorical effects and the problems it constitutes for the writing subject. Ultimately for me the challenge of the critic is to avoid becoming the all-knowing subject, a quasi-imperialist possessor of authorial logos, capable of transcending the constraints of what is sometimes inexpressible.

Reading psychoanalytically has enabled me to register the shifting energies of unconscious desire as they are elaborated in a literary field where the many discourses of love transcribe, through intertextual references, the enigma of love itself. In a way, each of the chapters in this book constitutes an effort to explore how, in a particular text, the play of forces creates a syntax of meaning that can only be produced by the dialogic relationship established between reading and writing. In my own readings I have therefore attempted to delineate the complexity of the writing project as a phenomenon implicitly derived from the creation of a textual memory that cannot be dissociated from the question of intertextuality itself. What this actually implies is that the "history" of the subject represented in the texts analyzed here is inextricably bound to a rewriting process through which the writer re-members, and is simultaneously spoken by fragments of a pre-existent cultural *corpus*; the "I" of the text is invented through a series of images, figures of desire, that inscribe the subject in a discursive space from which emerges the symptomatic obsession that engenders literary production. Following the theoretical assumption that the text, like the subject, is a *locus* where knowledge and meaning reside, the act of rhetorical analysis exercised by me in this book must indeed be regarded as a critical gesture that constructs meaning through "listening," and in that process, shows that fantasy is "in relation to the real," but does not reveal precisely what that relation is.

The Rhetoric of Sexuality is not a mere application of psychoanalytic theory to texts of the French Renaissance. Quite clearly it takes as its point of departure the presupposition that psychoanalysis is an interpretative discipline operating within a continual dialectic of cross-fertilization with literature. Perhaps better than anyone else Shoshana Felman has formulated this problematic in her attempt to demystify the essentialized differences between literature and psychoanalysis. By calling into question the temptation to reduce this polarity to positions of mastery, Felman forestalls the threat of creating unnatural distinctions between literature and psychoanalysis.

Psychoanalysis tells us that fantasy is a fiction, and that consciousness is itself, in a sense, a fantasy-effect. In the same way, literature tells us that authority is a language effect, the product or the creation of its own rhetorical power: that authority is the *power of fiction*; that authority, therefore, is likewise a fiction.[3]

In essence, the theoretical perspectives put forward in the individual case studies that constitute this book arise equally from the rhetorical play figured in the individual texts studied as from the psychoanalytic models that form the "fictional backdrop" through which the literary critic processes the writer's narrative. I have therefore tried to identify and observe the rhetorical strategies of each of the texts studied by submitting my analyses to a process that critically engages the dialectics of desire in a meaningful dialogue with the hermeneutics of an eclectically conceived psychoanalysis.

While this book has many agendas, its most conspicuous preoccupation has been the attempt to contextualize a strategy of reading that focuses on the issue of object relations in texts. This conceptual framework designates theories or aspects of theories – both literary and psychoanalytic – concerned with exploring the relationship between the image of the narrative subject as it is figured in the text and the representation of the other as generator of psychic functioning. So far as my own reading practice is concerned, particularly in the chapters treating love as a form of discourse, I have tried to consider the desiring subject's amorous ties as a form of narcissistic reflexivity. Accordingly, the notion of desire, a concept to which I return frequently throughout this study, must be understood as a play of subjectivities realized through a figural field of perceptions and cognitions. The questions toward which this book ultimately moves, as it "essays" the issues of gender, the body, and the dynamics of repression, examine the rhetorical structures through which desire binds to an object and plays itself out as the other's desire. The end point of such a project is to elucidate how the text represents intersubjective relations that denote the cause and effects of these fictions of desire, manifested as either a drive for recognition or a need to satisfy an inadequate or damaged relation with a binding ideal. If, as Jacques Lacan claims, it is from the other that the desiring subject transmits the signifiers of his or her desire, then the figural representation of these relations can only be realized in the intrapersonal fantasy underlying the text.[4]

The relationship between the sexes and the attempt to delineate the status of women and men was a major *topos* in French Renaissance texts. At the core of this controversy is the question of gender identity and the rapport between sexuality and the narrative representation of the desiring subject. Part I of this book, "Rhetorics of Gender," explores gender as both a rhetoric and thematic preoccupation in some major sixteenth-century texts. It deals with both female and male gender identity in terms of the established codes of the Renaissance, and analyzes how the historical myths of gender roles, bound up with the cultural institutions that frame texts discursively, are interrogated. In using the term "gender" I not only refer to the differences between and within the sexes themselves, but also to the question of power relations and the ways in which they problematize patriarchal myths.

The essays in this section are concerned with the symbolic representation of gender identity in text production, and the rhetorical strategies through which sexual difference subverts and challenges the fantasy of a unitary subject rooted in the myth of biological partition. Like Naomi Schor, I have adopted as ideological presupposition for this study the idea that only the dissymmetry of difference can undermine repetition, but going even further, I argue that the politics of representation can only become powerful when producing fictions of identity whose fundamental trope is one of gender revision.[5] The five essays grouped together in part I therefore function as cultural discourses revealing the contingency of gender roles by engaging texts in agonistic encounters with patrilineal and matrilineal sources.

In "Pernette du Guillet and a voice of one's own," I examine the question of female autonomy and its articulation through a revisionist rhetoric that transcends the dominance–submission paradigm of petrarchism and instead theorizes in figurative language a utopian discourse of equals derived from the neo-platonic tradition. In the next chapter, the concept of manliness is explored in a case study analysis of the Rondibilis episode in Rabelais' *Tiers Livre* where the construction of a male gender identity emerges as the result of a misogynistic discourse representing the very negative qualities attributed to female narcissism. Reading with attention to the anxiety associated with the marriage question and its contextualization through references to the controversy between two opposing schools of spermatology (the teaching of Claudius Galen and the Platonico-Hippocratic school), I have tried to focus here on the question of male sexuality and its representation in the character Panurge. The essay on Marguerite de Navarre, centered on the tenth *nouvelle* of *L'Heptaméron,* examines woman's place in a world where, beyond being an invisible support for male desire, she would transcend the tension of indifference and affirm her autonomy in the paradoxical language of female silence.

The last chapters in part I examine two of the most typically anthologized pieces from Montaigne's *Essais* as masculine modes of creativity: "De l'institution des enfans" (I, 26) and "De l'affection des peres aux enfans" (II, 8). In "Pedagogical graffiti and the rhetoric of conceit," I delineate the figural representation of the genesis of the male ego and its relationship to the marks of gender that are inscribed in the text. Most particularly, what is analyzed rhetorically is the enigma of male sexuality as allegorized through a panoply of intertextual references, ranging from Horace and Ovid to Ariosto. The chapter "Montaigne's Family Romance," on the other hand, unravels the myth concerning the origins of the creative act and the tensions derived from the conflict between the aesthetic and the biological. Out of the field of perception figured in "De l'affection des peres aux enfans," emerges the representation of an exemplary bond of nurturance which functions as a reparative gesture in terms of the dynamics of the "family romance."

Part II, "Figures of the Body," addresses the question of how the body is represented in the *blasons,* love poetry, and prose of the period. In portraying the female body, Petrarch's description of Laura not only informs the Renaissance model of womanly beauty, but also becomes a descriptive system through which male writers fetishize the female body and dismember it through their scriptural practices. This rhetoric of fragmentation in French Renaissance texts unveils the phallocentric biases and conflicts of the male writer whose particularized descriptions represent the female as either a beloved maternal object or one of sheer abjection.

The first two chapters of part II deal with the disfiguration of the female body. In "Architecture of the Utopian Body," the *blasons* of both Marot and Ronsard are studied in an attempt to elucidate the signifying practices through which the desiring subject's representation of the ideal body is revealed as resistant to the ravaging force of temporality. The chapter on Ronsard's 1552 sonnet cycle reveals how fictions of the body, ranging from the pseudo-Anacreon of *The Greek Anthology* and Horace to Petrarch and Ariosto, are rewritten, and in that process create a lover's discourse in which the sexuality of the desiring male is both affirmed and interrogated.

In the essay on the rhetoric of Montaigne's self-portraiture, the metaphoric relationship between text and body as mimetic mode is studied in "Sur des vers de Virgile" (III, 5). What emerges from my analysis is not only a demonstration of how rhetoric and sexuality are interchangeable *topoi* in the montaignian essay, but far more importantly how textual representation is but a mere simulacrum of a lost ideal.

Part III of this book, "Allegories of Repression," examines how figural language suggests libidinal, political or social tensions at work in texts that are rhetorical analogues of compulsive and obsessional behavior. In "Scève: the rhetoric of dream and the language of love," I explore how the dream poem's multiple descriptive systems converge in an allegorical narrative that transcribes the amorous subject's struggle between eros and the intellect. Drawing partially on the image of woman inherited from both petrarchan and biblical traditions, Scève's dream of love is inextricably linked to a scenario whose principle motivator is the figure of the phallic mother.

The final chapter on "Sexuality and the Political Unconscious in Rabelais' *Quart Livre*," studies in detail three key sections of that book: the prologue, the *Chiquanous,* and the *Papimanes* episodes. The concept of allegory as used here refers to a process whereby the rabelaisian narrative transcribes "social material" in the form of theatrically motivated fictions that stage repressed desires and fears. At stake are the figural representations of power relationships and the ways in which they overdetermine the writer's scriptural practice and subjugate textual production to the political rule of Law, a phenomenon culminating in the representation of the 1551–2 Gallican crisis in the Papimane episode.

Through this book my concern is with the function of sexuality as rhetorical trope. The heterogeneity of the texts and issues discussed are meant to contribute to the volume's overall interest by providing reading models for investigating the taboo subject of the sexuality underlying the rhetorical practices of the French Renaissance literary canon.

Part I

RHETORICS OF GENDER

1

PERNETTE DU GUILLET AND A VOICE OF ONE'S OWN

Et li savi dicono che 'l vero ricco e quello che si contenta di quel che
possiede.
(Leone Ebreo)

Pernette du Guillet's *Rymes* offer an interesting case study of
woman's writing in which we witness the construction of a female
subject caught between the submission to a masculine ideal
represented by Maurice Scève, and the exigencies of *équité*
(mutual companionship) transcending the essentialized gender
differences inscribed in a patriarchal power structure. Although
now and then du Guillet draws on elements of the neo-petrarchan tradition, the dominant tone of her scriptural quest emanates from the love theory of Leone Ebreo's *I Dialoghi d'amore*.[1]
In an effort to de-emphasize the anguish associated with the
dominance–submission paradigm of petrarchan poetics, du Guillet's text constructs woman as a "writing effect," represents the
textuality of gender through the reconstitution of subject–object
relations conceived as a utopian discourse of equals.

If Pernette draws on *I Dialoghi* perhaps more than any other
work, it is because it enables her to seek refuge in a discourse that
assures her protection from the objectification and surrender of
"le mal d'aymer." Quite clearly, the petrarchan discursive mode
is based on a psychology of love in which the lover is the victim of
the omnipotence attributed to the desired object. Within this
code the idea of omnipotence can only emerge in the context of
impotence and helplessness. In Scève's *Délie*, for example, it
functions as a fantasy derived from a feeling of despair and
helplessness. The imaginary withholding of love privileges a

11

singular *locus* in the spatial configuration of affectivity, and in so doing reinforces the perception of the desired object's power as a defensive wish.

But du Guillet is in search of something quite different; her quest for love as *amytié* projects language as curative affect and knowledge as confirmation of the loved object's being.[2]

> O vraye amour, dont je suis prise,
> Comment m'as-tu si bien apprise,
> Que de mon Jour tant me contente,
> Que je n'en espere autre attente,
> Que celle de ce doulx amer,
> Pour me guerir du mal d'aymer?
>   Du bien j'ay eu la jouyssance,
> Dont il m'a donné congnoissance
> Pour m'asseurer de l'amytié,
> De laquelle il tient la moytié:
> Doncques est il plus doux, qu'amer,
> Pour me guerir du mal d'aymer.   (Ch. III)

True love, as it is figured in the text, offers as its foundation an intersubjective mode that emphasizes the joy of spiritual union. However free this may be from the ravaging passion of love, du Guillet's amorous discourse manifests an inner psychic world of object relations in which the ability to differentiate between self and other is subsumed by a linguistic fiction that is suggestively phallocentric. In refusing to rely on the authority of patriarchy in the dynamics of amorous exchange, du Guillet nevertheless discreetly reinstitutes it on a symbolic level by failing to think the absence of origin. For du Guillet, to write as a woman raises the question of the relationship between sexual difference and the amorous contract as it is bound up with the ontological idea of language.

In the *Rymes*, Pernette becomes the object of an exchange sanctioned by the power of language itself; her identity is bound up in a representational order that supports the epistemological power of phallocentric discourse. To be sure, Scève's example is Pernette's magic *want*: a wish that gives her access to the authority of language. "Preste-moy donc ton eloquent sçavoir/Pour te louer ainsi que tu me loues!" (Epig. VI). Much like the character Sofia in Ebreo's *I Dialoghi,* du Guillet is attracted to Scève for both his learning and his Apollinian-like eloquence.

> Esprit celeste, et des Dieux transformé
> En corps mortel transmis en ce bas Monde,
> A Apollo peulx estre conformé
> Pour la vertu, dont est la source, et l'onde.
> Ton eloquence, avecques ta faconde,
> Et hault sçavoir, auquel tu es appris,
> Demonstre assez le bien en toy compris:
> Car en doulceur ta plume tant fluante
> A merité d'emporter gloire, et prys,
> Voyant ta veine en hault stille affluante. (Epig. IV)

If Pernette's narrative gives pointed significance to the *logos* as a demonstration of Scève's artistic perfection, it is because she sees in it virtuosity, etymologically derived from *vertu,* exemplifying knowledge and truth. Yet on another level *vertu,* incorporating the notion of virility, can be seen as a fitting embodiment of masculine values. The glorious image of aesthetic achievement put forward here emanates from symbols of culture in which the representation of perfection is quintessentially male. The phallic, therefore, receives its inscription at the level of the identity of a masculine subject that fixes it as point of reference for the female writer. The scèvian figure "de nom et de faict, trop severe" (Epig. XXXIV) becomes a "poet–pedagogue" whose only truly worthy object of linguistic "penetration" is du Guillet in her role as dutiful disciple.[3] "Mais advis m'est que ton sainct entretien/Ne peult si bien en ces autres empraindre/Tes motz dorez, comme au cueur, qui est tien" (Epig. XXXIV).

The specular image of virtue, the imaginary rule of law, reduces du Guillet's poetic mentor to a play of language.[4] The body of the "poet–pedagogue" takes the form of two anagrams of the name Scève – "vice à se muer" and "ce vice mueras" – with which the female subject is spiritually impregnated and consequently undergoes metamorphosis.[5]

> Puis qu'il t'a pleu de me faire congnoistre,
> Et par ta main, le VICE A SE MUER,

13

Je tascheray faire en moy ce bien croistre,
Qui seul en toy me pourra transmuer:
C'est à sçavoir de tant m'esvertuer
Que congnoistras, que par esgal office
Je fuiray loing d'ignorance le vice,
Puis que desir de me transmuer as
De noire en blanche, et par si hault service
En mon erreur CE VICE MUERAS.   (Epig. v)

What this epigram seems to reveal is du Guillet's propensity for an ideal love in which she submits to a moral order that she tries to adumbrate; the drive to goodness – the transubstantiated form of Scève's desire for knowledge and lucidity – transforms the poetess into a simulacrum of the poet. As Scève's *idole* (image), the object of "la plus haulte vertu" through which he has forced vice to reform, the female figure represented in the text refers to a subject outside itself, a subject that is the subject of speech (the imaginary ideal of goodness inscribed in Scève's name) and subservient to that order. The seductive power of language not only confirms Scève's function as a quasi-divine force, but also makes the poetess believe that it can transform her into an ideal being capable of securing access to the glory and the power of the other. "Par sa vertu, qui à l'aimer m'attire/Plus que beaulté: car sa grace, et faconde/Me fond cuyder la premiere du monde" (Epig. xvii). Du Guillet's desire is not the desire of the inner self, but is rather the transubstantiated image of what the poetess believes his desire to be. The magical figure with whom du Guillet identifies possesses the rhetorical skill necessary – "sa grace et faconde " – to make her believe that she is worthy of praise.

However, du Guillet describes herself as being linguistically inadequate, the victim of an ontological alienation from language. As a sign, and as a generator of signs, the poetess describes herself as unable to match the aesthetic model she would like to emulate. Incapable of engaging in an encomiastic discourse that echoes the master's praise for her, du Guillet stages a discursive drama in which the symbolic contract between self and other is based on a debt that cannot be reciprocated.[6]

Pernette du Guillet and a voice of one's own

Par ce dizain clerement je m'accuse
De ne sçavoir tes vertus honnorer,
Fors du vouloir, qui est bien maigre excuse:
Mais qui pourroit par escript decorer
Ce qui de soy se peult faire adorer?
  Je ne dy pas, si j'avois ton pouvoir,
Qu'à m'acquicter ne feisse mon debvoir,
A tout le moins du bien que tu m'advoues.   (Epig. vi)

In idealizing the loved object, du Guillet finds herself in an imaginary relation which demands circumscribing the emptiness identified with the perceived "lack" of what the other possesses. She adores another whom she believes she cannot be: "ce grand renom de ton meslé sçavoir" (Epig. iii). For a man – "ce qui de soy se peult faire adorer" – du Guillet can only hope to elicit, in return for her love, the recognition of he who embodies the agency of universal cathexis. In this perspective, the object of the poetess's desire is described as incarnating the magical mirror that gives access to the world. Accordingly, the voice which permits du Guillet to say "I" enables her to model an ego that is a simulacrum of the ideal. By abstracting *journée* from *jour* in chanson x – a symbolic gesture of splitting the word into its derivative form – du Guillet's text expels the very subject it represents into a gender-marked otherness that appears as the embodiment of its very being.[7] "Je suis la Journee,/Vous, Amy, le Jour/Qui m'a destournee/Du fascheux sejour" (Ch. ix).

If du Guillet offers herself to the light of day, it is in order to bathe in the luminosity of an ideal that subordinates her to the astrological syntax of patriarchy. Identification of an object world is thus grounded in this imaginary vision of refracted light whereby du Guillet's subjecthood takes shape in the amorphous space of a signifier represented by the specter of temporality (*la journée*). The dawn of the subject and the origin of knowledge (luminosity) is masculine while that of the object, the image of the mirror, is feminine and essentially passive. "Ainsi esclairee/ De si heureux jour,/Seray asseuree/De plaisant sejour" (Ch. ix). This process of idealization unquestionably becomes the basis for ascribing the imaginary role of intellectual liberator to the

15

philosopher–poet onto whom du Guillet projects a fantasy of omnipotence. "O heureux jour, bien te doit estimer/Celle qu'ainsi as voulu allumer" (Ch. IX). The spiritual perception that she believes her "creator" endows her with is far greater than that which she sees with her own eyes. Engaged in a form of magical thinking generated by Scève's intellectual nurturance, du Guillet's ocular power emphasizes a certain cognitive dependence and a willingness to offer recognition.

> Puis que mon Jour par clarté adoulcie
> M'esclaire toute, et tant, qu'à la mynuict
> En mon esprit me faict appercevoir
> Ce que mes yeulx ne sceurent oncques veoir.   (Epig. VIII)

In epigram II du Guillet rewrites the neo-petrarchan *topos* of the coming of dawn. Du Guillet situates herself in an unconscious state – "la nuit d'ignorance" (Epig. XXXIX) – the victim of a cognitive blindness that prevents her from recognizing the beauty of knowledge.[8]

> La nuict estoit pour moy si tresobscure
> Que Terre, et Ciel elle m'obscurcissoit,
> Tant qu'à Midy de discerner figure
> N'avoit pouvoir, qui fort me marrissoit:
>   Mais quand je vis que l'aulbe apparoissoit
> En couleurs mille et diverse, et seraine,
> Je me trouvay de liesse si pleine
> (Voyant desjà la clarté à la ronde)
> Que commençay louer à voix haultaine
> Celuy qui feit pour moy ce Jour au Monde.   (Epig. II)

The semiotic gesture through which the beauty of the female beloved is depicted in the petrarchan lexicon now comes to signify the beauty of intelligibility associated with the magical unveiling of ignorance. In this context, Scève's luminosity becomes the *locus* of du Guillet's ecstasy; transcendence from the depressive state of a metaphoric night – "qui fort me marrissoit" – can only be realized through the light with which he impregnates her senses. The marks of gender in this scopic situation are thus represented by the viscosity of an ontologically

16

empty female subject who suddenly witnesses the arrival of the savior-like figure of the dawn to whom she owes her spiritual birth. Enacted by the incantatory drama of a poetic discourse that narrates the "coming into being" sanctioned by language, this spiritual awakening translates du Guillet's metamorphosis from an unconscious state to the illumination associated with the sense of self-recognition.[9] The figure of the scèvian dawn may be the motivating force here in the lucidity of its spirit, but du Guillet assigns herself an active role ("que commençay louer à voix haultaine") thus allowing the discovery of the joy to which she was previously blind. If the female figure becomes the spectator of her own pleasure it is because du Guillet's delivery into speech, through the rhythmic movement of a poetic chant, enables her to realize a relation to language that is a projection of creative lucidity.

Amongst the astrological metaphors du Guillet draws upon in the *Rymes* is that of the lofty power of the stars ("le hault pouvoir des Astres") used in the liminary epigram. This not only translates ideal love as an abstraction, but also draws our attention to the fatalistic nature of this amorous relationship. Scève is indeed du Guillet's destiny; and her happiness is based on a spiritual awakening that precipitates the emergence of a more autonomous self-image. The promise sealed at birth will ultimately enable her to pass into the experience of abstract subjectivity and become "a subject who knows."

> Le hault pouvoir des Astres a permis
> (Quand je nasquis) d'estre heureuse et servie:
> Dont, congnoissant celuy qui m'est promis,
> Restee suis sans sentyment de vie,
> Fors le sentir du mal, qui me convie
> A regraver ma dure impression
> D'amour cruelle, et doulce passion,
> Où s'apparut celle divinité,
> Qui me cause l'imagination
> A contempler si haulte qualité.   (Epig. I)

The dramatic apparition of this divine figure permits cognition through a contemplative activity that allows the movement from sensation to knowledge. But if this exemplary presence catalyzes du Guillet to act, it is through a self-conscious process that enables the female subject to invent its own history by transforming cognition into a performative act.

Quite clearly, it is through her ideal that du Guillet comes to see herself as a desiring subject. In a sense, Antoine du Moulin's strategic decision to prioritize this epigram amongst "ce petit amas de rymes" and place it in a liminary position is indeed revelatory. Du Guillet's declaration to "regraver ma dure impression/D'amour cruelle et doulce passion" translates writing as a hermeneutic act, as an attempt to inscribe *praxis* in *logos*, and in so doing to facilitate the re-cognition of an amorous discourse grounded in petrarchan conceits. In becoming the object of a divine presence ("qui me convie") du Guillet is converted into a script for self-edification ("à contempler si haulte qualité"). She submits to being so defined although she liberates herself in an act of engraving – a voice ironically articulated through the metaphor of imprinting – representing an effort to create rather than to be created. To write as a woman, to go beyond the dependence and order prescribed by the masculine, requires the writing subject to seek autonomy in the acquisition of a language whose symbolic register manifests itself not as self-sufficiency but rather as interaction or exchange.[10] "Vous me debvriez tel droict, que je vous doy" (Epig. xxvi). The development of this relation is the result of a discursive break – the reinscription of an unfavorable impression – whereby du Guillet realizes a way of writing that provides a measurement of difference as well as a support for its various manifestations. For du Guillet, then, this dialectic of seeing and writing, the relationship between the scopic and the textual, situates the female subject in the circuit of a verbal exchange that re-vises the constrained interaction emanating from the myth of origins. "Et toutesfois voicy un tresgrand poinct,/Lequel me rend ma pensee assouvie:/C'est que sans Dame Amour ne seroit point" (Epig. xxiv).

Yet before a more authentic discursive contract may be established, du Guillet must demystify the fiction of her being that is inscribed in Scève's *Délie*. "Quand est d'Amour, je croy que c'est un songe,/Ou fiction, qui se paist de mensonge" (Elégie I). To be sure, du Guillet's self-portraiture in the *Rymes* creates a narrative disjunction with Scève's description of this beloved in the *Délie*, where she is depicted as being distant, powerful, and terrifying. Created from a *corpus* of stereotypes derived from neo-Petrarchan discourse, Scève's representation of gender relations is one of female domination and male submission. In essence, Pernette–Délie becomes the object of a sadomasochistic fantasy that replicates a tension between self and other based on a longing for recognition from the "constituée Idole de [sa] vie" (D.1).[11] This narrative of the victimized male, too weak to resist domination, ironically targets as the object of its lament a cold and omnipotent female whose ability to discern his "silentes clameurs" functions as the very symbol of her potency. "Ie me taisois si pitoyablement/Que ma Déesse ouyt plaindre mon taire" (D. 8). For Scève, then, the intense pain caused by his beloved's mysterious power produces a linguistic impotence that actively attests to the tension created by the desire to write and the inability to do so. "O vain desir, ô folie evidente,/A qui de faict espere y paruenir" (D. 97). Scève's mistress is therefore portrayed as capable of inflicting aggression on a male subject whose desire for the other transcribes an anguished preoccupation with the need for domination.[12] "Tu fais soubdain, & deffais, moy viuant" (D. 25). This dynamic, then, creates an intersubjective rapport that ironically forecloses on the possibility of separation at the same time that it reinforces a perception of psychic distancing. "Elle me tient par ces cheueulx lyé/Et ie la tien pour ceulx là mesme prise" (D. 14). Thus if Pernette is led to proclaim "puis que mon Jour par clarté adoulcie/M'esclaire toute, et tant qu'à la mynuict" (Epig. VIII), she does this in the spirit of transforming Scève's phallocentric conception of power relations whereby the poet's anguish before the cruel figure of Délie is the result of abandonment in a state where "tout Mydi est nuit eternelle."

Not only does Pernette extricate herself from the image attributed to her by Scève, she also inevitably refuses to engage in an amorous relationship that posits the male author as primary *locus* of poetic fantasy. The goal of du Guillet's self-portraiture is thus implicitly to enter an intertextual dialogue with the neo-petrarchan tradition in order to diverge from it and thereby discover a means of expression that breaks with a rhetoric that depended on a projected sense of masochism for its very existence. This revisionist strategy blurs the perception of the suffering associated with gender relations and therefore renders du Guillet's image as writing subject somewhat more elusive. "Qu'errer je fais tout homme, qui me loue" (Epig. VII). By refusing to identify with the desire to surrender, du Guillet rejects the role reversal of the socially essentialized positions of amorous discourse as active and passive. If she is to acquire a voice of her own she must invent a discursive space in which the relations between the sexes transcend the logic that sees in love only potentially vulnerable victims.

> Si je ne suis telle que soulois estre,
> Prenez vous en au temps, qui m'a appris
> Qu'en me traictant rudement comme maistre,
> Jamais sur moy ne gaignerez le prys.   (Epig. XXVIII)

Yet this refusal does not signal an end to the pain of love, but only a pleasurable sense of shared feeling. It enables the amorous subject to experience her own autonomy and yet maintain the distinctiveness of the other.

> Pour contenter celuy, qui me tourmente,
> Chercher ne veulx remede à mon tourment:
> Car, en mon mal voyant qu'il se contente,
> Contente suis de son contentement.   (Epig. XV)

Through the use of a quasi-Ebrean language, du Guillet brings the high idealism of neo-platonic love down to the question of gender relations.[13] In using the feminist voice as an effect of language, du Guillet's *Rymes* represent her as a woman struggling to elevate herself to a higher form of love, and in that process to articulate a "discourse of equals" based on understanding and mutual recognition. The need for reciprocity presupposes a narrative contract beyond the self's inscription as an

absolute entity.[14] Du Guillet imagines authorship as a phenomenon derived from a structure of exchange in which the marks of
agency are shaped by the acknowledgment of the other and by
the imposition of a shared subjectivity grounded in virtuous love.

> Mais l'attente mienne
> Est le desir sien
> D'estre toute sienne,
> Comme il sera mien.
> Car quand Amour à Vertu est uny,
> Le cueur conçoit un desir infiny.   (Chanson VIII)

Du Guillet's desire is thus based on an idealized relationship
resulting from a utopian rhetoric that transcends the constraints
of gender splitting. "Prenez le cas que, comme je suis vostre/(Et
estre veulx) vous soyez tout à moy:/Certainement par ce commun bien nostre" (Epig. XXVI).

As writing subject, du Guillet establishes an ethics of love by
conceptualizing it as an act of generosity and not one of mere
narcissism. The reconstructive project produced by du Guillet's
critical reading of Scève's writing necessarily involves the figuration of an intersubjective mode liberated from the culture of
phallic symbolization. Unlike Scève, who in D. 136 celebrates
the erotic force of love, "le bien du mal en effet desirable," which
fosters gender opposition, du Guillet's amorous quest aims to
isolate and eternally solidify the *contentement* realized through
the shared unity of perfect love.

> Je n'oserois le penser veritable
> Si ce n'estoit pour un contentement,
> Qui faict sentir, et veoir ce bien durable
> Par la doulceur, qui en sort seulement.   (Epig. XLIII)

In a way, then, through her call for equality du Guillet rejects
selfish autonomy in the name of a paradoxically liberating dependency capable of modulating the exigencies of desire.

> L'on peult assés en servant requerir,
> Sans toutesfois par souffrir acquerir
> Ce que l'on pourchasse
> Par trop desirer.   (Chanson VIII)

21

By re-embodying the figure of Sofia drawn from Ebreo's *I Dialoghi,* du Guillet's text represents the nature of amorous experience as derived from the pursuit of knowledge. In this context love can arise only from the beauty that the soul knows; its desire, as T. A. Perry suggests, is "the reproduction of beauty ... (and the need) to be reduced to or united with the desired object."[15] If ideal love forces man and woman to seek each other out in the name of beauty and perfection, it is because goodness brings solid affection to amorous relationships based on an understanding of the beloved. "C'est pourquoy travaille/En moy cest espoir,/Qui desir me baille/Et veoir, et sçavoir" (Ch. VIII). Desire is thus represented as the logical consequence of knowledge; it is the result of an effort to go beyond the constraints of closure so that the pleasure of writing may be experienced as an act of commitment that is constantly reaffirmed.

> Si le servir merite recompense,
> Et recompense est la fin du desir,
> Tousjours vouldrois servir plus qu'on ne pense,
> Pour non venir au bout de mon plaisir.   (Epig. XXI)

However, to reduce du Guillet's conceptualization of love to the simple virtues of chastity, as Saulnier has suggested, would indeed be a mistake since the pleasure associated with libidinal drives is not absent from her poetry altogether.[16] In epigram XII, for instance, bodily pleasure has an effect on the soul; sexuality is absorbed into a spirituality that reaches epic proportions and inevitably encompasses the entire universe.

> Le Corps ravy, l'Ame s'en esmerveille
> Du grand plaisir, qui me vient entamer,
> Me ravissant d'Amour qui tout esveille
> Par ce seul bien, qui le faict Dieu nommer.   (Epig. XII)

Far beyond considering love simply as an ontological state of moral elevation in which truth is revealed, du Guillet represents the ecstasy of spiritual delight as emanating from the divine pleasures of the body. Cupid's turbulent passion, that "ardeur violente" (Epig. XLII), seeks an amorous negotiation with the other that precludes possession though not enjoyment.

It seems to me, therefore, that the staging of the drama of the female subject emerges precisely at the moment when the reconstitution of object relations allows for the intersection of sexuality and virtue in such a way that it permits the utopian fantasy of perfect love. To be cured from the "mal d'aymer," the writing subject must dissipate the anxiety associated with desire by regulating it in order to disrupt Scève's hold on the discourse of love. By losing *envie*, the amorous subject enters a new horizon of intersubjectivity that frees sexuality from genital supremacy, and through that process allows love to reach perfection.

> Mais si tu veulx son pouvoir consommer:
> Fault que par tout tu perdes cette envie:
> Tu le verras de ses traictz assommer,
> Et aux Amantz accroissement de vie.   (Epig. xii)

Physical desire must indeed be tempered so that pleasure may be maintained in a state of tranquility nurtured by a "sensuous chastity."[17] This movement away from sexuality as pure anatomical pleasure enables du Guillet to redefine love as *amytié*, and sensuality as the felicitous joining together of body and mind.

> Le grand desir du plaisir admirable
> Se doit nourrir par un contentement
> De souhaicter chose tant agreable,
> Que tout esprit peult ravir doulcement.
>   O que le faict doit estre grandement
> Remply de bien, quand pour la grande envie
> On veult mourir, s'on ne l'a promptement:
> Mais ce mourir engendre une autre vie.   (Epig. xiv)

For love to last it must transcend the need for fulfillment through the creation of a bond grounded in the solidity of affection. Du Guillet's quest offers refuge from the vicissitudes of desire in the sweet pleasure of understanding residing in the soul of the lover. "Car il luy engendre/Une ardeur de veoir,/Et toujours apprendre/Quelque hault sçavoir" (Chanson viii).

Du Guillet's second elegy offers a striking example of a text in which the poetess engages in a fantasy narrative where she

23

controls events and gains autonomy through the magnanimous
gesture of allowing Scève to retain the power of his poetic voice.
In this poem du Guillet situates herself in a pastoral landscape
and dreams of being alone with the object of her desire. She
imagines disrobing in a nearby stream to arouse the attraction of
her beloved, only to entice him into a dramatically playful
scenario coded for its erotic impact. Here is the vision so indis-
creetly portrayed:

> Combien de fois ay-je en moy souhaicté
> Me rencontrer sur la chaleur d'esté
> Tout tu plaisir pres de la clere fontaine,
> Où mon desir avec cil se pourmaine
> Qui exercite en sa philosophie
> Son gent esprit, duquel tant je me fie . . .
> Que dy-je: seule? ains bien accompaignee
> D'honnesteté que Vertu a gaignee
> A Apollo, Muses, et Nymphes maintes,
> Ne s'adonnantz qu'à toutes œuvres sainctes. . .
> Puis peu à de luy m'escarterois,
> Et toute nue en l'eau me gecterois:
> Mais je vouldrois lors quant, et quant avoir
> Mon petit Luth accordé au debvoir . . .
> J'entonnerois sur luy une chanson
> Pour un peu voir quels gestes il tiendroit.

(Elegie II)

While stressing the pleasures of womanhood, du Guillet performs the delightful music of the lute to test Scève's erotic
impulses.[18] The voice is used as a means of seduction, a euphoric
evocation that physically creates what Cixous terms "the song
before the Law."[19] Du Guillet imagines the possibility of a
female voice functioning as the generous dispenser of love,
nourishment, and poetic plenitude. Through the fluctuating
energy of music the poetess embodies the lyrical iconography of
a divine presence that is immensely powerful.

Du Guillet's text is framed by a narrative scene in which the
female subject simultaneously looks and desires to be looked at.
By imagining a hypothetical situation motivated more by the
desire to touch than by the concrete action itself, du Guillet

realizes a fantasy premised on the manipulation of the loved object.

> Mais si vers moy il s'en venoit tout droict,
> Je le lairrois hardyment approcher:
> Et s'il vouloit, tant soit peu, me toucher,
> Lui gecterois (pour le moins) ma main pleine
> De la pure eau de la clere fontaine,
> Lui gectant droict aux yeulx, ou à la face.

If du Guillet represents the power of the male gaze here as carrying within it the possibility for action and possession, she does so in order to affirm the potency of her beauty. Accordingly, the female body is characterized as the object of the gaze and the *locus* of male pleasure. In turning the erotic scene into a trap, du Guillet's text transcends the scopic model of sexual difference put forth in John Berger's *Ways of Seeing* where man scrutinizes woman who is reified within a phallocentric field of vision.[20] Most certainly, the repelling of the male gaze within this poem through the strategic positioning of the female figure reveals a feminine identity that equates ocular reception with power relations. The menace associated with the most material of the senses (touch) forces du Guillet to punish by temporarily impairing the most spiritual of the senses (sight), and this action thus dramatizes the phantasmatic power to forestall the possibility of sexual assault. Du Guillet's text creates an image in which the surveyor of woman in herself is a desiring male subject whose fantasy of corporeal possession is rejected.

In adapting the Ovidian intertext that recounts the tragic punishment for Actaeon's lascivious glance in the *Metamorphoses* (3, 193–8), du Guillet uses the curative baptism *topos* to depict the quest for female autonomy as inextricably linked to her own metamorphopsis into the figure of privileged interlocutor in the plot of gender relations.[21] Instead of changing Actaeon–Scève into a stag to be dismembered and scattered by his dogs, du Guillet's text reinvents the symbolic power of woman by enabling Pernette to splash him with water that has the power to cleanse and transform him into her slave. Unlike the narration of the traditional myth, the female figure represented here playfully teases the male subject and renders him the victim of a linguistic game (the play on the words "cerf/serf"). Du Guillet's account institutes telling as the logical result of the desiring subject's gaze, and with it transforms the Petrarchan version of the Actaeon myth by displacing the focus of self-conscious narration from the male to the female subject.

> O qu'alors eust l'onde telle efficace
> De le pouvoir en Acteon muer,
> Non toutefois pour le faire tuer,
> Et devorer à ses chiens, comme Cerf:
> Mais que de moy se sentist estre serf,
> Et serviteur transformé tellement
> Qu'ainsi cuydast en son entendement,
> Tant que Dyane en eust sur moy envie,
> De luy avoir sa puissance ravie.

If Pernette distances herself from the mythological figure of Diana, sister of Apollo and goddess of light, she does so in order to transcend the image ascribed to her by Scève so as to become Diana's very rival.

Du Guillet's daydream allows her to fantasize the possibility of arousing Diana's jealousy by enslaving Scève and taking pleasure in the separation of the lovers.[22] In robbing Diana of her power, du Guillet creates a region of autonomy activated by a principle of self-assertion that reveals a repressed content rooted more in a fantasy of power than in one of erotic impulses. But this gain in individual authority is vitiated by the loss of the principle of equal exchange. The structure of gender domination is figured here by a hypothetical situation in which subjugation is the necessary catalyst of a narcissistic drive capable of transforming du Guillet into a divinity of sorts. "Combien heureuse, et grande me dirois!/Certes Deesse estre me cuyderois" (Elegie II). The scripting of du Guillet's fantasy lies in the self-appointed task of representing a female subject beyond the vulnerability of the traditional subject–object confrontation. By becoming a goddess, du Guillet extricates herself from the laws of gender circu-

26

lation and ascribes to herself the solitary pleasure of emplotting a fiction of desire dependent on the logic of all or nothing.

Nevertheless, du Guillet enacts a true act of love in the aristotelian sense of a desire for the common good. Far beyond the constraints of what T. A. Perry has characterized as du Guillet's sheer "narcissistic satisfaction" in her relation to Scève, the female subject once again reveals her protean nature, and through the magnanimous gesture of enabling him to write, supports Scève's role as active servant to Apollo and the muses.[23] Instead of objectifying the male subject, the female voice gives the gift of voice back to the male poet, and thus restores him to his own subjectivity. The man no longer looks at the beloved; he must listen to the inflections of her voice before being able to embody his.

> Mais, pour me veoir contente à mon desir,
> Vouldrois je bien faire un tel deplaisir
> A Apollo, et aussi à ses Muses,
> De les laisser privees, et confuses
> D'un, qui les peult toutes servir à gré,
> Et faire honneur à leur hault choeur sacré?

In this text, then, woman becomes central to poetic creation through the sublimation of the erotic and the regendering of desire into a ritual of cultural production. In essence, the woman who has been sentenced to write by the scèvian example now ironically sentences herself to immortality by facilitating the establishment of a structure of exchange that undermines the totalizing effect of individual mastery.

At the moment of apparent retreat, du Guillet attributes to herself the power to endow Apollo with deity while at the same time permitting Scève to find the path to spiritual perfection as poet rather than as chaste lover. Du Guillet demonstrates that it is only through writing and the exchange of the letter that true satisfaction can be achieved.

> Ostez, ostez, mes souhaitz, si hault poinct
> D'avecques vous: il ne m'appartient point.
> Laissez le aller les neuf Muses servir,
> Sans se vouloir dessoubz moy asservir,

Soubz moy, qui suis sans grace, et sans merite.
   Laissez le aller, qu'Apollo je ne irrite,
Le remplissant de Deité profonde,
Pour contre moy susciter tout le Monde,
Lequel un jour par ses escriptz s'attend
D'estre avec moy et heureux, et content.

The so-called "submissive pose" that the poetess adopts here is merely a rhetorical stance that enacts an exemplary structure of exchange based on dependency and the recognition that is essential to subjectivity.[24] The illusion of subordination paradoxically allows du Guillet to empower Scève and thus realize her own sense of autonomy through the recognition of his: a creative talent that will immortalize the object of his desire.

The gift of the word is thus du Guillet's true gesture of reciprocity since it allows her to give voice to her desire, only for it to be echoed in the discourse of the beloved. Du Guillet's magic *want* has enabled her to keep the flow of language in circulation by imparting to the object of her affection its own separateness. In recognizing Scève's poetic virtuosity here, du Guillet still manages to narrate both the appeal and the necessity of individuality in a voice that assumes and articulates its self-difference. Through her own example, and not Scève's, du Guillet is led to demystify the illusion of mastery, and in so doing transcends the culture of phallic idealism. The poetess' vision strives to valorize her sacrifice for humanity, to control and yet to disengage from the object of her desire so that he can enter into a creative activity that is beneficial to all. In the end, du Guillet's example demonstrates that the confrontation with difference need not be resolved by representing the other as the narcissistic extension of one's own gratification, but rather as the result of the pro-duction of a generous love.

2

RABELAIS AND THE REPRESENTATION OF MALE SUBJECTIVITY: THE RONDIBILIS EPISODE AS CASE STUDY

The status of women and what may be characterized as a power struggle, the inevitable war between the sexes, is a seminal *topos* in French Renaissance literature.[1] The relationship between men and women, and the ideological implications that it entailed, had its roots well developed in the Middle Ages (for example, in Jean de Meung's *Roman de la Rose* [1398–1402]) when the discussion which focused on the institution of marriage portrayed woman as inferior to man both on physiological and theological grounds. In the France of the 1530s, this debate between feminist and antifeminist forces, known as the *Querelle des Femmes,* took on a new meaning when it concerned itself with the nature of love and the comportment of woman. Most clearly, the antifeminism of that period owed its existence to the universality of misogyny and gynophobia perhaps as much as it does today. As Jean de Marconville suggests, for example, in *De l'heur et malheur du mariage* (Paris, 1564), woman's insatiable sexual drives can only be characterized as a ploy to ruin man's health and drain him of his vitality.[2] In another, but equally revelatory, context François de Billon's work *Le fort inexpugnable de l'honneur du sexe femenin* portrays the delight of woman in the utter destruction of man "suivant la coustume d'icelles Amazones, qui (comme bien savez) se servoient des Hommes, seullement pour maintenir leurs puissance à engendrer des filles, pour leur rompre la teste."[3] Not only did the *Querelle* maintain that women were the lascivious corruptors of men, it also put forth counterarguments by feminist writers such as Henri Corneille Agrippa who refocused the debate on equality and the demystification of the prevailing misogynist notions concerning woman's nature.[4] The *Querelle* thus became a rhetorical battle that either exposed or critically challenged women's subjugation to men.

The subject examined in this chapter deals with the question of male gender identity, and both the anger and anxiety it creates within the confines of the amorous struggle. Implicit within my analysis is the presupposition that the figuration of male subjectivity in the text assumes a relation to the reproductive function of sexuality through a series of cultural mediations. Panurge's unmitigated quest for a faithful marriage partner in Rabelais' *Tiers Livre* (1546) provokes unquestionable hysteria on the part of this male figure since it was generally thought that women were naturally prone to deception because of their uncontrollable libidinal energy. I shall discuss in detail the Rondibilis episode of the *Tiers Livre* (chapters 31–4) as "case study" since it most clearly problematizes the quest to become a man, and with it the way in which gynophobic myths risk trapping men within the reified male/female dichotomy, rendering them angry victims of their own paranoia.

Throughout Rabelais' *Tiers Livre* there is a sustained discussion concerning the origin and the nature of semen, and both the moral and libidinal implications that it entails. The basis of this debate may be found in the controversy established between two opposing schools of spermatology: the teachings of Claudius Galen and those of the Platonic–Hippocratic school. According to the argument put forth in Galen's *De Spermate,* semen is produced in the testicles and it is the result of an involuntary drive liberated from the power of the will. For Renaissance followers of Galen, the responsibility for the survival of the species is assigned to Nature, and following the principles of Aristotelian philosophy it is generally regarded as unconnected with the fate of individual man.[5] The platonists, on the other hand, saw the problem in a far different light. They put forth a contradictory doctrine claiming that the production of semen could only be controlled by the will or what they characterized as man's power of reason. Nature, they claimed, was concerned with the perfection of individual manhood to the detriment of women, who were identified with the distortion of the senses and thought to possess the incorrigible moral flaws of sexual hysteria.

If these medico-philosophical intertexts function as backdrop to this episode, it is not, I believe, merely to prioritize the intrinsic value of either of these two positions. Instead they are used to help us identify misogyny as a discursive form that problematizes, through the process of rewriting, the question of male sexuality and the constraints challenging it. Rabelais' writing interrogates the repressive and essentialized notions of masculine and feminine as symbolic gender values caught in a network of historical power relations. In other words, his text depicts sexual difference as a phenomenon emanating from the difference of libidinal economies or drives; accordingly, this representational process is responsible for creating fictions of sexuality that investigate the very question of male gender identity.

The unifying *topos* underlying Rabelais' *Tiers Livre* is the marriage question.[6] Like the figure of Diogenes who futilely pushes his tub in the book's prologue, Panurge is represented as a comic anti-hero whose linguistic gyrations on the marriage question imprison him in a labyrinth of doubt. Throughout the divinations and consultations that structure the book we bear witness to Panurge's angry frustration, stemming from his complete inability to make up his mind. His remarks go back and forth between a desire for marriage and the fear of its consequences, in other words the dangers of cuckoldry. Panurge's desire for a definitive opinion on whether or not he should marry represents his quest to be in control, and this manifests itself as the need to domesticate female desire and sexual behavior and submit it to the imperatives of the phallocentric order. The rabelaisian text enacts a narrative account of the menace of female sexuality, a phenomenon which ultimately threatens the phallocentric figure with the imaginary loss of its being; the mythically omnipotent, uncontrolled, and luridly sexual woman poses an unmitigated threat to the patriarchal order. Consequently, as we shall see, Rabelais' text conceals not only an ambivalence towards women, but at the same time projects a profound sexual anxiety through the dynamics of a male figure depicted as thoroughly narcissistic and regressive in behavior.

The image of woman that emerges most clearly in the *Tiers Livre* is found in the Rondibilis episode where the female is portrayed as a protean being fated to the demands of an uncontrollable *jouissance*. In consultation with the doctor Rondibilis, Panurge learns the importance of the *topos animal avidum generandi* derived from Plato's *Timaeus*: woman is seen as the victim of an animal-like hunger for generation. She is regarded as a somewhat hysterical figure whose uncontrollable appetite makes her unstable, imperfect, and lustful. In adapting Plato's gynecology, the rabelaisian text attributes to the mythological functions of femininity the power of self-movement and the ability to differentiate between various odors. The mystery of hysteria which is the generative force of woman's sexuality reduces her to a shockingly independent figure whose desire for power, unlike the drive for perfection thought to be found in the male species, is motivated by a self-gratifying narcissism. In essence, woman's inability to control her sexual drives is but a form of womb disease (*hysteria*), an image of death represented by convulsive disorders that eloquently suggest the lack of any acceptable means of authentically repressing desire. Described as a sexually insatiable being, woman is therefore erotically doomed to live out a fate in which desire is forever unsatisfied, and because of this she is transformed into a monstrous figure who both shocks and frightens.

. . . à bon droict Platon le nomme animal, recongnoissant en luy mouvemens propres de suffocation, de praecipitation, de corrugation, de indignation, voire si violens que bien souvent par eulx est tollu à la femme tout aultre sens et mouvement, comme si feust lipothymie, syncope, epilepsie, apoplexie, et vraye ressemblance de mort. Oultre plus, nous voyons en icelluy discretion des odeurs manifeste, et le sentent les femmes fuyr les puantes suyvre les aromaticques.[7] (p. 540).

Anticipating Freud's etiology, the hysterical symptom used as a reproach against woman in the rabelaisian text is characterized as a form of physical conversion for which no organic cause can be truly identified.[8] Accordingly, Rondibilis looks into the mystery of female desire – the "dark continent" of sexuality as Lacan would later put it – only to discover even more mystery and lust. Female sexuality is portrayed as an enigma, as that which Rabelais, in quoting Virgil (*Aeneid*, VI), describes as "variable and so easily moved"; it consequently becomes an amorphous entity, the very figure of ambiguity, incapable of precise definition. Woman is thus conceptualized as an atrophied male or a fragmented creature who solicits desire.

Car Nature leurs a dedans le corps posé en lieu secret et intestin un animal, un membre, lequel n'est es hommes, on quelques foys sont engendrées certaines humeurs salses, nitreuses, bauracineuses, acres, mordicantes, lancinantes, chatouillantes amerement; par la poincture et fretillement douloureux des quelles (car ce membre est tout nerveux et de vif sentement) tout le corps est en elles esbranlé, tous les sens raviz, toutes affections interinées, tous pensemens confonduz. (pp. 539–40)

What makes female sexuality so threatening and anxiety-producing for men is their inability to apprehend what the narrative terms the secret and interior *locus* where the female sex organ is lodged. If, as Lacan claims, woman's place is outside of language ("Le sexe de la femme ne lui dit rien"), then man is inevitably fated to be incapable of taking hold of her discursively, or in any other manner. Woman's excessive fluidity thus transforms her into an elusive figure who can neither be controlled nor defined since it is beyond definition that her sexual identity lies. In essence, Rabelais' text puts forward the idea that an image is in some sense forbidden to woman. "Quand je diz femme [says Rondibilis] je diz un sexe tant fragil, tant variable, tant muable, tant inconstant et imperfaict" (p. 539). Yet to the extent to which woman may be defined within a phallocentric system – however limited it may be – it is always as lack or absence. Physiologically defective, she is seen as a scar against nature and a source of displeasure. Indeed, it is this equation of woman with the monstrous that identifies misogyny as a conflict between the awareness of woman as flawed and the desire for perfection expressed in the male exhortation to a kind of moral "virginity" on the part of the female. "Nature me semble (parlant en tout honneur et reverence) s'estre esguarée de ce bon sens par lequel elle avait créé et formé toutes choses, quand elle a basty la femme" (p. 539).

If women represent a sexual threat to Panurge, it is because they possess the power to anger and frighten men by revealing to them their potential source of weakness. The fear that is expressed stems, in large measure, from the myth associated with the insatiable desire of the vagina. And woman's libidinal power gives her the authority to call into question man's sexuality by raising the hypothesis that man might potentially be unable to contain the inexorable necessity of female lust. What is most striking, in this context, is the paradoxical tension that emerges in the representation of Panurge as a male figure hopelessly divided between a rigorously rendered drive for mastery (his repeated assertions of Priapic potency) and the anxious fear of being unable to meet those demands. As a figure, Panurge oscillates between overwhelming aggression and paralyzing defensiveness. And the effect of these fears and the mechanisms of its mitigation takes several forms within the episode.

On the one hand, Panurge expresses a self-gratifying narcissism that transforms him into a victim of dissipation.[9] The female threat to phallic potency is translated into a form of defensiveness that fetishizes the phallus and makes it the center of the symbolic order. In fact, Rabelais' text describes it as the "ferrement infatiguable" [the indefatigable tool], that exemplary figure of strength, which must come to terms with what Rondibilis describes as the threatening and self-consuming sexual desire of the female. Panurge's libidinal energy is gradually withdrawn from the "real world" and is projected onto a phallic figure that ascribes to itself the symbolic primacy of the self-image.

Si continuellement ne exercez ta mentule [says Frere Jan], elle perdra son laict et ne te servira que de pissotiere: les couilles pareillement ne te serviront que de laict et ne te servira que de pissotiere: les couilles pareillement ne te serviront que de gibbessiere. Je t'en advise, mon amy. J'en ay veu l'experience en plusieurs, qui ne l'ont peu quand ilz vouloient, car ne l'avoient faict quand le povoient. Aussi par non usaige sont perduz tous privileges, ce disent les clercs. Pourtant, fillol, maintiens tout ce bas et menu populaire troglodyte en estat de labouraige sempiternel. Donne ordre qu'ilz ne vivent en gentilz hommes, de leurs rantes sans rien faire . . . [Panurge:] Je te prie croyre (et ne croyras chose que ne soit vraye) mon naturel, le sacre Ithyphalle, messer Cotal d'Albingues, estre le *prime del monde.*   (pp. 516–18)

Any threat to phallic potency must thus be seen as a threat to the male mystique, to the virile self-image, and the ability to remain in control. In confronting this threat love for the other can only become self-love, or what might be termed in this context a form of phallic conceit. The Galenic imperative to valorize the function of the genitals imprisons Panurge within the domain of male delusion and conceals a profound sexual anxiety, a threat to phallocentric power. The need to maximize sexual activity is not only a way to assure permanence or immortality, as Terence Cave claims, but it can also be viewed as a "hysterial" male reaction to an epistemological anxiety about the ideals of male hegemony and paternity.[10]

Tu me semblez aulcunement doubter, voyre deffier, de ma paternité, comme ayant peu favorable le roydde dieu des jardins . . . Depuys lui [Solomon] Aristoteles a declairé l'estre des femmes estre de soy insatiable; mais je veulx qu'on saiche que, de mesmes qualibre, j'ay le ferrement infatiguable.   (pp. 517–18)

The battle of the sexes is reflected here through the symbolic play of power interests: the phallus is narcissistically invested through this declaration of self-defense, serving as a reminder that woman's indefatigable biological power enables her to call into question male sexuality.

But in the attempt to phallicize the female–Panurge's ironic claim to have an instrument as powerful as the woman's "ferrement infatiguable" [the "indefatigable tool" or, literally, the "iron rod"] – the rabelaisian text abdicates to the "lustier sex" the sexual potency necessary for domination, by inscribing the female within a masculine system of representation. Yet ironically, Rabelais' text maintains at the same time the need to put

35

forward the image of a phallically potent male, through the symbol of the "tonneau inexpuisable," and consequently to project a sense of mastery. One last remark is pertinent here concerning an anecdote in this episode which relates the story of the frock of the monk of Castres, a piece of clothing known for its occult properties.

> Escoute ça, couillette. Veidz tu oncques le froc du moine de Castres? Quand on le posoit en quelque maison, feust à descouvert, feust à cachettes, soubdain, par sa vertus horrificque, tous les manens et habitans du lieu entroient en ruyt, bestes et gens, hommes et femmes, jusques aux ratz et aux chatz. Je te jure qu'en ma braguette j'ay aultres fois congneu certaine energie encore plus anormale.   (p. 518)

In addressing his "couillette" [his "cock"], Panurge demonstrates the exemplary virtues of the frock belonging to the monk of Castres, attributing to it the power to cure cowardice in men. In reality, the myth associated with this garment demonstrates the need to re-establish the phallocentric, hierarchal principle of an order based upon an ontologically pure male essence in which the idealized cock – as Rabelais' text puts it – transcends the power of the frock that is figured in the text.

The counterargument to the assertion of potency in Rabelais' text is based on the threat of impotency or the inability to satisfy female sexuality, thus making man a potential victim of cuckoldry. Panurge appears unable to recognize his own limitations. By comically deforming Galenic theory for the benefit of Panurge's libidinal impulses, the rabelaisian text magnifies the potential consequences of an inflationary economy of desire based on a principle of dissipation that risks transforming narcissism into libidinal bankruptcy. Panurge refuses to acknowledge any threat to the integrity and stability of the self as a biopsychological entity subject to the decline associated with old age.

> Je t'entends (dist frere Jan) mais le temps matte toutes choses. Il n'est le marbre, ny le porphyre qui n'ayt sa viellesse et decadence. Si tu ne en est là pour ceste heure, peu d'années après subsequentes, je te oiray confessant que les couilles pendent à plusieurs par faulte de gibbessiere. Desja voy je ton poil grisonner en teste. Ta barbe, par les distinctions du

36

gris, du blanc, du tanné et du noir, me semble une mappemonde . . . Ce touppet icy, tout blanc, sont les monts Hyperborées. Par ma soif, mon amy, quand les neiges sont es montaignes, je diz la teste et le menton, il n'y a pas grand chaleur par les valées de la braguette. Tes males mules (respondit Panurge). Tu n'entends pas les topiques. Quand la neige est sus les montaignes, la fouldre, l'esclair, les lanciz, le maulubec, le rouge grenat, le tonnoirre, la tempeste, tous les diables sont par les vallées . . . Je crains que par quelque longue absence de nostre roy Pantagruel auquel force est que je face compaignie, voire allast il à tous les diables, ma femme me face coqu. Voy là le mot peremptoire.   (pp. 519–21)

The threat to virility is translated here by the shift in focus from the physiological decay of man to the moral or ethical flaws of the female. In essence, impotency manifests itself in terms of man's inability to control the female who, in her non-conformity to the phantasmatic masculine standard of fidelity, threatens the dominance of phallocentric culture. The myopia of male logic denies the inevitability of self-loss at the same time that it calls into question the so-called "mastery" of the Master. "Car tous ceulx à qui j'en ay parlé me en menassent et afferment qu'il me est ainsi praedestiné des cieulx" (p. 521). Man's fate is thus subject to a desire that shows no pity. If male impotency announces itself as a possibility in Rabelais' text, it must take the form of an imaginary servitude to female capriciousness that not only reveals a generalized feeling of misogyny but also underscores the moral superiority in man based on a feeling of weakness.

Throughout Rabelais' book, and especially in the Rondibilis episode, woman is represented as a creature who is not to be trusted. Morally weak because of her innate ability to deceive, she must paradoxically hide herself in order to show herself. The image of woman as moon put forth by Rondibilis marks poignantly the effect of this paradox since the condition of her visibility depends on the absence of man.

Mon amy, le naturel des femmes nous est figuré par la Lune, et en aultres choses et en ceste qu'elles se mussent, elles se constraignent, et dissimulent en la veue et praesence de leurs mariz. Iceulx absens, elles prennent leur adventaige, se donnent du bon temps, vaguent, trotent, deposent leur hypocrisie et se declairent: comme la lune, en conjunction du soleil, n'apparoist on ciel, ne en terre; mais, en son opposition, estant, au plus du soleil esloingnée, reluist en sa plenitude et apparoist toute, notamment on temps de nuyct. Ainsi sont toutes femmes femmes. (p. 539)

The sexual desire of the female thus finally exposes itself in the silence of the "dark continent of sexuality" where it distances itself from the reign of phallocentric law. In so doing, woman positions herself in a space of liberation functioning as a shining presence that takes shape through the possibility of separation. Not only is woman regarded as a figure capable of draining man's health (the production of semen was seen as producing a distillation of the blood), but her immoderate sexual appetite ostensibly enables her to blossom fully as a source of light through dissimulative behavior. From Panurge's angry and anguished perspective, what makes a woman truly a woman is her ability to execute acts of deception calculated to perpetuate her "difference." The fact that women lay aside their pretenses in the absence of their husbands suggests that entry into the conjugal pact is both dangerous and unpredictable.

Panurge's existential dilemma concerning the marriage question not only demonstrates that desire is inseparable from generation, it also makes clear that manliness is dependent on the power to provide legitimate posterity. If desire is at stake in the male species, it must be modulated in relation to the issues of marriage, sexuality, and generation. Now Rabelais' critics have stressed a somewhat different perspective in their analyses of the Rondibilis consultation. For example, Michael Screech asserts that the consultation with Rondibilis is essentially "scientific" in nature but that Rabelais "does not exploit this scientific data in the spirit of the *Querelle des Femmes*."[11] To be sure, Screech's reading of the Platonic intertext in relation to this episode implies that man does not function through the generative act merely as a blind tool of nature dedicated to the preservation of the species. He subtly suggests the moral superiority of man in exercising the freedom to contain libidinal instincts, a phenomenon realized thanks to the intervention of divine guidance. In a quite different perspective I would argue that Ravelais' text strikingly challenges this particular ethico-religious tradition in

38

the representation of Panurge by raising the crucial question of what it takes to become a man, and how manliness is contingent upon the power of woman to give man what he wants: a child, a *pierre vive* (TL, 6) or a living monument. Consequently, the only redemptive quality associated with woman's intrinsic value as woman appears to lie in her ability to constitute man as a patriarchal figure, as *pater familias*. And, ironically, the marriage bond which affords the very possibility of paternity might, in the end, only provide an institutional framework in which the machinations of a deceptive wife can challenge the security of phallocentric law.

When Panurge visits Rondibilis, instead of ascertaining a definitive answer to the marriage question, Rondibilis prescribes five methods of controlling desire and quelling lust. In the methods proposed the restraint of concupiscence is associated with dissipation of the generative seed, a phenomenon that undermines masculinity or the so-called "male mystique." In a first example, for instance, the immoderate use of wine creates a "refroidisse-ment de sang, resolution des nerfs, dissipation de semence generative, hebetation des sens, perversion des mouvemens, qui sont toutes impertinences à l'acte de generation" (p. 533). Drinking, we are told, deadens vigor and strength and undermines the biological desire for mastery. The containment of aggression as a characteristic of sexual instinct damages the priapic potency of masculinity. And this is figured in the text through a reference to Bacchus "dieu des yvroignes, sans barbe et en habit de femme, comme tout effoeminé, comme eunuche et escouillé" (p. 533). The second method of restraint is the taking of certain drugs which not only quell incontinence but render man frigid and incapable of the act of generation.

The third remedy – hard labor – once again underscores the threat to manliness by equating hard work with a slackening of the power to make a seminal secretion. Here the reference to Diana, goddess of the hunt, ostensibly links chastity to a symbolic form of castration.

Ainsi est dicte Diane chaste, laquelle continuellement travaille à la chasse. Ainsí jadis estoient dictz les castres, comme castes, es quelz continuellement travailloient les athletes et soubdars. Ainsi escript Hippocrates, *lib, de aere aqua et locis,* de quelques peuples en Scythie, les quelz, de son temps, plus estoient impotens que eunuches à l'esbatement venerien, parce que continuellement ilz estoient à cheval et au travail, comme au contraire disent les philosophes, oysiveté estre mere de luxure.   (p. 534)

The tropological and phonological acrobatics in Rabelais' text create an association amongst the words "chaste/chase/castra" and furnish the textual evidence necessary for the assumption that impotency stems from overwork and functions as a castrative gesture, a sign of lack that deprives man of the regenerative privilege associated with the symbolic value of the phallus. In this way, then, Rabelais' text suggests that repression of male desire leads to a kind of entropy that blurs the distinction between the masculine and the feminine.

The fourth means of restraining lust is through fervent study. In playing on the Ciceronian adage that to philosophize is to learn how to die, Rabelais' text shows that study leads to the renunciation of desire and the concomittant menace of death, be it real or spiritual. The consent to sacrifice life for contemplative ideals does not impel the generative secretion to its destined place and "de quoy pousser aux lieux destinez ceste resudation générative et enfler le nerf caverneux, duquel l'office est hors la projecter, pour la propopation d'humaine nature" (p. 535). It is this renunciation of reproductive power for what metaphorically might be termed a kind of "murderous knowledge" that unquestionably subverts the libidinal and procreative affirmation of life.

It is, however, Rondibilis' fifth solution that is the most revealing. When he proposes the veneral act itself to Panurge, he responds by saying: "Je vous attendois là ... et le prens pour moy. Use des praecedens qui vouldra ... Je le [to get married] seray, n'en doubtez, et bien toust" (p. 537). Panurge's choice is more than merely comic; it is indeed more than just an ironic cure for the malady of sensuality by the malady itself. When Panurge raises the marriage question with Rondibilis, the power to reproduce hovers underneath it, with the sensuality issue acting as its ostensible pretext. What makes a man a man is the

40

power to reproduce. And marriage, following the Paulinian tradition (I, Cor., vii 9) not only serves as a divinely-appointed remedy for those whose lust demands an outlet, but more importantly, it affords man the power to fulfill his own sense of masculinity and adhere to a socially prescribed gender identity.[12] In effect, desire becomes part of fathering and reproduction and, as such, the repression of lust is ostensibly a repression of manliness. However, as Rabelais' text makes quite clear, if procreation captures the essence of the paternal function, it is only through the symbolic gift of the woman that man's sense of masculinity may be guaranteed. Accordingly, the generative power through which masculinity is affirmed is caught in a paradox in which the pleasures of manly satisfaction give rise to potential conflict that takes the form of an angry and nightmarish vision of cuckoldry; the quest for potency announces itself as a form of servitude. Entrance into the marriage contract thus affords Panurge an ambivalent brand of sexuality that has the potential both to satisfy and to endanger phallocentric power. The woman that giveth also has the power to take away. In essence, the Aristotelian tradition, which portrayed woman as a receptacle for the paternal seed, is interrogated here in that she becomes responsible for the biological fate of the species as well as for the realization of the masculinity of man. Panurge's state of indecision is the result of a precarious tension and a paralytic anger that situates him on the precipice of unresolved fear, and reveals a profound sexual anxiety emanating from the image of an uncontrollable but powerful female figure who declares her independence from the confines of male desire. The endless repetition of Panurge's question "Shan't I be a cuckold?" transforms his skepticism into a kind of declarative utterance that paradoxically affirms the certainty of his doubt, and, because of it, reveals an angry hysteria emanating from the inability to decide.

Nevertheless, Panurge's quest for a monogamous relationship is based upon his inability to recognize woman as separate and other, and the narcissistic desire passively to enjoy his own male pleasure. In essence, his endless demand for the exclusivity of

41

object relations reveals the need for a kind of symbiotic dependency based on the ideal of becoming one with the female figure. Female *jouissance,* regarded as a deficiency, threatens the integrity of the matrimonial bond as well as the idealized interdependency and the adherence to the principle of exchange – "celle grand ame de l'univers" – put forward by Panurge. In spite of Panurge's inability to enter into a competitive or threatening relationship with another male, he is obliged, nevertheless, to enagage in an imaginary struggle for sexual power with an imaginary female figure who refuses to subsume femininity within the repressive parameters of paternal law. Women are therefore regarded as a threat to the male mystique and, more particularly here, to Panurge's sense of gender identity. Depicted as easy prey for the savagery of desire, they represent for men the terrifying image of a world in which women would be independent and self-sufficient.

Now, as we have seen within the context of the episode, any threat to phallic potency is indeed a threat to Panurge's self-image as mediated by the constraints of the so-called patriarchal marriage system. If, as Jean Laplanche claims, castration is not a reality, but rather "a thematization of reality based on the perception of potential loss," then the fantasized withdrawal of female nurturance and security produces a "hysterial" reaction, stemming from Panurge's perceived inability to domesticate and control female sexual behavior.[13] Indeed, Panurge runs the risk of being unable to fulfill that demand, and the comforting belief in the ideal of the omnipotent male disappears. The potential loss of control over a mythological woman is thus akin to a narcissistically invested object loss that figuratively takes the form of a disease that Rondibilis is asked to cure. Panurge's anger is directed against what I would term the image of a phallic woman whose "ferrement infatiguable" ["indefatigable tool" or "iron rod"] transforms the mythological weakness of the uterus into a libidinal machine that man has not always "de quoy payer et satisfaire au contentement" (p. 541). Quite clearly, the so-called moral hypothesis put forward by Screech on the Rondibilis consultation suggests that the episode is "concerned with the perfection of man as an individual person." This interpretation thus avoids the whole question of vulnerability to which the phallic body is exposed. In fact, everything in Rabelais' text ultimately points to Panurge's inability to sustain the permanent calling into question of the ideological solidarity of the notions *phallus*, father, power, and man. The angst or anger (from the same Latin root *angere*, to strangle) that paralyzes the male subject here essentially anticipates those mythologically negative qualities of female narcissism put forward by Freud (sensuality and independence) that Panurge believes he is unable to counterbalance.[14]

However, Rondibilis offers a solution to the threat of cuckoldry with a moral drawn from Plutarch (*Opera*, I, 122) in which man is able to restrain female desire by granting woman the freedom to engage in the pleasures of the body. If Panurge's original desire for female "propriety" was but a cover for the fear of his own powerlessness, then the phallic fantasy of female liberation that Rondibilis proposes as a cure carries within it an attempt to obfuscate a blatant sense of impotency by transforming it and making fear the pretext for a seemingly benevolent act. Rabelais' text presents a rewritten version of Plutarch's fable in which the allegorical figure representing Grief and/or Mourning in the original is changed into the God of Cukoldry. The moral of the fable is quite clear. As in the case of the representation of Grief, Cuckoldry is described as a fate that comes to those who worship it. In this perspective, the prohibition of desire (the interdiction of woman's freedom) not only makes it more appealing, it becomes the very cause of the deception that it seeks to avoid. To be sure, jealousy increases the potential of female sexual activity by moving women beyond the boundaries of the patriarchal order and the constraints of its prohibitive laws.

Comme la fouldre ne brise et ne brusle, sinon les matieres dures, solides, resistentes, elle ne se arreste es choses molles, vuides et cedentes . . . elle consumera les os des corps sans entommer la chair qui les couvre: ainsi ne bendent les femmes jamais la contention, subtilité, et contradiction de leurs espritz, sinon envers ce que congnoistront leur estre prohibé et defendu.   (p. 545)

43

In essence, the text transcribes female sexuality as a phenomenon to be both expressed and repressed. Misogyny is indeed allegorized in this fable in that the so-called submission to female desire merely constitutes a sublimated form of patriarchal control from which the apparent "softness" or lack of rigidity on the part of the male subject veils a secret plan to gain access to a position of power. If man pushes this manipulative strategy to an extreme, it is only to be able to conceal himself from the endless threats to his sense of manliness. In the end, security in Rabelais' text is sought after not just for the love of women, but unquestionably for the satisfaction derived from man's attempt to shield himself from an anxiety-producing threat to gender hegemony.

3

VERBA EROTICA: MARGUERITE DE NAVARRE AND THE RHETORIC OF SILENCE

The feminine has had to be deciphered as forbidden [*interdit*], in between signs, between the realized meanings, between the lines.
Luce Irigaray, *Speculum de l'autre femme* (1974)

"Female sexuality," claims Luce Irigaray, "has always been theorized within masculine parameters."[1] Under the phallocentric order, the riddle of feminine sexuality has solicited desire to a dualistic tension between exhibition and pudic retreat. For Irigaray, woman, according to classical psychoanalytic theory, is conceptualized as a "lack"; seen through men's eyes, she has always been effaced in order to act as a blank canvas for the working out of his fantasies. And female desire, which is emblematized by the elusive figure of the clitoris, is characterized as "the negative, the opposite, the reverse, the counterpart of the only visible, morphologically designate sex organ: the penis."[2] In a culture that privileges phallomorphism, the presence of woman, according to Irigaray, is inscribed in a blank space, in the "nothing to be seen" already admitted in Greek statuary representation where the female sex organ is "both absent and sewn up."[3]

One must bear in mind this critical perspective, I believe, if one wishes to understand how feminist theory is thematized in the representation of female desire in the tenth *nouvelle* of Marguerite de Navarre's *L'Heptaméron*. Within this context it comes as no surprise, as the historian Joan Kelly explains, that Renaissance women's writing was "the metaphorical projection of her woman's state," and from the male point of view it would be conceived as an idealized form of silence.[4] Here let us not forget that Francesco Barbaro set forth the ideal of the chaste and silent woman in his conduct book, *De Re Uxoria* (Paris, 1513, 1553): "It is proper that not only arms but indeed also the speech of woman never be made public; for the speech of a noble woman can be no less dangerous than the nakedness of her limbs."[5] The question that therefore arises is what would woman's place be in a world where she functioned as the invisible support for male desire? How does the inaudible language of female silence give rise to a representational mode in which woman's difference is no longer regarded as the inverse figure of an essentialized view of man?

The tenth *nouvelle* of Marguerite de Navarre's *L'Heptaméron* presents an interesting case study in which the motifs of courtly love and the ethics of *parfaicte amitye* are thematized.[6] The perfect young courtier–knight and courtly lover Amadour, esteemed for his "grande hardiesse," falls desperately in love with an *exempla* of female beauty and honor, Floride, whom he has known since the age of nine. But because of the difference in their social stature, not to mention Floride's untempered quest to remain true to her honor and self-respect, Amadour is forced to conceal, at least initially, his erotic impulses behind the mask of virtue. Floride, it appears, is committed to an abstract ideal of perfection, although the text increasingly characterizes her as having an unstable identity arising from the tension created by the forces of passion. What emerges, little by little, is the image of the woman as the bearer of guilt, as one who knows the truth of her apparent crime (the sin of desire), but who, nevertheless, refuses to divulge her passion and recognize the consequences of the potential loss of self. The trajectory of Floride's desire moves from "ung tres grand contentement" (p. 61) to "joye" (p. 70) and "affection" (p. 73) which finally overwhelms Floride and forces her to commit herself to God so that she can be preserved from "toute meschenté."[7] Not only does this exemplary tale depict the relationship between men and women as a war between the sexes threatening the moral degeneration of ideal love, it characterizes female desire from the point of view of its repression.

Throughout the tale, Floride is constrained to adhere to an abstract code of virtue which bars her access to the pleasure sought by masculine desire and which consequently forces her to remain "une femme de bien, victorieuse de son cueur, de son corps, d'amour et de son amy" (p. 54). To be sure, Floride possesses all of the qualities demanded by the civilized world, but as a woman she becomes the victim of "une peste" (p. 65), something which she cannot describe but which, nevertheless, takes hold of her and articulates the imperatives of unconscious desire through her silence and non-verbal language. In spite of trying to find a space in which she can exist as something other than an idealized object of perfection, Floride is destined to engage in a battle against the futile rebellion of the body and speak in the only voice sanctioned by the rules of a social code that allows her to keep her honor intact: "elle l'aymoit comme s'il eust été son propre frere" (p. 60).

From the beginning of the narrative, Floride is defined in terms of Amadour's perception of her as an icon of beauty and grace functioning as the sign of rhetorical convention. The narrator marks the precise moment at which the desiring subject's gaze captures the image as pure idea:

Ce gentil homme . . . en regardant la beaulté et bonne grace de sa fille Floride . . . se pensa en luy-mesme que c'estoit bien la plus honneste personne qu'il avoit jamais veue, et que, s'il pouvoit avoir sa bonne grace, il en seroit plus satisfaict que de tous les biens et plaisirs qu'il pourroit avoir d'une autre.   (p. 56)

The image of the other is presented here as a prototype of perfection that completely absorbs the beholder in the founding perception. Floride's *persona* thus conforms to an idealization whereby female identity is subsumed as the tool for Amadour's narcissistic satisfaction and accordingly privileges the viewing subject and establishes a transcendent point of vision.

At the outset, Floride's sense of self is defined in terms of a prehistory dominated by a maternal authority adhering to the exigencies of phallocentric culture. The Countess of Aranda devotes herself to her daughter's education. She is concerned with inculcating Floride with the love of virtue and self-restraint. This pedagogical imperative ironically traps her within an undifferentiated masculine structure of exchange, requiring the obedience of a female subject who is taught to disguise her true desires, which she does even before the threatening gaze of her mother: ". . . jamais, devant sa mere ne nul autre, n'en feit ung seul semblant" (p. 69).

In effect, Marguerite's text returns the representation of Floride to a point of origin where the moral imperatives of masculine exemplarity take the place of female difference. Throughout the narrative, the courtly code traces Floride's identity back to the will of a dominant male culture. "La dicte dame meyt peine de nourrir ses enfans en toutes les vertuz et honnestetez qui appartiennent à seigneurs et gentilz hommes" (p. 55). The Countess of Aranda facilitates the erasure of Floride's female identity so that she may act as a canvas on which the code of the courtier may be inscribed. Floride's *persona* is thus sustained through a reflexive game that is indeed rhetorical; she is obliged to don the mask of chastity and thereby engage in a dramatic performance that is fundamentally a mimesis of courtly law. This spectacle of *bienséance* imposes silence on the troubling rapport between the sexes, a place where phallocentric privilege thrives and where female identity, at best, is the simulacrum of an ideal.

If Floride's mother obliges her to marry "le jeune duc de Cardonne," it is not only to realize the king's preference concerning a husband for her daughter, but also acts as a means of pleasing Amadour. Marriage serves as a cover, an institution that enables the desiring subject to love and yet to sustain the illusion of chastity.

> Avant que fussiez mariée [Floride], j'ay sceu si bien vaincre mon cueur, que vous n'avez sceu congnoistre ma volunté; mais, maintenant que vous l'estes, et que vostre honneur peult estre couvert, quel tort vous tiens-je de demander ce qui est mien? (p. 73)

Within the context of this matriarchal strategy, then, Floride's role tends to be passive and reactive as she adheres to an "aristocratic marriage game" in which her symbolic identification with the phallus can only be understood as her identification with the mother's desire. If the marks of the maternal are inscribed in Floride's behavior here, they come to signify a martyred subject who identifies with the desire of the mother rather than with the desire of woman. "Ceste jeune dame doncques se delibera de mectre Dieu et l'honneur devant ses oeilz, et dissimulla si bien ses ennuyz, que jamais nul des siens ne s'apparceut que son mary luy despleust" (p. 69). Accordingly, Floride dissimulates her pleasure as a woman by declining to tell what she knows, that is, through her silence. "Floride s'estonnast de le veoir sans response, si est-ce qu'elle l'attribua plustost à quelque sottise, que à la force d'amour, et passa oultre, sans parler davantaige" (p. 58). In order to keep from being conquered by passion, Floride's sense of being must be mediated by the will of her mother. The mother becomes an agent capable of making her daughter the victim of a social code designed to reflect her own ambivalence. "Elle est si saige, dist Avanturade, que pour rien elle ne confesseroit avoir autre volunté que celle de sa mere" (p. 58).

Amadour's desire for Floride catalyzes the narrative, forcing it to move forward through a series of amorous conflicts in which Floride's virtue and honor are challenged. Phallocentric desire overdetermines the plot and accounts for the successive dissimulative maneuvers that Amadour undertakes to achieve his goal. Amadour fashions a self in response to what he thinks the female other requires of him "comme celluy qui n'estoit jamais desporveu d'inventions" (p. 79). He must become an expert in theatrics and manipulation so that he may project the illusion of a convincing drama. Amadour's hypocritical self-fashioning advocates inauthenticity as the only acceptable *modus operandi* to secure male supremacy in the quest for the inaccessible woman. In order to gain access to Floride, Amadour creates various fictive strategies whereby she becomes the victim of a blindness that forbids the exposure of his "real motives." Amadour's narrative is therefore carefully prepared and sustained through manipulative tactics such as the marriage arranged by the Countess of Aranda to Floride's friend Avanturade ("ce mariage lui estoit très heureuse couverture" [p. 60]) and his creation of an "angelic essence" as trusted family friend and advisor ("comme ung sainct ou ung ange" [p. 61]). He even begins to flirt with Poline, a woman of the court, so that he may better conceal his hidden agenda: "Amadour, entendant bien par ces parolles qu'elle avoit envye de remedier à sa necessité, luy en tient les meilleurs propos qu'il fut possible, pensant que en luy faisant acroyre une mensonge, il luy couvriroit une verité" (pp. 61–2). Amadour thus navigates his public *persona* according to the exigencies of instinctive response so that his desire is constituted in response to what he believes the other demands of him; he speaks the fantasized discourse of the other as his very own. "Mais entendez, ma dame, que celluy qui veult bastir ung edifice perpetuel, il doibt regarder à prendre ung seur et ferme fondement: parquoy, moy, qui desire perpetuellement demorer en vostre service" (p. 64).

In this tale, the architectural metaphor of strength and solidity characterizing ideal love ("ung ediffice perpetuel") soon becomes one of moral collapse, an "ediffice . . . sur sablon legier ou sur la fange infame" (p. 74), based as it is on the emptiness of lies. Amadour's initial pursuit of Floride in terms of the stereotypical maxims of the courtier degenerates; he subsequently engages in increasingly belligerent behavior in an attempt to undermine what he perceives to be the female role of hypocritical resistance. A psychological confrontation mediated by images of war and sustained by the repetition of the verbs *guerroyer* and *deliberer* in the narrative delineates the interaction between the sexes as a form of battle in which men conquer and women are vanquished.[8] "Au bout de deux ou trois ans après avoir faict tant de belles choses . . . [Amadour] imagina une invention très grande, non pour gainger le cueur de Floride . . . mais pour avoir la victoire de son ennemye" (p. 77). Represented as a form of repressed desire, the phenomenology of love is recorded here as a battle designed to disengage woman from the abstract ideals of perfect love.

Par Dieu! Floride, le fruict de mon labeur ne me sera poinct osté par vos scrupules; car, puis que amour, patience et humble priere ne servent de riens, je n'espargneray poinct ma force pour acquerir le bien qui, sans l'avoir, me la feroit perdre. (p. 78)

Yet Floride's inability to transcend the paralysis of a cloistered discourse eloquently translates her refusal to recognize an erotic self within the context of a masculine definition of desire. Propriety is but a pretense; it is founded on a conception of honor functioning only to temper Amadour's lust. Floride's public *persona* is thus the result of the power of the male gaze to transform the female subject into a performing artist whose tropes of identity are symptomatic of a concealed structure of imaginary reception; desire as want-to-be settles into a behavior that satisfies. "Ma dame, quelle contenance me faictes-vous? – Telle que je pense que vous la voulez, respondit Floride" (p. 65). The lack of any acceptable resolution to the conflict between sexual impulses and the coded laws of *parfaicte amytié* therefore reveals an essential duplicity arising from the discrepancy between appearance and reality.

Floride, tant contante qu'elle n'en pouvoit plus porter, commencea en son cueur à sentir quelque chose plus qu'elle n'avoit accoustumé; et voyant les honnestes raisons qu'il luy alleguoit, luy dist que la vertu et l'honnesteté repondroient pour elle, et lui accordoit ce qu'il demandoit ... Mais Floride creut trop plus son conseil qu'il ne vouloit; car elle, qui estoit crainctifve non seullement devant Poline, mais en tous autres lieux, commencea à ne le chercher pas, comme elle avoit accoustumé.
(p. 65)

Marguerite's text thus translates the enigma of female desire as an exiled signifier which no longer has a proper signified. The representation of desire as a nameless thing – the narrative reference to "sentir quelque chose" – characterizes female sexuality as something elusive yet always present; it is, in fact, an obscure object of perception which no consciousness can ever completely master. On learning of her arranged marriage to the Duc de Cardonne she "se contraingnit si fort, que les larmes, par force retirées en son cueur, feirent sortir le sang par le nez en telle abondance, que la vie fut en dangier de s'en aller quant et quant" (p. 69). Ultimately, Floride's happiness is destined for

51

conversion into guilt and with it the fatal power of love transforms the exemplary femininity associated with perfect love into the perception of a negatively conceived desiring self. Victim of a maternal pedagogy located within the conventions of the courtly code, Floride can neither fully explore her passion nor let it develop freely.

In the course of the story, a semiotics of repressed sexuality takes shape and opens a narrative space where the question of female desire is articulated with force through non-verbal means.[9] Although Floride struggles violently to preserve her honor by adhering to a concept of love desexualized through the exercise of virtue, her facial expressions, nevertheless, deceive her and represent an unspeakable female language that causes embarrassment and must be masked. The multiple references in the text to Floride's "visaige" function as figures of the silence out of which female repression speaks: they express the inexpressible. The face is the *locus* on which is inscribed the enigma of female desire; Floride's gesticulations disrupt the misleading idealization established by the code of virtue and gentility that the maternal superego identifies with "truth." Accordingly, the text dramatizes a split between seeming and being, the reality of self-contradiction that is so vigorously repressed in Floride. In essence, the female body becomes the ostensible vehicle of expression when all else fails; the woman-in-love figured here is thus led to involuntarily drop her mask and no longer hide behind the fictions that enable her virtue to survive. "La jeune dame, oyant ung propos non accoustumé, commencea à changer de couleur et baisser les oeils comme femme estonnée . . . Amadour s'apparceut bientost de la contenance de Floride" (pp. 64, 65). And when her mother, the Countess of Aranda, wants to know what Floride is thinking or feeling she tries, in spite of her inadequacies, to decipher her daughter's facial hieroglyphics so as to translate the integers of her moral and psychological expression. "La contesse luy en parloit souvent, mais jamais ne sceut tirer contenance où elle peust asseoir jugement . . . La mere, qui regardoit sa contenance, n'y sceut rien juger" (pp. 68, 81).

Quite clearly, Floride fears the monstrousness of female

desire; she recognizes in herself an image that she does not wish to recognize. It is only with the emergence of her so-called "illicit" feelings that Floride begins to develop what might be termed an identity of her own. Upon Amadour's return from battle, Floride attempts to isolate herself from the object of her desire. In fact her vulnerability is underscored through a narrative commentary that delineates the discrepancy between the idealized female of *parfaicte amytié* and the power of sexuality to ignite erotic desire and push her further and further away from the socially sanctioned paragon of female honor.

> [Floride] ... craingnant que la joye qu'elle avoit de le veoir luy fist changer de visaige, et que ceulx qui ne la congnoissoient poinct en prinssent mauvaise opinion, se tint à une fenestre, pour le veoir venir de loing. Et, si tost qu'elle l'advisa, descendit par ung escallier tant obscur que nul ne pouvoit cognoistre si elle changeoit de couleur.
>
> (p. 70)

Thus the narration of Floride's desire appears to emerge out of desire's loss of authority over itself and its apparent incapacity to name itself. In fact this paradoxical moment of mute expression carries within it the plot's generative power, or what Lucien Febvre has characterized, in another context, as the story's "psychological oscillation."[10] Floride's ambivalent expression of love for Amadour increasingly allows him to reveal his true desires and ultimately to transcend the game of ideal love. "Toutesfoys, il guanga la bataille, tant qu'elle luy promeit" (p. 64).

In spite of Floride's insistence that the love between her and Amadour be founded on the "pierre d'honnesteté" (p. 74), "le fils de l'Infant Fortune" is inevitably obliged to confess his physical desire and with it to unleash the potential for violence. The two protagonists engage in Tetel's notion of a platonic, albeit suggestive, *marivaudage* sanctioned by the friendship between Floride and Amadour's wife.[11] However, with the death of the latter, Floride's passion is once again kindled. Nevertheless, Amadour's quest for the "dernieres faveurs" is rejected when Floride refuses to yield to his libidinal impulses, and this is met with the protagonist's "meschante affection" (p. 77).

Near the end of the story Floride is told by her mother of Amadour's return from military duty after an absence of several years. The fact that Amadour, victim of an uncontrollable lust, had already made an unsuccessful attempt to violate Floride's honor a few years earlier motivates her to disfigure herself with a stone rather than engage in another such confrontation.[12] In a way, the "pierre d'honnesté" saves her and carries within it the power of action that is lacking in the dynamics of courtly exchange.

Floride, qui n'estoit pas encores asseurée de sa premiere paour, n'en feyt semblant à sa mere, mais s'en alla ung oratoire se recommander à Nostre Seigneur, et luy priant vouloir conserver son cueur de toute meschante affection, pensa que souvent Amadour l'avoit louée de sa beaulté ... parquoy, aymant mieulx faire tort à son visaige, en le diminuant, que de souffrir par elle le cueur d'un si honneste homme brusler d'un si meschant feu, print une pierre qui estoit en la chappelle, et s'en donna par le visaige si grand coup, que la bouche, le nez et les oeilz en estoient tout difformez. (p. 77)

Floride's act of disfiguration points to the lack of any acceptable resolution to the conflict between active sexual impulses and the exigencies of the society in which she must live. Throughout the story, female sexuality is represented as synonymous with a kind of shameful criminality as evidenced by Floride's dissimulative lowering of her eyes, her turning away or her hiding in obscurity from the menacing gaze of the other. In contrast, Amadour's "visaige," a trope of the male gaze, projects a highly transparent and visually perceptible sexuality that is the incarnation of masculine desire and its potential for violence. "Le feu caché en son cueur [that of Amadour] le brusloit si fort qu'il ne pouvoit empeshcer que la couleur ne luy montast au visaige, et que les estincelles saillissent par ses oeilz" (p. 61).

But what does Floride's self-mutilation imply? Quite clearly it is a gesture that produces a critical difference within the structure of gender relations; it acts as a means of effacing the visceral figure of female desire which is immolated to the apparent virtues of *parfaicte amytié*. Finding herself in the oxymoronic state of avoidance and recognition, Floride is caught between the unmitigated power associated with masculine passion and the need to dominate ("amour, patience et humble priere ne servent de riens, je [Amadour] n'espargneray poinct ma force pour acquerir le bien qui, sans l'avoir, me la feroit perdre" [p. 78]), and the necessity of renunciation. In this incident the disfiguration is a symbolic gesture, an enactment of a female fantasy of empowerment and self-determination that represents the image of a woman as she might exist beyond the constraints of an uncritical idealization. The erasure of desire and the subsequent bandaging of the wound – "pansée et bandée par tout le visaige" (p. 78) – permits Floride to abstract herself from a power structure in which men conquer and women fall.

To return to Irigaray's theory and to consider it from another angle, if women's language is based on the nature of her sexuality as it is seen through men's eyes, then the visually absent affect that resists representation here acknowledges sexual difference at the same time that it disrupts phallocentric values. Female desire is no longer described as being strictly reactive. On the contrary, desire resides within woman and can only be realized by the paradoxical refusal to represent it, a curious phenomenon that has the felicitous consequences of protecting Floride from the excesses of "toute meschante affection." To be sure, Floride's martyrdom – emblematized by the hyperbolic use of the wound image – is less than indifferent to masculine desire: "aymant mieulx faire tort à son visaige que de souffrir . . . le cueur d'un si honnete homme" (p. 77). In this interaction her sexuality is deprived of the transparency of its proper meaning so that the face that transcribes the dynamics of female desire will speak no more. The bandaging of the deformed face therefore suggests the unspeakable women's language that must remain concealed. But if female desire is capable of producing monsters it can only flourish in a libidinal economy in which the desire of the other cannot be seen. The quest to conceal the other's wish results in a foreclosure on the relation between narrative desire and the scopic field.

In essence, the effacement of desire for Floride is an act of renunciation and a declaration of autonomy; it is a sign of ambivalence that is reinforced by the renewed failure to denounce Amadour to her mother who believes that Floride "fust si desraisonnable qu'elle haïst toutes les choses qu'elle [the mother] aymoit" (p. 81). Indeed, Floride is a divided being situated between the exigencies of sexual expression and the refusal to be assimilated to a mode of relations conceived in terms of masculine desire. By exploring the regenderization of the female subject here, Marguerite de Navarre's text depicts a re-vision of Floride's self-image through the paradox of its effacement and its non-coincidence with an idealized representation of self. If chastity (the female ideal) is but a cover-up for repressed desire, one has only to discover the manner in which this socially disguised sexual energy will be released. Even at the end of the narrative we learn of Floride's attempt to escape her mother's harshness when she "delibera de tromper Amadour" (p. 81) by surreptitiously focusing his attention on Lorette, a married lady, as a last attempt to deflect the desire of the other. Yet Floride does not refuse desire merely for her own self-protection; instead, she displaces it and enacts a fantasy of empowerment through which silence gives her the strength to resist domination and to rescue something of her own desire. Having removed herself from circulation in the public domain by retreating to a convent, Floride chooses to become the self-sufficient woman who knows the truth of her own passion but refuses to divulge it. In Jacques Derrida's terms, Floride becomes the "third woman" who recognizes and affirms her power as a dissimulatress by allowing herself the privilege of refusing to enter into complicity with the demands of phallocentric culture. "Elle n'est pas affirmée par l'homme mais s'affirme elle-même, en elle-même."[13]

4

PEDAGOGICAL GRAFFITI AND THE RHETORIC OF CONCEIT

Co-naître, pour tout, c'est naître. Toute connaissance est une naissance.
Paul Claudel, *Art poétique* (1915)

Most, if not all, of Montaigne's critics of the essay "De l'institution des enfans" read that text quite literally as a statement of the essayist's pedagogical imperative.[1] Undoubtedly Montaigne sets out to define an idealized education that challenges the exigencies of medieval scholasticism in the name of a pedagogy aiming at the formation of judgment and wisdom. But on another level Montaigne's text problematizes the figural birth of the ego. "Je ne vise icy qu'à découvrir moy-mesmes."[2] The allegorical instruction underlying Montaigne's essay demonstrates that his pedagogical theory transcends its exemplary status; it is a rhetoric that projects the desire of an ego struggling to establish its sense of mastery.[3] Montaigne's pedagogical graffiti engender a rhetoric of conceit, a term which I use both in its etymological and secondary significations: conceptualization, taking hold of, and vanity.[4] Indeed, the crucial epistemological challenge of how to know what we know includes within it a speculative response that portrays the writing process as a linguistic apprenticeship unveiling latent configurations of narcissism.

Montaigne's text transcribes unconscious fantasies through figures of the self within the rhetoric of the essay; like the text of the dream, the text of the essay is "articulated through secondary elaboration," an activity that displaces "the scriptural process of representation to the representation of the scriptural process."[5] The significance of Montaigne's pedagogical performance is less in the epistemological model that he proposes than in the choreographics of his desire. This compels us to consider the figural representation of the self as both the repression and the transformation of knowledge not totally conscious of itself. In short, the subject is symbolically figured by substitute objects that correspond to the unraveling of unconscious desires, ec-centric to the text's ostensible meaning.[6] Like the painter "qu'il eschappe par fois des traits de la main . . . surpassans sa conception et sa science" (p. 126), the essayist's self-image eludes him and private reflections become public knowledge; and yet this self turned "inside-out" renders total confusion an ontological impossibility. "Quel que je soye, je le veux estre ailleurs qu'en papier" (p. 764).

At the level of analysis, Montaigne ascribes a special function to his "suffisant lecteur" who "descouvre souvant ès escrits d'autruy des perfections autres que celles que l'autheur y a mises et apperceües, et y preste des sens et des visages plus riches" (p. 126). Montaigne's text suggests here the hermeneutic process in which the reader is engaged when he deciphers the content of the essay. Reading becomes a pedagogical adventure that yields new knowledge when the traces of the unconscious gain access to signifiers, those metaphoric barometers that are a source of blindness as well as of cognition. "Joint qu'à l'adventure ay-je quelque obligation particuliere à ne dire qu'à demy, à dire confusément, à dire discordamment" (p. 974). But the rhetorical analysis of the psychic processes that constitute the writing of conceit enables the reader to play out his assigned role as transcriber of Montaigne's fiction of desire. The reader becomes, in effect, the postmodernist figure of the archeologist whose narratological quest both elaborates and alters the lacunae within the essayist's very own story. "Il s'en trouvera tousjours en un coing quelque mot qui ne laisse pas d'estre bastant quoy qu'il soit serré" (p. 973).

The figure of the father and the birth of the text

Montaigne's anti-oratorical *exordium* to the essay "De l'institution des enfans" situates the text within the Ovidian tradition of the *Tristia* where the author is father of a poem which ostensibly becomes his child.[7] From the start, Montaigne portrays himself as a Father who paradoxically possesses – through the aberrant logic of fiction – the maternal capacity to reproduce. But this unnatural desire to give birth is capable only of engendering something of a monster. "Je ne vis jamais pere, pour teigneux ou bossé que fut son fils, qui laissast de l'avoüer" (p. 144).[8] Ironically the figure of the father reconstitutes itself on another level (the displaced version of an imagined other) and provisionally localizes the ontological dream to coincide with the son and shape a life in one's very own self-image. Paternity obliges the author to father a beginning to which he has but a metaphoric bond.

In a sense, Montaigne commits himself to the temptation to create a text that reflects the narcissistic satisfaction of self-conceptualization. He inevitably abandons the symbolic position of the powerful father and adapts the voice of one who lacks sufficient control over what he engenders. The essayist projects his weakness onto the figure of the son by depicting himself as a writer at work confessing his inability to take hold of his *conceptions*. The presentation of the authorial self ironically represents Montaigne's refusal to become author and assume the position of absolute authority which is indeed the place of the Father; the fathering of the text, however, forecloses on the priority of the father and underscores the abdication of mastery to which the essayist voluntarily submits himself:

Aussi moy, je voy, mieux que tout autre, que ce ne sont icy que resveries d'homme qui n'a gousté des sciences que la crouste premiere, en son enfance, et n'en a retenu qu'un general et informe visage; un peu de chaque chose, et rien du tout, à la Françoise.   (p. 144)

Montaigne opts for ignorance, the impulse to forget, which as Lacan suggests is a passion to resist knowledge.[9] And this cognitive repression, more than just a mere rewriting of the *topos* of self-depreciation, is but the inverse face of Montaigne's so-called reflexive lucidity. Accordingly, Montaigne's text proclaims the defectiveness of its epistemological ground, and yet it remains strikingly legislative in its adamant refusal of authority. "Ce sont icy mes humeurs et opinions; je les donne pour ce qui est en ma creance, non pour ce qui est à croire . . . Je n'ay point l'authorité d'estre creu, ny ne le desire, me sentant trop mal instruit pour instruire autruy" (p. 147). The montaignian text thus occludes the idealized consubstantiality between being and knowing, if we are to accept the fundamental premise that to know is to possess substantialized knowledge that operates under the guise of mastery. So Montaigne's pedagogue paradoxically becomes an anti-pedagogue who unwittingly declares the self-consciousness of that which he does not know. "Et n'est enfant des classes moyennes qui ne se puisse dire plus sçavant que moy, qui n'ay seulement pas dequoy l'examiner sur sa premier leçon, au moins selon icelle" (p. 144).

Not only does the book/child *topos* function, as Curtius suggests, as an example of the figure of writing as self-perpetuation, it also stands for the hyperkinetic energy characterizing the life of the signifier, a semination that is a seed spilled in vain "remplissant et versant sans cesse" (p. 144).[10] The son or the seed engendered by the Father is destined never to return to its embryonic stage or moment of insemination. One might, in fact, conceive of the text as the symbolic representation of a prodigal son, a textual procreation that departs in quest of an unattainable goal. Montaigne's *conceptions* seem to signify beyond what they could possibly designate since writing is wandering without end, an outward movement now reduced to the manifest destiny of an insatiable epistemological quest:

Mes conceptions et mon jugement ne marche qu'à tastons, chancelant, bronchant et chopant; et quand je suis allé le plus avant que je puis, si ne me suis-je aucunement satisfaict; je voy encore du païs au delà, mais d'une veuë trouble et en nuage, que je ne puis desmeler.　(p. 145)

Montaigne's essay thus begins with a wish to displace the singularity of authority, the need to carve out of language a filial *corpus* that represents a desperate affirmation of life through the inscription of temporality in the space of desire.

The essays are written in the shadow of a powerful, albeit

absent, other. And in that context Latin plays a symbolic role. Not only is it the language that bears the imprint of the Father (Montaigne's tutor was instructed to speak to the yet uncultivated child in no other language than Latin) but it is also the language of virile figures such as Cato and solid writers such as Plutarch and Seneca. "Les anciens me semblent plus pleins et plus roides" (p. 389).[11] The idealized other who is "pleinement homme" (the ideal "I") is contrasted with the inadequacy of the montaignian self ("sa defaillance") whose insufficient Gallic ideolect is "si exangues, si descharnées et si vuides de matiere et de sens" (p. 145). Montaigne's defensive posture is thus the product of both a linguistic and intertextual situation of writerly inferiority. The inadequacy of the vernacular "I" in relation to the Latin superego transcribes the narrative of the discovery of difference, that dominating image of a phallic other who exemplifies the rule of desire and functions as a source of alienation in the essayist:

s'il m'advient, comme il faict souvent, de rencontrer de fortune dans les bons autheurs ces mesmes lieux que j'ay entrepris de traiter . . . à me reconnoistre, au prix de ces gens là, si foible et si chetif, si poisant et si endormy, je me fay pitié ou desdain à moy mesmes . . . Aussi que j'ay cela . . . de connoistre l'extreme difference d'entre eux et moy.

(p. 145)

In practice Montaigne is unable to maintain self-sufficiency, since his protean writing traces out the image of an authorial self in endless pursuit of a textual anchor, a *langage plus ferme*. Latin, the language of manliness, becomes an idealized object and the source of secret pleasures surreptitiously pursued "à la desrobée gourmander ces livres" (p. 175).

Near the end of this essay, an interesting anecdote is recounted concerning Montaigne's student days at the Collège de Guyenne where he took particular delight in playing leading parts in Latin tragedies and in re-covering the texts of his "langue maternelle." This narrative detail seems to underscore one of the most significant tensions to emerge in the *Essais*. Montaigne's quest for consubstantiality is endlessly betrayed by the representation of an identity characterized by separation from the self. For the pleasure of acting at school leads him into subsequent dissimulative plays of identity and difference in which the subject is subordinated to the pleasures of the loved object to the point of ostensibly being absorbed by it. The text enacts here a scene in which the subject confronts a linguistic memory of the past and yet at the same time finds himself in an imaginary situation of otherness: "Mettray-je en compte cette faculté de mon enfance: une à asseurance de visage, et souplesse de voix et de geste, à m'appliquer aux rolles que j'entreprenois? Car, avant l'aage . . . j'ai soustenu les premiers personnages és tragedies latines" (p. 176). It is through the image-making apparatus of play, then, that Montaigne is able to attain a paradoxical freedom by confronting the ghost of the past through a language that articulates traces of paternity but never authentically projects a sense of "coming-into-being."[12]

In Montaigne's discussion of childhood in this essay the pleasures of the self are analeptically evoked in the pre-oedipal delights of the primary object of nurturance: the symbolic mother tongue of Latin. But if to speak Latin was to satisfy the desire of the Father, then the acquired appetite of the younger Montaigne for his furtive escapades into the paternal domain of bookish culture is but a symbolic enactment of the desire to introject the Father. The guilt-ridden appetite for the object of filial fantasizing is but the specular representation of Montaigne's libidinal attachment to the image of the Father. No doubt, the metaphors of appetite within the text translate the need for fiction to supplant reality and permit the essayist to enact a fantasy of transgression:

Le premier goust que j'eus aux livres, il me vient du plaisir des fables de la *Metamorphose* d'Ovide. Car, environ, l'aage de sept ou huict ans, je me desrobois de tout autre plaisir pour les lire; d'autant que cette langue estoit la mienne maternelle . . . Faisant semblant de n'en voir rien, il [Montaigne's tutor] aiguisoit ma faim, ne me laissant que à la desrobée gourmander ces livres.   (p. 175)

This retreat from the outer world to the realm of the imaginary transcribes a semiotic inversion whereby the child is able to resist the anticipated exigencies of the schoolmaster and lapse into more primitive reveries. This withdrawal into the world of magical thinking ironically provided him with the illusion of having abandoned the Law (the illusion of mastery) while at the same time still adhering to it.

A good part of "De l'institution des enfans" is devoted to the inevitable threats of unmastery and impotence. From the beginning the text transcribes the quest of the student–essayist as a linguistic apprenticeship if, in fact, we are to accept the Latin word for child (*infans > enfans*) inscribed in the title: one incapable of speaking. Montaigne's search for a language of his own moves from a gesture of reverence for his pre-history (the intertextual fathers) to one of aggression toward the loved object. Montaigne conceives of writing as a cathartic process of separation from idealized figures through which he may liberate himself from his literary forefathers and engender a book of his own. The essayist describes his *clinamen* from tradition as the imperative for self-definition. "Je ne dis les autres, sinon pour d'autant plus me dire" (p. 146). And scriptural warfare, although not yet an act of textual violence, expresses itself through a tempered deference to authority whereby the essayist can articulate only a fragment of what he wishes to say:

Si sçay-je bien combien audacieusement j'entreprens moy mesmes à tous coups de m'esgaler à mes larrecins, d'aller pair à pair quand et eux, non sans une temeraire esperance que je puisse tromper les yeux des juges à les discerner ... Et puis, je ne luitte point en gros ces vieux champions là, et corps à corps: c'est par reprinses, menues et legieres attaintes. Je ne m'y aheurte pas; je ne fay que les taster; et ne vais point tant comme je marchande d'aller. (p. 146)

The desire to displace the Father and to transform – through the genealogy of the word – his semination of the text into a disseminative act is realized on the level of writerly fantasy as the need to resist passivity and escape the debilitating effects that characterize the theological rule of paternal culture.

Throughout Montaigne's epistemological critique he reveals a preference for judgment rather than memory; acquired or pro-

63

mulgated knowledge ("the rule of Law") is unfavorably contrasted with the wisdom developed through the exercise of judgment. And the essayist insists that the ideal student must transform and digest knowledge rather than merely swallow it in the
crudest possible form: "il ne faut pas seulement loger chez soi, il
la [la science] faut espouser" (p. 177). As such, Montaigne's
essay teaches only insofar as it obviates the monolithic force of
knowledge. To be sure, the goal of learning, like that of writing,
is not merely to retrieve and venerate cultural models of the past.
Instead it is to reflect a new epistemological practice that is not
based on memorizing – "redire ce qu'on nous a dict" (p. 149) –
but on the process of the re-membering of old signs, a patricidal
gesture that is essentially a dis-figuration ("informe visage") of
"master" texts: "C'est tesmoignage de crudité et indigestion que
de regorger la viande comme on l'a avalée. L'estomac n'a pas
faict son operation s'il n'a faict changer la facon et la forme à ce
qu'on lui avoit donné à cuire" (p. 150). The process of introjection and assimilation is one that effaces the origin of knowledge
while sublating it into an object of flesh and blood. Montaigne
gives new life, a veritable re-naissance, to ancient texts in the
form of a reprieve that "esleve et enfle les parolles" (p. 851) of
the literary figures that he has devoured.

As this chapter strikingly reveals, knowledge is indeed a function of desire and operates as a figural symptom in which the
physiological is presented as a bridge to the psychological. Montaigne's text undergoes a series of tropological substitutions that
activate the passage from *bios* to *logos,* the biological representation of the symbolic. In this context, William Kerrigan points
out that Renaissance physicians in the tradition of Galen organized all physiology on the model of digestion.[13] And in Freud
the concept under which the ego develops is anatomical in
nature. Accordingly desire, as it is represented in this essay, is
translated through images of nutrition and nurturing, digestion
and incorporation. Appetite functions as a mediator between
inside and outside and reveals the libidinal nature of Montaigne's
desiring energy. The initiation to the *corpus* (the great works of
antiquity) becomes a form of sublimated desire that reduces

learning to a form of carnal knowledge. "Le premier *goust* que j'eus aux livres . . . il n'y a tel que d'allécher l'appétit et l'affection" (pp. 175, 177). Tasting the text – "gouster les choses, les choisir et discerner d'elle meme" – is a metonymic figure of the reading process through which desire is directed towards that obscure object of interpretation. The pleasure that the student–essayist seeks is realized through the incorporation of knowledge within the body, the introjection or the drinking in of the external object.[14] "Il fault qu'il emboive leurs humeurs, non qu'il aprenne leurs preceptes" (p. 150). And the veritable objects of desire are bodies of knowledge which, like Plutarch's text, foreclose on the possibility of total satisfaction. "Il [Plutarch] ayme mieux nous laisser desir de soy que satiété" (p. 156). In the final analysis, then, the goal of desire must remain the refusal to saturate objects of knowledge and hypostatize them with meaning.

From a psychoanalytical standpoint, the metaphors of consumption in Montaigne's essay allegorize the symbolic relationship that the subject maintains with the absent, albeit omnipotent, father. We already know that in Quintilian, as Terence Cave points out, the images of nature represent the process whereby transference functions as a regenerative process.[15] But on another level the thematics of incorporation is a gesture of mourning that traces out the figural passage of the ego from self-conception to conceit or narcissism.

In Montaigne's adaptation of the Horatian image of the bee that makes honey, the text represents the *innutrition* metaphor of learning and writing as an organic process of metamorphosis.[16] Like the pollen that the bee gathers, the act of writing is conceived as a process of gathering, a weaving together of disparate fragments in which the intertexts themselves undergo a renewal and birth through the dynamics of cross-fertilization. The body of the Father is subsumed by the word of the writer and ultimately becomes the body of the son, a paradoxical *corpus* in which the paternal body continues to be invisibly present in a transubstantiated form: "Les abeilles pillotent deçà delà les fleurs, mais elles en font après le miel, qui est tout leur; ce n'est plus thin ny marjolaine: ainsi les pieces empruntées d'autruy, il les transformera et confondera, pour en faire un ouvrage tout sien" (pp. 150–1). The self that emerges from this metaphoric description of individuality is produced by a form of cannibalism, the anatomical correlate of eating the other which, in effect, engenders an imaginary re-citation of Father in the opacity of the text: "qu'il cele tout ce dequoy il a esté secouru, et ne produise que ce qu'il en a faict" (p. 151).

Freud's *Mourning and Melancholia* has drawn our attention to the inextricable relationship between ego formation and the loss of a loved object.[17] Now we know that the wound inflicted on the subject due to the disappearance of idealized models of virility (such as the Father and La Boétie) characterize Montaigne's self-portrait, and this can be read, as Derrida suggests, as a sign of mourning for the irretrievable loss of the name of the Father, one's "word thing."[18] Freud situates introjection within an oedipal context as a process emanating from primitive fantasies of cannibalistic incorporation, and as a defense against destruction and loss. But the introjection he describes, as Karl Abraham points out, defines itself by a certain ambivalence toward the loved object.[19] To return to the Horatian intertext – in the context of Montaigne's essay – is not only to become aware of the equivocal relationship that the textual unconscious establishes with the abandoned object, it also permits us to understand better the unequivocal satisfaction derived from an uncanny assertion of self. Here a remark of Richard Regosin is pertinent. He tells us that "Montaigne's use of *confondre* as synonymous with *transformer* communicates a sense of . . . negation for it retained into the 16th century its medieval meaning of 'destroy' as well as that of 'mix' and 'blend.' "[20] In a sense, Montaigne's "reader's digest" not only provides the locus for the projection of the missing signifier but also involves the subject's revenge or violence against the object it has lost. If the activity of mourning is realized at the level of the *logos* and "the shadow of the lost object falls back upon the ego," then the relentless self-depreciation that characterizes the rhetoric of Montaigne's self-portrait is but a scornful attack on the degraded product of an object that is devoured, destroyed, and expelled: those *crotesques* (p. 181) and *excremens d'un vieil esprit* (p. 923).[21] Thus the story of the birth of the book is both a representation of filial imperfection (the deformed end-product of an ingested paternal *corpus*) and a defense against loss (the retention of the desired object in another form). Narcissism results from a naive form of self-love that in itself is a specular reflexion of the text's very own sense of insufficiency. "Non pourtant, s'il n'est du tout enyvré de cet'affection, qu'il ne s'aperçoive de sa defaillance; mais tant y a qu'il est sien" (p. 144).[22]

The gender of the text

Throughout "De l'institution des enfans" the text appears to juxtapose essentialized notions of both the masculine and the feminine. This play on sexual difference is articulated by references to the conventional male/female dichotomy that structures the metaphorical discourses of love and war. In this light, writing functions as the semiotic gauge of sexual difference by ascribing to rhetoric anatomical features that define social roles and behavior. Without question, Montaigne seeks to valorize the language of Plutarch and Seneca as models of virility, toughness, and repression of emotion with which he contrasts the effeminate writing associated with Ciceronian rhetoric. The language of masculinity elevates the substance of rhetoric and projects the image of a muscular body:

Le parler que j'ayme c'est ... un parler succulent et nerveux, court et serré, (c) non tant delicat et peigné comme vehement et brusque ... plustost difficile qu'ennuieux, esloingné d'affectation, desreglé, descousu et hardy, chaque lopin y face son corps; non pedantesque, non fratesque, non pleideresque, mais plustost soldatesque.   (p. 171)

If the self-portrait is mediated by figures of the body, as I have delineated elsewhere, then Montaigne's text recognizes in this symbolic image of an idealized masculine language an inverse image of the essayist.[23] "L'esprit, je l'avois lent ... l'apprehension tardive, l'invention lasche ... aussi n'avoit la mienne autre

67

vice que langueur et paresse" (pp. 174–5). The image of being "si foible et si chetif, si poisant et si endormy" suggests a state of passivity and serves to describe a sense of "lack" in opposition to the order prescribed by the aesthetics of the masculine. But what I shall argue is that the work of language that the essay traces out in its quest for filial authorship reveals a bitextuality or the traces of the feminine in the masculine mode. This phenomenon is directly related to the apparent unwillingness to accept oedipalization (the refusal of desire) and the need to remain cathected onto a figure of female nurturance who inspires love for knowledge more by "affection" than by "reverence." More importantly, the struggle for individuality is one of liberation from virile models of representation through the travesties or shadows ("ombrages") of female desire. Here Lacan's philological examination of the notion of separation is quite pertinent:

Separare, to separate – I would point out at once the equivocation of the *se parare,* of the *se parer,* in all the fluctuating meanings it has in French. It means not only to dress oneself, but also to defend oneself, to provide oneself with what one needs to be on one's guard, and I will go still further . . . to the *se parere,* the *s'engendrer,* the to be engendered which is involved here.[24]

Montaigne's rhetoric of conceit inscribes the biographical sense of alterity, the figure of a man "writing in drag" who leaves an unmistakable mark of indecision on a textual *corpus* forever in search of self-definition. The essayist's "conceptions informes" are "sur le point de l'enfanter . . . leur travail n'est point à l'accouchement, (c) mais à la conception" (pp. 168–9). The *corpus* (the text) that transcribes figures of the self adorns itself (*se pare*) in the equivocal garb of those two androgynous heroines, the Bradamante and Angelica of Ariosto's *Orlando Furioso* and thus delineates identity in terms of the enigma of sexuality.[25]

The pedagogical model that Montaigne formulates is destined for a male student who must "roidir l'ame" and "roidir les muscles" (p. 152). But instead of having his student adhere exclusively to the phallocentric code of masculinity, the figures in

68

the text project the image of a student whose sexuality is unquestionably nurtured by the power of a female assimilated into a male body. Not only must the learning process be characterized by vigor and strength, it must also be associated with ease and pleasure so that virtue may become a metonymy of philosophy (love of wisdom). "Combien leurs classes seroient plus decemment jonchées de fleurs et de feuilles que de tronçons d'osier sanglants!" (p. 165).[26] By transforming philosophy into an anthropomorphic figure, an actor of writing who "a pour son but la vertu," the montaignian text disfigures the traditional face of virtue: *virtu*, the essential masculine quality to be demonstrated in life rather than in writing.[27] In activating this metamorphosis, the text transcribes the sexual indecision of Montaigne's pedagogical imperative. The essay thus disassociates virtue from the masculine ideology of the heroic by inscribing the figures of sexuality in the text within a metonymic confusion of gender.[28] Virtue is situated in an eroticized textual space occupied by an archetypal seductive female: "cette vertu supreme, belle, triumfante, amoureuse, délicieuse, pareillement et courageuse" (p. 161). And the lesson of virtue is taught at the site of pleasure from which a self emerges that is anything but autonomous. Like Socrates, who "quitte à escient sa force" (p. 161) in order to come into contact with virtue, the ideal student must also abandon his strength and direct all his desires toward a fantasmatic object of maternal nurturance, "la mere nourrice des plaisirs humains" (p. 161). This feminizing effect produces a subject whose instability and self-dissipation projects an image of both gentleness and ecstasy (from the Greek "to put out of place"): "pour glisser [the subject] en la naïveté et aisance de son progrez" (p. 161).

It is significant, therefore, that within the context of these remarks the text enacts a passage from the essayist's very own sense of insufficiency (the awareness of not being significantly male enough) to an anticipated image of a renewed, although sexually ambiguous, notion of strength – "riche et puissante et sçavante, et coucher dans des matelats musquez (p. 162) – transcribed by a man "incapable de se rendre à la force et violence" (p. 176). If the quest for pleasure is regarded as being quintessentially female, then Montaigne's text attempts to revise what it is to be a man, for the male who chooses love and desire is no less masculine. In this context one detail is particularly relevant in the rapport between self-definition and sexual difference. We are told that when the pupil comes of age and a choice in love is offered him, his tutor "jugera masle son amour mesme, s'il choisit tout diversement à cet effeminé pasteur de Phrygie" (p. 161). The text establishes new limits here on what is conceived as being manly. In judging his pupil "masle," even if he chooses other than that "effeminate shepherd," the tutor will, according to the text, break down the dichotomy between love and ambition so that being a man is re-conceptualized beyond the boundaries of these essentialized categories. The reference to Paris is, of course, to that mythological figure incarnating weakness and inconstancy before the seductive forces of desire. The effeminate shepherd who chose Aphrodite (the fairest woman) sacrificed the ambition to become lord of Europe and Asia as well as the possible victory over the Greeks. The text recognizes in this bookish image of the past a reflection of Montaigne's inclination to be "lurré tousjours par la douceur de subject" (p. 175). Indeed Paris's refusal to repress desire and acquiescence to a homogenized view of manliness depicts the prejudice of the writing subject as a textual effect moralized by an exemplary anecdotal mirror. Here the power of repression and the kinetic energy of eros unite and inscribe themselves in a defensive posture that puts forward the hypothesis that desire can be just as anxiety-producing as either reason or ambition. "Les Dieux ont mis plustost la sueur aux advenues des cabinetz de Venus que de Pallas" (p. 161).

If "virtue allies herself with nature," as Lapp suggests, it is indeed to defend the so-called naturalness of this androgynous figure of beauty, a textual excrescence born rather "de l'acointance des muses que de l'acointance de [sa] femme" (p. 383).[29] This artificial creation, a synecdochic cross-dressing of a composite ideal, embodies a figure of womanly strength whose lesson in moderation sustains the exigencies of pleasure in both appetite and breath. "Retranchant ceux qu'elle refuse, elle nous aiguise envers ceux qu'elle nous laisse; et nous laisse abondamment tous ceux que veut nature, et jusques à la satiété, maternellement" (p. 161). Like the intellectual eros that links Socrates to his students, the essayist appears to be attracted to the poetic essence of femininity while remaining subject to the holder of the Law. Perhaps the oxymoronic structure of the Montaignian admonition to treat the model student with "severe douceur" (p. 165) is nothing other than an emblem of the unresolved tension between the masculine and the feminine, a sign of ambivalence within the textual subject.

5

MONTAIGNE'S FAMILY ROMANCE

Perhaps more than any other essay, Montaigne's "De l'affection des Peres aux enfans" (II, 8) delineates a myth concerning the origins of the creative act and strikingly prefigures Freud's 1909 essay "Family Romances."[1] In that paper Freud discusses the "works of fiction" that the child creates to free himself from the authority of his parents; he constructs a fictive genealogy in which the biological parents are replaced by imaginary figures of "higher birth." To be sure, the enactment of the family romance does not stem exclusively from estrangement from one's parents; it is the phantasmatic fulfillment of wishes as a correction or antidote to the infelicities of actual life. If, as Freud claims, these fantasies are enacted at a time when "one doubts the incomparable and unique qualities" attributed to one's parents, it is in an attempt to salvage the theoretical fiction of parental perfection and omnipotence through the imaginative activity associated with pre-oedipal bliss.[2]

What is striking about Montaigne's family romance is its inverted structure. The narrative does not recount the child's fantasy about his parents, but rather the parental fantasy about the engendering of the child. Although Freud does not discuss a genre of family romance emanating from the parental perspective, such a genre does, however, seem appropriate for a writer whose linguistic apprenticeship produces a scriptural offspring that is a self-projection. The text is essentially a reflective object in which the essayist can affectionately contemplate the figuration of his self-image and admire his "unique" qualities in "le seul livre au monde de son espece" (p. 364c); the invention of the child is but an imitation of the parental figure functioning as an act of unmitigated affection. To write the fiction of the self as other is thus merely an inverse way of inventing the fiction of one's origin in the specular image of the text, or what Erasmus terms *mentis imago pictura, pictura sive speculum animi.*[3] Montaigne becomes both the subject and object of his creation, and as such the representation of the self is dependent upon the narcissism that Lacan equated with the Imaginary; he speaks as if he were reading the writing of his birth as an act of love produced only by virtue of his giving.[4] In a way, then, Montaigne transforms the writing of the text into a life-giving force that weighs both aesthetic and moral questions.

In Montaigne's family romance the essayist enacts a fantasy of parentage in which the act of writing is a substitute for copulation, a corrective measure that reshapes the world according to the essayist's satisfaction.[5] The birth of the subject as it is represented by the text is an immaculate one. Montaigne's text elaborates a mode of reproduction belonging to civilization and art, not one associated with women and the body. As in the Freudian model, the plot of Montaigne's family romance creates something more perfect and noble than nature itself since it attempts to transcend the limitations of biological law. In essence, art is regarded as capable of producing offspring that are quintessentially superior to those engendered by the body. By fictionalizing the origins of the self, life becomes an artistic construction that reshapes what is lacking in reality. This creation of a child of the mind is an exemplary gesture of affection which, in one of its etymological meanings derived from the Latin *afficere,* signifies to act upon, to dispose, and to constitute.[6] The writing of the book is indeed an act of love which links the essayist to a discursive object that has the status of myth. The generative act is an exercise of the mind aimed at repairing the deficiencies of life and demonstrating that the other in the text is only a figure of language simulating the real. "Tout ouvrier [aime] mieux son ouvrage qu'il n'en seroit aimé, si l'ouvrage avoit du sentiment" (p. 366c). But what in fact are these deficiencies of life?

Michel Butor and other critics have maintained that the loss of

La Boétie for Montaigne as intimate and perfect friend stimulated a writing project that permitted the essayist to compensate for this absence by transforming loss into a dialogic project.[7] La Boétie was more than a symbol of friendship for Montaigne; he represented, as a letter to his father revealed, that obscure object of desire, an exemplary figure of linguistic nurturance who bestowed on the essayist a literary vocation. On his deathbed, La Boétie proclaimed to Montaigne: "Je vous supplie pour signal de mon *affection* envers vous, vouloir estre successeur de ma Bibliothecque & de mes livres, que je vous donne: present bien petit, mais qui de bon cueur: & qui vous est convenable pour *l'affection* que vous avez aux lettres" (p. 1352). If the gift of the book is indeed a quintessential sign of affection then the writing of the essay in its turn is an "acting out" of this legacy of friendship.

Privé de l'ami le plus doux, le plus cher et le plus intime, et tel que notre siècle n'en a vu de meilleur, de plus docte, de plus agréable et de plus parfait, Michel de Montaigne, voulant consacrer le souvenir de ce mutuel amour par un témoignage unique de sa reconnaissance, et ne pouvant le faire de manière qui l'exprimât mieux, a voué à cette mémoire ce studieux appareil dont il fait ses délices.
(Inscription in Montaigne's library, "Chronologie de Montaigne," pp. xvi–xvii)

Language therefore gives shape to the voice of bereavement and functions as a symbolic reenactment of La Boétie's will, a repetition of the amorous act itself, realized through the dynamics of reading and writing. This gesture of affection is but a re-presentation of the gift of the book as a catalyzer of desire, and accordingly situates the affective experience of loss in an attempted mastery of language. As I have attempted to demonstrate in another context, the friendship between Montaigne and La Boétie was linguistically fated and the proper name became the object through which that sacred union, the mystical joining together of the souls, took place and symbolically assumed the idea of affection.[8] "(c) Nous nous cherchions avant que de nous estre veus, et par des rapports que nous oyïons l'un de l'autre, qui faisoient en nostre affection plus d'effort que ne porte la raison des rapports, je croy par quelque ordonnance du ciel: nous nous embrassions par noz noms" (p. 187). In a sense, then, Montaigne and La Boétie are copies of one another; they become an exemplary model of friendship and bestow their names upon it.

Melancholy pervades the *Essais* and is a symptom of the mourning accomplished at the level of the language.[9] The subject who dons the cloak of sorrow finds himself in a situation in which the object he has lost becomes the cause of his desire in a quest that is indeed endless. Because of the beloved's absence, the figuration of the ego transcribes, as Freud would have put it, a state of deprivation, "poor, empty ... behaving like an open wound ... totally impoverished."[10] The melancholic subject, as portrayed by Montaigne, is therefore not only one who is divorced from the affairs of the world, isolated, and living in solitude, but is also the victim of a spiritual malaise plagued by "phantasmes" and "ombres" which set the very work in motion.[11] "(a) C'est une humeur melancolique, et une humeur par consequent très ennemie de ma complexion naturelle, produite par le chagrin de la solitude en laquelle il y a quelques années que je m'estoy jetté, qui m'a mis premierement en este cette resverie de me mesler d'escrire" (p. 364). The affective disorder that the text describes can only be overcome through the work of mourning which in itself might constitute a form of bliss that no longer corresponds to anything seemingly tangible. The essay ostensibly re-presents the order of being of the other and suggests that the writing of amorous discourse might be an appropriate substitute for an original presence. "Est-ce pas un pieux et plaisant office de ma vie, d'en faire à tout jamais les obsèques? Est-il jouyssance qui vaille cette privation?" (note 2 to p. 376, ed. 1595).

The question of narcissism is intimately bound up with the workings of mourning and melancholia as Freud and others have claimed, often taking the form of a regression from narcissistic object choice to pure narcissism.[12] By identifying himself with the abandoned object, "the melancholic," Freud wrote, "permitted the shadow of that object to fall back upon the ego."[13] If the object no longer corresponds to anything in reality,

76

and this phenomenon is translated in the text by obsessive images of emptiness, then the writing subject must find a substitute object capable of reconstituting the lost unity of symbiotic love in which "[nos ames] se meslent et confondent l'une en l'autre, d'un melange si universel, qu'elles effacent et ne retrouvent plus la couture qui les jointes" (p. 186). The melancholic retreat into narcissism permits Montaigne to transfer the bond between himself and La Boétie into a bond between writer and text and thereby encrypt the deceased in the "monumen des muses." The text is transformed into an object worthy of attention with the will of the essayist determining its outcome; the figure Montaigne creates is rendered living. "(a) Et puis, me trovant entierement despourveu et vuide de toute autre matiere, je me suis presenté moy-mesme à moy, pour argument et pour subject . . . ayant à m'y pourtraire au vif" (p. 364).

The inscription of the narcissistic body in the text functions as the ground from which all the re-creative activities of the mind take shape. The writing of the essays is therefore an attempt to recuperate "(a) une parfaite et entiere communication" (p. 376) or what Cicero termed *est . . . tanquam alter idem* (*De Amicitia,* XXI); and this can only be accomplished in a fictional mirror in which poetic composition is allegorized as a sharing so complete that it fuses its partners into a synthetic communion of souls that mimetically reproduces the ephemeral. What I am suggesting here is that the representation of the self as "argument and subject" constitutes an effort to endure the anxiety of separation and triumph over the nothingness of death through the narcissistic illusion of giving life to art; melancholy plays a decisive role in the generation of a book in which the essayist's inclination for the imaginary substitutes fiction for reality and allows "resveries" to fill the virgin space of writing.[14] The body forged in the text transcribes a subject in whom the movement of desire is but a re-presentation of the self in literary performance. "(c) Parquoy chascun est aucunement en son ouvrage" (p. 366). To present oneself to oneself reveals a self-nurturing textuality created from an initial dual unity and which expresses, in its course, the problematics of giving and receiving as implied in the succession of generations. By willing the self-portrait, Montaigne is able to maintain the life-giving force that the other can no longer provide through the dispossession of the self's riches and its transference onto a scriptural space where the work fashions the workman's narcissistic object-choice. The gift of the book as self-abandonment exemplifies the very notion of writing as inheritance and consecrates the essay as the *locus* of counter investment.

At the core of Montaigne's essay is the Aristotelian *topos* which suggests that after the instinct for self-preservation the love of parents for children is the most powerful of all natural laws.[15] The idealized parental image is characterized not only by an unselfish tenderness, but also by a sustained process of nurturing that serves children's needs; the act of giving situates the parent in a completely self-satisfying love relation which furnishes him with constant gratification. The power of affection that the engenderer bears for that which he has engendered represents an exceptional universal.

(a) S'il y a quelque loy vrayement naturelle, c'est à dire quelque instinct qui si voye universellement et perpetuellement empreinct aux bestes et en nous ... je puis dire, à mon advis, qu'après le soing que chasque animal a de sa conservation et de fuir ce qui nuit, l'affection que l'engendrant porte à son engeance tient le second lieu en ce rang ... (c) Joint cette autre consideration Aristotelique, que celuy qui bien faict à quelcun, l'aime mieux qu'il n'est aime, et celui à qui il est deu, aime mieus que celui qui doibt.   (pp. 365–6)

If it is better to give than to receive, it is because "qui bien faict, exerce une action belle et honneste" (p. 366). The ideal parent, so it seems, has no interest of its own other than the unequivocal pleasures of the will.

However, the essay proceeds otherwise; it problematizes the very notion of natural affection as pure instinct by declaring that it must be tempered with judgment and reason. "(a) Puisqu'il a pleu à Dieu nous doüer de quelque capacité de discours, affin que, comme les bestes, nous ne fussions pas servilement assujectis aux lois communes ... nous devons bien prester un peu à la simple authorité de nature, mais non pas nous laisser tyrranniquement emporter à elle; la seule raison doit avoir la conduite de nos inclinations" (p. 366). That which is foreign to nature becomes an example of what Jean Starobinski, following the humanist tradition of the Renaissance, terms the *dignitas hominis*; and it can only attain such a status through the machinations of the will.[16] Indeed, nature must be improved upon and reason and judgment fulfill that function as a line of defense against the potential deficiencies of instinct. This activity corresponds to the desire for mastery as an antidote to the vicissitudes of nature. "D'autant que nous avons cher, estre; elle consiste en mouvement et action" (p. 366). What is ironic here is the essay's tendency to pervert unequivocally the myth of perfection attributed to the biological family of origins. In essence, love for one's child must be substantially regulated otherwise the symbolic legacy of affection risks disassociating the potential beneficiary from the natural bond that it maintains with the child's progenitor. "(a) Une vraye affection et bien reglée devroit naistre et s'augmenter avec la connoissance qu'ils nous donnent d'eux; et lors, s'ils le valent, la propension naturelle marchant quant et la raison, les cherir d'une amitié vrayment paternelle" (p. 366).

The dangers of the patriarchal order and its inclination for excessive control are examined in relation to growing children and inheritance practices. Quite clearly, parents who manifest jealousy as their children grow into adulthood forbid them to share in family prosperity and attempt to maintain filial affection by withholding what is significantly theirs. Unlike Natalie Davis, who reads this essay from the perspective of a cultural historian, in terms of the notarial acts and family documents which underlie it, I contend that Montaigne's strategy here is to use these texts metaphorically to focus on the question of money as a representation of the parental economy of desire.[17] If the text refers to *testaments* and *donations entre vifs* it is in order to examine the fictions concerning the power of the will as mediator of affection, and the potential tyranny it can engender by ascribing to it the rule of law.

79

Montaigne's text puts forward the hypothesis that cruelty and rigor of avarice lead to the child's potential depravity because of excessive control, and this strikingly reveals that innate parental benevolence is anything but universal.

(a) Quant à moy, je trouve que c'est cruauté et injustice de ne les recevoir au partage et société de nos biens, et compaignons en l'intelligence de nos affaires domestiques quand ils ne sont capables ... C'est injustice de voir qu'un pere vieil, cassé et demi-mort, jouysse seul, à un coin du foyer, des biens qui suffiroient à l'avancement et entretien de plusieurs enfans ... Un pere est bien miserable, que ne tient l'affection de ses enfans que par le besoin qu'ils ont de son secours, si cela se doit nommer affection. Il faut se rendre respectable par sa vertu et par sa suffisance, et aymable par sa bonté et douceur de ses meurs. (pp. 367–8)

Speaking from the elocutionary position of the moralizing son, Montaigne extols paternity here as a medium of exchange which, like the gift of the book, has the potential to pass on wisdom to one's offspring; he is deeply suspicious of the worshipers of money who have no respect for true values and whose affective bonds are rooted in a bankrupt economy of desire that transcends the rhythm of temporality.[18]

If the gift of money is to play a substantive role in the semiotics of affection, it must exceed the status of self-contained property and possession and in exchange represent an economic principle of substitution and transference which enables the great chain of being to progress. The intersubjective relationship that the montaignian text transcribes forbids the begetter to become the oppressor of the begotten through violence and force. In place of the authoritarian patriarch, the essay invents the corrective image of a nurturing, reasonable father who subscribes to "l'usage du pais" in matters of inheritance. In terms of paternal affection, the text challenges the potential establishment of a prohibitive agency. It projects the image of a *pater familias* who no longer bars access to a naturally sought filial satisfaction by willing property as a living gift; the truly nurturant father refuses the unmitigated control associated with the male world of patriarchial law and order. Imagining himself as Father, Montaigne declares that he too would do everything in his power to flee the despot within him. "Quand je pourroy me faire craindre, j'aimeroy encore mieux me faire aymer" (p. 373). Accordingly, the narrative insistently returns to the latent hypothesis that the destiny of the family plot is, in a sense, a matter of aesthetic choice; it is more a function of artfulness than it is a question of natural disposition.

(a) La plus belle des actions de l'Empereur Charles cinquiesme fut celle-là (c) à l'imitation d'aucuns anciens de son calibre, (a) d'avoir sçeu reconnoistre que la raison nous commande assez de nous dépouiller, quand nos robes nous chargent et empeschent; et de nous coucher, quand les jambes nous faillent. Il resigna ses moyens, grandeur et puissance à son fils, lorsqu'il sentit defaillir en soy la fermeté et la force pour conduire les affaires avec la gloire qu'il y avoit acquise.   (pp. 370–1)

While examining the dangers of excessive control, this essay offers instead the image of the gift through which the text simultaneously inscribes both the idealization of the father and the symbolic idea of his very decline. The economic metaphor demonstrates that power can not only corrupt affection, but that the recirculation of property as inheritance functions as a transaction that conflates love and commodity and transcends the image of the withdrawn and distant father.

The authority of Montaigne's narrative derives from its capacity to evoke the dream of giving and receiving in which generations become interchangeable with one another, and which like the "parfaite et entiere communication" (p. 376) of friendship surrenders affectivity to the other. To be sure, the non-transmission of fatherly love has obvious links with the distribution of power in the fantasized plot of paternal imperfection since the silence of the father perpetuates the myth of masculine strength, a phenomenon produced more by fear than by love; it is a male defense against the threat of union and the dissolution of the self through fusion with the other. To this effect, Montaigne narrates the story of the Marshal of Monluc who, having lost his son before he reached manhood, laments the fact that he never communicated his love to him. If men exercise power by means of silence, it is only through the transmission and the sharing of the word that affection can indeed be realized.

(a) Feu Monsieur le Mareschal de Monluc, ayant perdu son filz . . . me faisoit fort valoir . . . le desplaisir et creve-coeur qu'il sentoit de ne s'estre jamais communiqué à luy . . . de luy declarer l'extreme amitié qu'il luy portoit et le digne jugement qu'il faisoit de sa vertu . . . [and he would say] A qui gardoy-je à découvrir cette singuliere affection que je luy portoy dans mon ame? . . . qu'il ne me peut avoir portee autre que bien froide, n'ayant jamais reçeu de moy que rudesse, ny senti qu'une facon tyrannique. (pp. 375–6)

The linguistic circulation that Montaigne proposes not only establishes a bond of nurturance between father and son, but also raises important questions concerning the illusory power of male gender identity through which filial desire is kept alive through need by the withholding of the desired object (the word) of the Father. However, the real power, the power to terminate the affective absence of the Father, can only be realized at the very moment when language and love intersect in a rare moment of joy as the alienated offspring is able to (re)cognize what is excluded from the impersonal authority of phallocentric cognition. Ironically, the failure to legitimize the law can be seen as the father's failure to become affectionate and transcend the conventional boundaries of the omnipotent and awe-inspiring male. Patriarchal control is but a performance necessitated by an inability to engage in the commerce of pleasure. "(a) Estoit-ce pas luy [the son] qui en devoit avoir tout le plaisir et toute l'obligation? Je me suis contraint et geiné pour maintenir ce vain masque; et y ay perdu le plaisir de sa conversation, et sa volonté quant et quant" (p. 376).

Although this essay is dedicated to the widowed Madame d'Estissac who Montaigne praises as a paragon of maternal affection and undaunted custodian of the conduct of her family's affairs, the text paradoxically reveals the inherent weaknesses of women in matters of judgment, particularly as executor of wills.[19] Unlike fathers who have the potential to correct their natural deficiencies through the use of reason, mothers are victims of a natural hysteria that prevents them from ever dominating their irrational impulses.

(a) Il est dangereux de laisser à leur jugement la dispensation de nostre

82

succession, selon le chois qu'elles feront des enfans, qui est à tous les coups inique et fantastique. Car cet appetit desreglé et goust malade qu'elles ont au temps de leurs groisses, elles l'ont en l'ame en tout temps ... car, n'ayant point assez de force de discours pour choisir et embrasser ce qui le vaut, elles se laissent plus volontiers aller ou les impressions de nature sont plus seules.   (p. 379)

If the will of the mother is capricious and therefore unpredictable, we are led to believe, at least initially, that women still possess an innate maternal instinct which inevitably draws them into a nurturing relationship. "Il me semble, je ne sçay comment, qu'en toutes facons la maistrise n'est aucunement deuë aux femmes sur des hommes, sauf la maternelle et naturelle, si ce n'est pour le chatiment de ceux qui, par quelque humeur fievreuse, se sont volontairement soubmis à elles" (p. 379a). Montaigne locates our perception of gender in terms of authority which fosters maternal power in a private world where the symbiotic bond acts as a cognitive barometer whose true potency is measured by the fusion of sensuality and sentiment. Like animals, whose affection is overdetermined by instinctive drives, mothers, "n'ont cognoissance de leurs petits, que pendant qu'ils tiennent à leur mamelle" (p. 379).

But the so-called "female mastery" in question constitutes no real sense of mastery at all. "Il est aisé à voir par experience que cette affection naturelle, à qui nous donnons tant d'authorité a les racines bien foibles" (pp. 379–80). Montaigne's text quite unambiguously damages here the image of instinctive maternal nurturance through the exemplary case of wet-nurses who willingly abandon their own children to mercenary nurses so as to nourish someone else's for money. By choosing to focus on the breast as symbolic object, the idealized mother–child relationship is demystified and replaced by what he terms "un'affection bastarde" (p. 380), a socially conditioned maternity that is not the agent of its own destiny.

(a) Pour un fort legier profit, nous arrachons tous les jours leurs propres enfans d'entre les bras des meres, et leur faisons prendre les nostres en charge; nous leur faisons abandonner les leurs à quelque chetive nourrisse à qui nous ne voulons pas commettre les nostres, ou à quelque chevre: leur defandant non seulement de les alaiter, quelque dangier qu'ils en puissent encourir, mais encore d'en avoir aucun soin, pour s'employer du tout au service des nostres. Et voit on, en la plus part d'entre elles, s'engendrer bien tost par accoustumance un'affection bastarde, plus vehemente que la naturelle, et plus grande sollicitude de la conservation des enfans empruntez que des leurs propres. (p. 380a)

The narrative transforms the maternal body into an object of submission that circulates between families for the perpetuation of culture with the breast functioning as the synecdochical representation of motherly affection. Montaigne questions the authority of the devotion of the biological mother and replaces it with an artificial replicant – the wet-nurse – whose bond of nurturance is described as being somewhat "unnatural," based as it is on habit and convention. The female figure is portrayed as one who does not express desire, but who functions instead according to the demands of an alien otherness rooted in an artificial object choice. What is most striking here is the apparent ease with which the mother is forcibly separated from the natural child, and with it the essay suggests a weak bond and perhaps an indifference to one's biological progeny. The negative image associated with the practice of wet-nursing was indeed propagated by moralists and physicians of the Renaissance who adhered to the arguments put forth by the second-century rhetorician, Aulus Gellius in *Noctes Atticae* (Book xii).[20] But what is at stake here in the practice of wet-nursing is more than the traditional concern for preserving the mother's health. The symbolic withdrawal of the breast from the natural child reveals an underlying male ambivalence about the power of affection emanating from the maternal body and the necessity of the single mother–infant relationship.[21]

When Montaigne evokes the instincts associated with the female body, it is because he is concerned with portraying the mother as a disinterested object of service not necessarily motivated by love. Following the psychoanalytical assumptions outlined by Melanie Klein, one could conceivably argue that the representation of the female body is a projection of the essayist's fantasy of it; only by acknowledging the imaginary power of the

84

breast can we finally understand the origins of both our desire and our ambivalence for it.[22] In a way, the essay damages the maternal image at the very *locus* of its symbolic value. Indeed, the life-giving environment that the wet-nurse supplies does not foster affection but rather denies the child the pleasure derived from the satisfaction of love. By demonstrating that maternal affection has very weak roots, the text suggests that nurturance may only be related to survival, and that the fantasized union with the mother is but a simulacrum of a natural but elusive love. The child's desire for nurturance can be satisfied through reflexive conditioning and need not depend upon the affection commonly associated with human attachment.

(a) Et ce que j'ay parlé des chevres, c'est d'autant qu'il est ordinaire autour de chez moy de voir les femmes de vilage, lors qu'elles ne peuvent nourrir les enfans de leur mamelles, appeller des chevres à leur secours . . . Ces chevres sont incontinant duites à venir alaitter ces petits enfans, reconoissent leur voix quand ils crient, et y accourent: si on leur presente un autre que leur nourrisson, elles le refusent; et l'enfant en faict de mesme d'une autre chevre . . . Les bestes alterent et abastardissent aussi aiséement que nous l'affection naturelle.   (p. 380)

While the child needs the maternal response in order to develop, he can ostensibly do so independently of the bond of affection. In short, the biological and the mechanical coalesce and become the very substance necessary for the satisfaction initiated through the repetition of desire.

Thus, throughout the essay, it appears that natural affection becomes increasingly problematized due to the innate deficiencies of the biological family. Not only must nature be supplemented by reason in order to assure paternal affection but, far more importantly, it is described as having a very weak foundation in terms of maternal love. As for the latter, the female body is represented in an equivocal way by revealing that object relations might just be more than the mere spectacle of a helpless infancy devoid of love. To be sure, the lack of affection derived from one's natural parents demands the symbolic repositioning of desire. As we shall see, the birth of the montaignian essay functions, in part, as a reparative gesture according to which art remodels and perfects the inadequacies of nature and life into a sublimated version of a lacking desire (true love); in place of the primal scene, the text constructs a fictional scenario of fulfillment. Once the natural object relations have been devalued, the text invents a surrogate object of nurturance and an idealized bond of affection. It constitutes itself as a work of art and an act of love which, according to Melanie Klein, is a recreation of the maternal body or a rediscovery in fantasy of the mother whom he "has lost actually or in his feelings."[23] In essence, then, the essay will have to create a more perfect relationship as a method of defense against the anxieties of nature.

To reach this end, Montaigne constructs a fiction of reproduction in which there is a stronger bond created with the children of the mind than with their biological counterpart. It is more worthy to show affection for one's spiritual progeny since the soul – the invisible mover of desire – is the highest part of man and more representative of him.

(a) Or, à considerer cette simple occasion d'aymer nos enfans pour les avoir engendrez, pour laquelle nous les appellons autres nous mesme, il semble qu'il y ait bien une autre production venant de nous, qui ne soit pas de moindre recommandation: car ce que nous engendrons par l'ame, les enfantemens de nostre esprit, de nostre courage et suffisance, sont produicts par une plus noble partie que la corporelle, et sont plus nostres. (p. 380)

By privileging the intellectual, the text puts forward a fantasy of engendering, a fictive genealogy which, through a generational inversion of the Freudian family romance, replaces biological offspring with those of a more noble birth; the progenitor's imagination becomes engaged in the task of finding an alternative to the biological parents of whom he has a less than perfect image. What matters above all else is love for one's work, which ironically engenders more passion in the Christian Saint Augustin and the pagan poet Virgil than do the natural drives of the *furor erotica*. Following a tradition that dates back to Aristotle's *Nicomachian Ethics,* the poet dotes on his works as if they were his children; he establishes a correspondence between the object of representation and the affective experience of beauty, one

86

which can only be generated by the energy of love. "(a) Il est peu d'hommes adonez à la poësie, qui ne se gratifiassent plus d'estre peres de *l'Eneide* que du plus beau garçon de Rome, et qui ne souffrissent plus aiséement l'une perte que l'autre" (p. 383a). Love's art is therefore an intellectual endeavor; it ennobles the generative act in such a way that it distances the creative from the carnal and effaces the memory of earthly origin. "Ceux cy [the children of the mind] nous coustent bien plus cher, et nous apportent plus d'honeur, s'ils ont quelque chose de bon" (pp. 380–1).

In this essay Montaigne becomes the progenitor of the text; he assumes the role of a hermaphroditic desexualized *persona* whose nurturing capacities are exemplary. The narrator speaks in a collective voice in an attempt to dramatize the power of this theoretical fiction in which maternity has been absorbed into the spiritual paternity of the affectionate writer. "Nous sommes pere et mere ensemble en cette generation" (p. 380a). In becoming both father and mother of his creation Montaigne embraces both power and authority, but he rejects the way in which gender is split under patriarchy and thereby links creativity and nurturance to productivity in the public domain. However, if sexual difference seems abandoned here it is because the author would have us believe that aesthetic production – the writing of the book – is a way to master it.

Montaigne thus invents a composite primal figure to generate his book, an origin of identity that is free of the determinants of procreation. In essence, he opts for an idealized state of omnipotence in which perfection is made possible by the refusal of separation and sexual difference. This artificial fusion incarnates perhaps "l'estrangeté . . . et la nouvelleté, qui ont accoustumé de donner pris aux choses" (p. 364) and consequently enables the essayist to realize an illusion of omnipotence based on a narcissistic drive.

The child of the mind figured in the book is constituted through a process of identification with images of the other as self and images of the self as other. Accordingly, the book is but the product of a desire that activates a repetition of the original in an effort to master the world. The text transcribes a rhetorical doubling; self and other are bound by the excessive love of the progenitor for his own work, which ostensibly functions as a form of narcissism. Indeed, love engenders art, and it is presented as affording the child, through the power of the word, the greatest potential for maintaining its relationship to the place of its origin of being. "Car la valeur de nos autres enfans [those of the body] est beaucoup plus leur que nostre; la part que nous y avons est bien legiere, mais de ceux cy [those of the mind] toute la beauté, toute la grace et pris est nostre. Par ainsin, ils nous representent et nous rapportent bien plus vivement que les autres" (p. 381). This act of self-duplication is an attempt to create something more real than nature itself and prefigures Montaigne's subsequent declaration (in "Sur des vers de Virgile" [III, 5]) that the writing process is the cause of imaginary fabulations which render fiction more potent than reality. "(b) Venus n'est pas si belle toute nue, et vive, et haletante, comme elle est icy chez Virgile" (p. 826). Quite clearly, the figure that Montaigne creates comes to life by willing onto the represented object the characteristics of the model whose real subject matter is the act of writing and whose creation is its own author. "Je l'eusse faict meilleur ailleurs, mais l'ouvrage eust esté moins mien; et sa fin principale et perfection, c'est d'estre exactement mien ... me represente-je pas vivement? ... J'ay faict ce que j'ay voulu: tout le monde me reconnoit en mon livre, et mon livre en moy" (p. 853).

Thus, reproduction is essentially imitation with a difference since it creates the illusion of giving life to an inanimate object through an intellectual act in which the essayist continues to mirror himself. In effect, the text unveils an apparent hesitance in the degree of pleasure derived from the conflict between the aesthetic and the biological. "(b) Et je ne sçay si je n'aimerois pas mieux beaucoup en avoir produict ung [a child], parfaictement bien forme, de l'acointance des muses, que de l'acointance de ma femme" (p. 383). However, to be able "to represent and report oneself more to life" (p. 381) in writing through the coupling of the artist and the muse not only implies that art is more authentic and perfect than reality, but also that the discourse of identity is marked by a rhetoric predicated on the realm of the imaginary. If Montaigne attributes the worth of "nos autres enfans" [our biological children] more to them than to their progenitors, it is because what has been created aesthetically has been crafted more in his own image than would otherwise be the case. Yet, the wish for a more perfect representation of self in other must remain a fiction (*fictum,* made up object) because the represented other can only be a mere approximation of a narcissistic subject whose body is transfigured in the text.[24]

The dialectic between the natural and the aesthetic is perhaps most poignantly delineated in the clausal reference to Ovid's *Metamorphoses* (XI, 11, 261–98) where Montaigne utilizes the Pygmalion myth to demonstrate how the power of love makes art come alive.[25] In Ovid's narrative, when the sculptor feels the stone under his fingers soften the narcissist fuses the aesthetic with the erotic and is overcome with unmitigated pleasure. In showing female life in its exemplary form, Pygmalion has produced an exquisite work of art in which desire enacts a fantasy of omnipotence; the aesthetic experience is so strong that the Gods enable art to be transformed into life.

Et, quant à ces passions vitieuses et furieuses qui ont eschauffé quelque fois les pere à l'amour de leurs filles, ou les mere envers leurs fils, encore s'en trouve il de pareilles en cette autre sorte de parenté; tesmoing ce que l'on recite de Pygmalion, qui, ayant basty une statue de femme de beauté singuliere, il devint si éperduement espris de l'amour forcené de ce sien ouvrage, qu'il falut qu'en faveur de sa rage les dieux la luy vivifiassent, Tentatum mollescit ebur, positóque rigore/Subsedit digitis.
OVID   (p. 383)

It is therefore not surprising that in this essay, sometimes considered to be Montaigne's most explicitly misogynistic, the love of Pygmalion for Galatea plays such an exemplary part in the creative process. In its mythological context Pygmalion was a woman-hater who resolved never to marry but who created, nevertheless, an "excellent statue" in the idealized form of a perfect woman designed to show men the deficiencies of the kind they had to tolerate. In the apparent shift of emphasis from

biological to spiritual procreation, the role of the body is, however, not excluded altogether; it is but a product of the imagination, a symbolic reworking of nature destined for the use of man.
Not only has Pygmalion engendered life, he has created it in the
form of a pliable and responsive other. But if the extreme degree
of affection associated with incest enters the picture here, it is
because artistic procreation is but a tool in the drive for narcissistic fulfillment; the statue of the female body that Pygmalion
creates out of stone is a mere re-presentation of the order of
being of an artist who reshapes the world according to his own
needs.[26] In a sense, the statue constitutes the female body from
which Pygmalion metaphorically emerges and with which he falls
in love. Analogously, just as Pygmalion's self is mediated by the
stone of the statue, Montaigne finds his self-expression in the
transubstantiated form of the essay, the mirror in which he
inscribes the (re)figuration of his very being as a mode of desire.

If, as Roland Barthes claims, the writer is someone who plays
with the mother's body, then the attempt to reproduce oneself in
the text can be regarded as a reparative gesture, a redemptive
duplication of the primal bond, not only in terms of the mother–
child relationship, but with respect to the entire family
romance.[27] The tendency of progenitor and offspring to fuse
somewhat with one another dissipates the ambivalence of parental love and ironically demonstrates that the bond of affection
becomes more authentic in creative endeavors which are sublimated versions of the gift of nurturance. However, this blurring
of boundaries between parent and child is only made possible by
a loss of control, comparable in intensity to incest, and which
paradoxically transforms the identification with the child to a
libidinal investment in it. "(c) Car, selon Aristote, de tous les
ouvriers, le poëte nomméement est le plus amoureux de son
ouvrage" (p. 383). If to love is to write, then the creation of the
essay is indeed the equivalent of the sexualizing gaze of the
narcissist who, as in the case of Pygmalion's passion, can metaphorically transform words into flesh and thereby realize a fantasy of incest; the artist's other is indeed the prize he seeks in the
amorous quest for erotic attachment. Montaigne's family

romance is therefore rooted in the refusal to abandon the perfection and omnipotence associated with the bliss of attachment derived from presenting "moy-mesmes à moy, pour argument et pour subject" (p. 364).

To the very end, Montaigne's text maintains a tension between the self and his spiritual other, the child of the mind, and to such a degree that one could characterize the transitional quality of the offspring state as neither completely separate from nor united with the other; the book is seen as both containing and withholding the self.[28] The text assimilates the knowledge that its wise progenitor is presumed to have had and thereby becomes a transitional *locus* suffused with the freedom to become; there is a progressive effacing of the parent through the emergence of the figure of the child in a space that acts as an epistemological receptacle capable of merging the affective with the cognitive. Ironically, the so-called activity of self-creation is to be achieved through a process that borders on a form of self-alienation.

(c) A cettuy cy, tel qu'il est, ce que je donne, je le donne purement et irrevocablement, comme on donne aux enfans corporels; ce peu de bien que je luy ay faict, il n'est plus en ma disposition; il peut sçavoir assez de choses que je ne sçay plus, et tenir de moy ce que je n'ay point retenu et qu'il faudroit que, tout ainsi qu'un estranger, j'empruntasse de luy, si besoin m'en venoit. Il est plus riche que moy, si je suis plus sage que luy.
(p. 383)

To give purely and irrevocably to the child of the mind is to liberate it symbolically from phallic authority and to create an externalized otherness functioning as a projection of the fantasy of separation. But the separation in question here, however illusory it may be, is not one based on oedipalization since the progenitor of the text appears to relinquish the very notion of absolute authority. If the generator of the essay has figuratively become a "stranger" in relation to the book, it is because he sees in it an image of otherness that "holds from the subject what he no longer retains" and yet permits the object of nurturance to become a reservoir of riches through which poetic composition takes shape. "Je n'ay pas plus faict mon livre que mon livre m'a faict" (p. 648). The child who masters the parent's desire is but a mere reflection of its creator's sense of mastery. Unquestionably, this figuration transcribes a dialectical process of giving and borrowing back, a phenomenon that incarnates the essaying act as *philautia* and which produces the re-naissance of the author fashioned in the image of its creator. Montaigne wishes to create the illusion that "to write" is a transitive verb and that birth is indeed produced as a gift of writing; it is indeed an immortal creation which in turn deifies its progenitor. "(c) Platon adjouste que ce sont icy des enfans immortels [the children of the mind] qui immortalisent leurs peres, voire et les deïfient, comme à Lycurgus, à Solon, à Minos" (p. 381).

Like La Boétie's gift of his library, "d'une si amoureuse recommandation," Montaigne's gift of the book can be interpreted, as Natalie Davis suggests, as an example of the Augustinian notion of *caritas,* a metaphor for the succession of generations and the inevitable loss of parental control.[29] Yet, on another level, this desire to promote virtue in others, the legacy of the book, is but a recirculation of the self in language, a phenomenon which reenacts the symbolic inheritance from La Boétie in the form of an exemplary bond of nurturance – a work of art – generated by the family romance. The attempt to render a substitute for the lost friend simply adds yet another substitute, an exemplary parental figure whose act of dispossession, like that of La Boétie, catalyzes the generative force which gives birth to the book. Montaigne's *donation entre vifs* is thus a narcissistic gesture, an imaginary narrative of self-creation that has as its goal "aucune fin, que domestique et privée" (*Au lecteur*, p. 9) and which constitutes for the essayist a way to defend himself against death by transforming the text into a living will, a "monumens des Muses" (p. 381) destined for posterity.[30] "Je l'ay voué [my book] à la commodité particuliere de mes parens et amis: à ce que m'ayant perdu (ce qu'ils ont à faire bien tost) ils y puisent retrouver aucuns traits de mes conditions et humeurs, et que par ce moyen ils nourrissent plus entiere et plus vifve la connoissance qu'ils ont eu de moy" (p. 9).

Part II

FIGURES OF THE BODY

A. DISFIGURING THE FEMININE

6

ARCHITECTURE OF THE UTOPIAN BODY: THE *BLASONS* OF MAROT AND RONSARD

The Renaissance genre of the *blason anatomique* constructs an architecture of love derived from the morphology of the female body.[1] This architecture of the body produces a poetics of detail: the construction is composed of fragmentary elements organized in enumerative groups. The image of the woman is represented by a series of part objects whose variety imposes an anatomically fragmented representation. In most cases the poet's *encomium,* ironic or not, is addressed to those parts of the body that are most noble according to Ficinian doctrine (eyes, ears, eyebrows), or to those considered most sensual within the satiric tradition (breasts, genitals, buttocks, thighs).[2] The *blasonneur's* work is that of a *homo faber,* reducing the female body to strokes of the pen through the creation of a textual pointillism invoking precious metals as well as more prosaic objects. The text functions as a descriptive catalogue; it imitates, and indeed becomes, a construction, one that reveals, through its mass of words, the hand of a poet–architect. The *blasonneur* becomes the virtuoso of a corporeal rhetoric which translates the sublime joy of a writing project, producing a series of verbal monuments dedicated to becoming privileged *loci* of physical celebration.[3]

In the *blason anatomique* the female body becomes consubstantial with the body of writing; the representation of the woman depicts that of the poet's imaginary projection of the reality of his desire onto an object that is narcissistically subjectivized. "Le langage n'est pas immatériel," Lacan maintains, "il est corps subtil, mais il est corps. Les mots sont pris dans toutes les images corporelles qui captivent le sujet."[4] If the body is to be found in words, it is because it is a means of signification constituted in language itself. The poetic *blason* is thus the articulation of man's discourse on woman's body. Indeed, bodily representation, realized in the scriptural space onto which the effects of the subject's desire is portrayed, is disclosed as a consequence of the masculine gaze on the represented object.

My aim here is to analyze not only the architecture of the utopian body, but also the text's underlying architecture that constructs the sexuality of the desiring subject and that of the object of his desire. The bodily metaphor is delineated by the desiring subject's fantasy relations to perceptible objects, determined by a particular type of drive. The transposition of the libido as instinctual energy into language reveals that the representation of the body functions as a reservoir of rhetorical fantasies, a point of intertextual recall from which stem all the investments of an ego positioned among a multiplicity of poetic pronouncements. Construction of the female body thus takes the form of a libidinal quest elaborating fictions that assimilate the representation of woman into that of poetic production. Although they make reference to an intertextual tradition, the physical objects inscribed in that text are in no way objective; they live only by virtue of their symbolic signification in a sphere in which the female body is broken up and fetishized by a voyeuristic masculine gaze.

If such an anatomical discourse represents a fragmented body behind which the feminine subject effectively disappears, it is because the *blasonneur* depicts both the violence of the subject's relation to a fetishized body and the sadism linked to the manipulation of textual material. The poet attempts to evoke the woman's presence by means of a text that manipulates the architecture of the body into a synecdochical collage of the desired object; idealization entails a fetishism of the object in the form of a succession of disjunctive images. If, as Roland Barthes suggests, the writer is one who "joue avec le corps de la mère . . . pour le glorifier, l'embellir, ou pour le dépercer," in turn the *blasonneur* expresses the joy and anguish of a subject faced with the body of the primal Mother.[5] The fetishized body captures the subject's sense of self while at the same time transforming the material of the text into a disfigured maternal body. "Material," from the Latin *materia,* includes within it the word *mater*; the female body as represented assumes the very form of the desire that generates it and transports it to the very limits of what is cognitively perceptible.

This fragmentation of the woman paradoxically lends itself to a blurring of the desired object because of its protean nature. In effect, the *blasonneur* is attracted by parts of the woman which the text represents as detachable and subject to multiple metamorphoses. Once fragmented, the female body paradoxically becomes the *locus* of a decentering of the object of desire which, in turn, creates an obstacle to the image of the body as totality. What is ostensibly symbolized here is a phenomenology of desire that entails a dismemberment of the female body, one that conjures up detached body parts or fetishized objects, whose wholeness is entirely phantasmatic. In the end, this distancing produces an imaginary anatomical representation essentially generated by a *lack.*

The architecture of the breast in Clément Marot's *blason* and *contreblason* reflects the aesthetic preoccupations of a particular literary culture. As V.-L. Saulnier has observed: "Ils suivent une tradition médiévale, celle du catalogue; une tradition littéraire, morale et decorative, celle des emblèmes."[6] Each of Marot's texts constitutes a rhetorical exercise in which the *blason* stands as monument of desire, situated between the name that the anatomical part designates and the litany of its positive and negative scriptural meanings. By virtue of the conventionality of the *blason*'s imagery, Marot's text transcribes an intertextual tradition that dates back to Coquillart's *Droits Nouveaux,* in which the poet describes both the beauty and ugliness of the breast.[7] This sort of binary opposition on a corporeal level imposes a dual symbolism whose nature changes according to the fantasized relations of the poet to the representational modes these objects take. If the "good" maternal images correspond to the plenitude associated with the ideal object, the "bad" accordingly must take on a repugnant quality.[8] The breast (the *blason* of the beautiful breast) and its double (the *contreblason*) together represent an object that is both highly sexualized and profoundly divided along aesthetic lines. On the one hand, praise of the desired object's perfection acts as a mechanism against the possibility of unhappiness; but on the other hand, the *contreblason* implies a disgust at seeing the object decay, which would seem to move the desiring subject to idealize the breast by lending it a whole and global nature: "Faisant d'un tetin de pucelle – tetin de femme entiere et belle."

Marot represents the image of the utopian breast as possessing a white, pink, and sensual form.[9] The development of this form suggests, through rhetorical figures of amplification, a hyperbole of desire. The text circles its physical object, makes the breast into an object of veneration, and celebrates a bodily ideal whose perfection is a synonym for beauty.

> Tetin refect, plus blanc qu'un œuf,
> Tetin de satin blanc tout neuf,
> Tout qui fais honte à la Rose,
> Tetin plus beau que nulle chose,
> Tetin dur, non pas Tetin, voyre,
> Mais petite boule d'Ivoyre,
> Au milieu duquel est assise
> Une Fraize ou une Cerise
> Que nul ne voit ne touche aussi,
> Mais je gage qu'il est ainsi;
> Tetin doncq au petit bout rouge,
> Tetin qui jamais ne se bouge,
> Soit pour venir, soit pour aller,
> Soit pour courir, soit pour baller;
> Tetin gaulche, Tetin mignon
> Tousjours loing de son compaignon.[10]

For mimetic reasons, the richness associated with this *topos* – the roundness and softness that date back to the *Salut d'amour du XIIIe siècle* – demands a language that must signify plenitude.[11] In this context, the repetition of the word *tetin* engenders an exhaustive collection of heterogeneous characteristics fas-

hioned out of references to intertextual material. What transpires here is the genesis of a verbal icon produced by a synco-
pated rhythm, one whose very essence signifies the strength and
endurance of the poem as construction. To be sure, the *poeta
faber*'s allusions to workmanship (the plastic image of the ivory
ball) along with details that reveal the architectural peculiarities
of manual creation (the strawberry sitting in the middle of the
breast), mark the triumph of craftsmanship over the natural.
Accordingly, the architecture of the breast represented in the
text imposes itself as a verbal mass, a *copia verborum* whose
proliferation of details mimetically reflects the artisan-like attention that links it to the aesthetic.

Marot rewrites various clichés derived from the medieval
tradition ranging from Guillaume de Lorris to Gratien du Pont,
and seeks to animate them through the creation of an erotic
language; he unveils the figure of the female breast only to assign
to it the function of awakening forbidden desire. The desiring
subject's erotic investment situates him in terms of sexual difference, and at the same time identifies the speech act with sexualization and gender. Accordingly, the breast becomes an object of
narcissistic beauty that paradoxically endows the male figure
with the power to impregnate the woman and transform her into
an ideal maternal object.

> Tetin qui portes tesmoignage
> Du demourant du personnage;
> Quand on te voit, il vient à mainctz,
> Une envie dedans les mains
> De te taster, de te tenir:
> Mais il se fault bien contenir
> D'en approcher, bon gré, ma vie,
> Car il viendroit une autre envie.
> O Tetin, ne grand, ne petit,
> Tetin meur, Tetin d'appetit,
> Tetin qui nuict & jour criez:
> Mariez moy tost, mariez!
> Tetin qui t'enfles & repoulses
> Ton Gorgerin de deux bons poulses;
> A bon droict heureux on dira
> Celluy qui de laict t'emplira,

101

Faisant d'ung Tetin de pucelle,
Tetin de femme entiere & belle.

The breast functions as a partial sign of woman, a synecdochic representation of the female body, which simultaneously supplants the woman herself and yet ironically paves the way to a dream of wholeness. In effect, the text attributes the desired object's metamorphosis into a woman to the male's libidinal power to "fill the woman" (*d'emplir la femelle*), and in this manner allows the "virile" subject to appropriate the power of female biology. In a sense, gender roles are reversed here: man takes it upon himself to nourish the virgin (the *pucelle*), to fill her with milk, while at the same time assuming the capacity of according her the fullness associated with the "good" maternal image.

In the *contreblason,* Marot's text engages in a destructive spectacle generated by the ludic possibilities of a physical description dramatically foregrounding the poem's chiastic matter and manner in terms of the ideal. The figuration of erotic desire that had been revealed up to this point henceforth becomes problematic and is transformed into a writing activity that verges on a kind of perverse and sadistic pleasure.[12] Now represented as a maternal body that is depleted and "used up," the object correlative of the subject's desire (the *beau tetin*) changes into a veritable locus of abjection.[13] The breast becomes an object of putrefaction realized through a sort of lyricism that resembles what Freud termed "the cannibal feast of mania." The metaphoric associations suggested here introduce fantasies of destruction manifesting the impotence of Marot's writing to depict the female body otherwise than through the brutal annihilation produced by the written word. Indeed, the rewriting of the original *blason* emphasizes the violence that language perpetrates on the female body in forcing it into the realm of decay. Therefore the description contained in the *contreblason* not only signifies the death of erotic desire, but also constructs the architecture of a female figure who is henceforth represented as anatomically "empty."

Architecture of the utopian body

Tetin qui n'as rien que la peau,
Tetin flac, tetin de drappeau,
Grand'Tetine, longue Tetasse,
Tetin, doy-je dire: bezasse?
Tetin au grand vilain bout noir
Comme celuy d'ung Entonnoir,
Tetin qui brimballe à tous coups,
Sans estre esbranlé ne secoux.
Bien se peult vanter qui te taste
D'avoir mis la main à la paste.
Tetin grillé, Tetin pendant,
Tetin flestry, tetin rendant
Villaine bourbe en lieu de laict,
Le Diable te feit bien si laid!
Tetin pour trippe reputé,
Tetin, ce cuide je, emprunté
Ou desrobé en quelque sorte
De quelque vieille Chevre morte.
Tetin propre pour en Enfer
Nourrir l'enfant de Lucifer,
Tetin boyau long d'une Gaule,
Tetasse à jecter sur l'espaule
Pour faire (tout bien compassé)
Ung chapperon du temps passé.

This poetic celebration of ugliness depicts a playfully grotesque image of nature in decline; it defines woman by means of verbal disfigurations through which the poem acquires an immanent authorial agency appropriate to its representational mode.

As a result of this lyrical defacement, what remains of the figuration of the breast is the image of a "sack" (a *besace*) in which the beauty of fullness has been destroyed by the description of decay often associated with the figure of the aged and emaciated mother. This quintessentially "bad" object is now given over to the perverse pleasures of decomposition. The mother's breast has been refigured and endowed with all the details of anatomical decadence. The ugliness in question here is a limit and, more particularly, it represents a point beyond which the poem's rhetoric is performatively implicated in the decomposition that it reports.

Quand on te voit, il vient à maintz

103

Une envie dedans les mains
De te prendre avec des gans doubles,
Pour en donner cinq ou six couples
De souffletz sur le nez de celle
Qui te cache soubz son esselle.
Va, grand vilain Tetin puant,
Tu fourniroys bien en suant
De civettes & de parfuns
Pour faire cent mille defunctz.
Tetin de laydeur despiteuse,
Tetin dont Nature est honteuse,
Tetin des villains le plus brave,
Tetin dont le bout tousjous bave,
Tetin faict de poix & de glus,
Bren, ma plume n'en parlez plus!
Laissez-le là, ventre sainct George,
Vous me feriez rendre ma gorge.

The unpleasant and infelicitous nature of this image submits the plastic architecture of the utopian body to the formidable ravage exercised by the force of temporality. As a result, this visceral deformation renders the maternal body a living cadaver and thereby threatens the perfection of the oral object. In its realization, the power of abjection conveys, despite its ludic character, a disgust for the impure body, depicted as that of the intolerable old mother. This obsession with the body in decay is thus represented as the fantasy of a disfigured breast, a bodily architecture in ruins, animated by the destructive will of poetic mastery and revealed in the way the poem rhetorically unfolds.

The poets of the Pléïade did not take Marot's *Beau tetin* as the intertextual model for their descriptions of the female body, but rather worked with a tradition which extends from Petrarch to Ariosto. In Belleau's poetry, for example, the enumeration of female beauty constructs the portrait of a utopian body belonging to the realm of dreams. The elements of this architecture are represented by a series of anatomical monuments situated on the landscape of desire, a figural topography that grants the body a place in all its material density. Paraphrasing the biblical tradition associated with the *Song of Songs*, the description con-

104

veyed here through a series of erotic clichés, whose very nature goes beyond the constraints of Nature itself, enforces a strangely performative correspondence between text and architecture. The body becomes the site of an ideal geometry. Each image is part of a metaphoric field and thereby constitutes an architectural emblem that amplifies the desired object's total beauty. Yet at the same time, this process lends each separate element a life of its own as part of a material phenomenality whose ekphrastic movement transforms the imaginary work into an architectural performance.

> Ton nombril delicat, qui sert comme d'un centre
> Sur un arc arrondi, marque de ce beau ventre,
> Resemble à la rondeur d'un vase fait au tour,
> Tousjours plein de parfum & de flueurs à l'entour . . .
> Le petit mont jumeau de tes deux mammelettes
> Semblen deux petis Fans, qui parmi les fleurettes
> Folâtrement à l'envi. L'yvoire blanc & mol
> Qui flotte à menus plis par dessus ton beau col,
> Est semblable à la tour en rondeur eslevee,
> Toute d'yvoire blanc richement achevee . . .
> Le profil de ton nez est semblable à la Tour
> Assise au mont Liban, qui découvre à l'entour
> La ville de Damas & les champs de Syrie.[14]

Many of the Pléïade's *blasons anatomiques* that celebrate the beloved's beauty, based either on neo-Petrarchan models or on Ariosto's portraits of Alcina and Olympia, are characterized by an architecture of the *non-finito,* a phenomenon that reproduces mimetically an image of the body in movement. In Ronsard's sonnet "Ce beau coral, ce marbre qui souspire," for example, the juxtaposition of bodily images with groups of precious metals and stones implies a sense of physical fragmentation. The architecture of the body articulates a desired presence, a textual phantom, revealed through the poem's discursive breaks. The description of the woman's beauty takes shape through a series of discrete attributes that metaphorically elicit hunger and thirst. Derived from the activity of sensual contemplation, the desired object is represented as capable of arousing the imagination of the poet who sees her in a variety of forms. This visionary aesthetic allows the body to realize its libidinal potential and thereby to acquire a rhetorical density through the splitting of the female image. The figuration of the poet's desire is thus manifested by detachable parts of the anatomy that are subject to a metamorphosis into micro-portraits.

These visually iconic images of lips red as coral, stomach white as marble, ebony eyebrows, alabaster foreheads, and eyes that sparkle like sapphires presuppose the specular ideal conventionally deployed in Renaissance texts. The various elements which constitute this anatomical discourse construct a linguistic edifice held together by metaphors that implicitly evoke the penetration of art into the domain of the "real"; they create a specular mimetics that blurs the distinction between representation and that which it represents.

> Ce beau coral, ce marbre qui souspire,
> Et cest ébénne ornement d'un sourci,
> Et cest albastre en vouste racourci,
> Et ces zaphirs, ce jaspe, & ce porphyre,
> Ces diaments, ces rubis qu'un zephyre
> Tient animez d'un souspir adouci,
> Et ces oeilletz, & ces roses aussi,
> Et ce fin or, où l'or mesme se mire,
> Me sont au cuoeur en si profond esmoy,
> Qu'un autre object ne se présente à moy,
> Si non le beau de leur beau que j'adore,
> Et le plaisir qui ne se peult passer
> De les songer, penser, & repenser
> Songer, penser, & repenser encore.[15]

Yielding to the power of the male gaze, these physical images are transcribed through the movement of the imaginary which confers on the body a resonance capable of transforming it – "le plaisir ... de les songer, penser et repenser encore" – into a veritable object of contemplation. The image of the woman is not represented by a static portrait, but rather by the spectacle of heterogeneous characteristics manifested as a sum of movable parts. Desire as it is expressed in many of Ronsard's anatomical *blasons* is thus transcribed as movement, insofar as the mental activity of the architectural work in progress engenders multiple fantasies of the feminine ideal. Belonging to the universe of unstable matter and contingent effects, desire is depicted as repeatedly disengaging itself from its object of cathexis in order to construct new representations of the body and rediscover the woman whom he imagines as enslaved to the exigencies of his pleasure.

> Vous avez tant appasté mon desir,
>> Que pour souler la faim de son plaisir,
>> Et nuict & jour il fault qu'il vous revoye.
> Comme un oyseau, qui ne peult sejourner,
>> Sans revoler, tourner & retourner,
>> Aux bordz congneux pour y trouver sa proye.
>
> (p. 82)

Through its dynamic functioning, then, Ronsard's text registers a list of the part objects to which the subject is drawn, and in that process it embodies the architecture of the desired object by allowing the amorous subject to construct an imaginary order in whose image he has fashioned his own desire.

If the female body projects the image of fragmentation whose principal theme is one of absence, then Ronsard's sonnet "Petit nombril, que mon penser adore" suggests the lack from which the desiring subject suffers. In this context, the navel takes on a symbolic value that communicates to the lover what he does not have; it is the architectural "scar" inscribed on an anatomical surface, representing the rupture of the physical link to the mother from whom the self was formed. The amorous quest is thus motivated by the wound that imprints on the body of the woman the sign of separation, and with it comes the hope of a possible reunion. The amorous object becomes a metaphorical emblem evoking a divided self since the figure of the navel comes to signify the traces of a fragmented being uprooted from its anatomical vortex. The fantasy of androgyny alluded to here thus recalls the name of both sexes (andro[man]/gyny[woman]) in order to better evoke an ideal body from which nothing would ever be missing.

> Petit nombril, que mon penser adore,

Non pas mon œil, qui n'eut oncques ce bien,
Nombril de qui l'honneur merite bien,
Qu'une grand'ville on luy bastisse encore:
Signe divin, qui divinement ore
  Retiens encore l'Androgyne lien,
  Combien & toy, mon mignon, & combien
Tes flancs jumeaulx follastrement j'honore!

(pp. 45–6)

The *encomium* to the divine sign representing the *petit nombril* conveys a sense of nostalgia emanating from a loss rooted in a myth referring to the bliss of symbiotic relations. In its way, the desire to retain the "Androgyne lien" represents the quest for the maternal other who has caused the subject to be deprived of a sense of wholeness and totality. The lover is fascinated by the possibility of this regression which, from the perspective of the nostalgic lover, leads him to recognize the ecstatic joy that consecrates their union through the two halves of this composite ideal.

The representation of the navel as idealized *locus* is thus conceived in terms of a lost relationship, designating an anatomical rapport that is now ontologically deficient; it is determined by a negative *copia verborum* that succeeds in valorizing the edenic fusion of male and female by evoking the absence of magical power associated with other bodily parts. The anaphoric litany chanted here is interrupted by the phantasmatic hope of eventually joining with the other in order to reconstitute the architectural wholeness of the mutilated body. In its way, then, the dream of sexual pleasure paradoxically leads to the desire for wholeness and comfort as well as to a nostalgic quest to reconstruct the lost paradise of the primal dyad.

Ny ce beau chef, ny ces yeulx, ny ce front,
  Ny ce doulx ris; ny ceste main qui fond
  Mon cuoeur ne source, & de pleurs me fait riche,
Ne me sçauroyent de leur beau contenter,
  Sans esperer quelque foys de taster
  Ton paradis, où mon plaisir se niche.

If happiness is to be found, it is only at the point at which the navel becomes the object correlative of desire, the *locus amoenus* in which the amorous subject is engaged in the memory of prenatal life. The drive to find a "nest" reveals an empty space destined to be desired and perhaps once again occupied. The navel is therefore represented as a broken-off fragment, a bodily part flawed by its very detachment. As a result, the metonymic object of desire – the navel – incorporates a tactile fantasy destined to evoke an imaginary, or indeed utopian, wholeness through fusion with the female body. The amorous subject thus exists in the hope of renewing this symbolic sense of belonging that makes him "subject to love" while allowing him to invent the imaginary object that constitutes an architecture of ideal love.

In the sonnet "Madame se levoit au beau matin d'Esté," the Ronsardian text once again makes use of the *blason anatomique* and the *topos* of "due pome acerbe" derived from Ariosto; the poem transforms the Medusa myth into an allegory of the creative act that represents an architecture of the female body.[16] Rather than allowing for the decline associated with old age, the figure of the poet accedes to an aesthetic transcendence that guarantees the permanence of the beautiful and ephemeral female body.[17]

This sonnet represents Hélène's breast as an artistic object, an icon of female beauty, distinguished by its plastic form. Through repeated references to the noble materials of the sculptor (gold, ivory, porphyry, and marble), Ronsard's text describes two "pommes de beauté" that recall those belonging to the garden of the Hesperides in the *Greek Anthology*. But in this revised narrative context, the sonnet to Hélène focuses on what the sculptor Phidias created, and in so doing freezes his desire into an exemplary gesture.[18] Ronsard's amorous discourse enervates the female figure by reifying it in the form of a part object. The fetishized breast, turned into a monument of sorts, captures the ungraspable reality of physical beauty's ephemeral presence. The poet imagines himself as sculptor and dreams of the metamorphosis of flesh into eternal marble; the perceiving subject turns the object of his gaze into a reified image.

J'entre-vy dans son sein deux pommes de beauté,
Telles qu'on ne voit point au verger Hesperide:
Telles ne porte point la Deesse de Gnide,
Ny celle qui a Mars des siennes allaité.
   Telle enflure d'yvoire en sa voute arrondie,
Tel relief de Porphyre ouvrage de Phidie,
Eut Andromede alors que Persee passa,
   Quand il la vit liée à des roches marines,
Et quand la peur de mort tout le corps luy glassa,
Transformant ses tétins en deux boules marbrines.   (p. 417)

It appears, then, that the permanence of female beauty can only be conceptualized through images designating a body whose essence consists precisely of the deprivation of its existential being.

Whereas the classical myth speaks of Medusa's face and its deadly power of petrification, this poem is concerned with the stiffening of the female body as it is depicted in the figure of Hélène/Andromeda. But the deliverance by Ronsard–Perseus is surely an ironic salvation at best, since the statuary metamorphosis effected here produces a symbolic paralysis of the woman. The transformation accomplished by this act of love evokes an aesthetic "mastery" whose function is to stave off the fatality inscribed in the aging body; ironically, the poem dedicated to an idealized mistress-reader glorifies the master's art. Such, then, is the miracle of the creative act: it saves the female body from its own decline to make its architecture the object of a utopian gaze that paradoxically confers on it the immortality that is the result of an antimetamorphosis.

If this poem reveals the power that statuary material has in the semiotics of female representation, it marks all the more clearly the poet's desire to establish a symbolic link between writing and the sculptural as a way to memorialize his verbal art.

Donne moy l'encre, & le papier aussi
   En cent papiers tesmoingz de mon souci,
   Je veux tracer la peine que j'endure:
En cent papiers plus dures que diamant,
   A celle fin que la race future
   Juge du mal que je soufre en aymant.   (p. 122)

The woman's symbolic metamorphosis becomes the necessary condition for the birth of a writerly act that curiously converts life into art; the petrification of the woman emblematizes the narration that motivates it. The statuary symbol conveys the image of writing as the constructing of a poetic tombstone whose rhetorical power signifies the triumph over the movement of oblivion. Ironically, the re-membering of the female beauty reassures the poet's own fear of loss and shifts the emphasis from the desired object's body to the subject's poetic *corpus* and the fascination with his own representation.

The architecture of the utopian body is thus depicted as one of absence and fragmentation. Generated by a rhetoric that is based on the partial erasure of the desired object, the *blason anatomique* produces an amorous discourse that either distances itself from woman in her wholeness or demonstrates rather spectacularly that the relationship to the feminine operates through the representation of a woman whose vital, and indeed sexual, force may be destroyed. In any case, the female body is always conceptualized as being elsewhere; in its most idealized form it must remain an aesthetic creation resistant to the ravages of nature's pitiless temporality. The *blasonneur* thus evokes a fantasy based on nostalgia for what has been lost through a scriptural process producing aesthetic transcendence. As a result, the creative effort consists in constructing a utopian architecture of the body that goes beyond the constraints of reality and transforms the text into the privileged locus of the desirable.

7

FICTIONS OF THE BODY AND THE GENDER OF THE TEXT IN RONSARD'S 1552 *AMOURS*

In most classical analyses of Ronsard's *Amours* one encounters a certain critical reductiveness, the temptation to reduce the passion of the desiring subject to the Petrarchan dialectic of conquest and servitude. Although this assessment can undoubtedly be substantiated, it must certainly be nuanced by situating Ronsard's poetry within the framework of a discourse on sexuality. Let us begin with a basic hypothesis: the ronsardian text problematizes male sexuality; it takes the liberty of putting into question certain aspects of the so-called "masculinity" of the desiring subject in order to uncover the phallocentric masquerade that is inscribed in the text. If Ronsard disarms man and strips him of his power, it is because the fiction of amorous conquest is nothing more than a charade that dissimulates a profound sexual ambivalence. My reading of the ronsardian text does not deny the importance of cultural stereotypes such as those found, for example, in the intertextual traditions of Plato, Petrarch, Horace, and Ariosto; on the contrary, it aims to demonstrate how the inscription of the corporeal *topos* functions within poetic discourse (what codes are responsible for meaning) and creates fictions of the body in the symbolic tapestry of the text. And as in the case of dreams, this network is destined to constitute a corporeal object whose language is its subject in the ontological meaning of the term. If a narrative articulates nothing more than the absence of the subject in a text for which it acts as a substitute, it is because all love stories are defined, as Michel de Certeau claims, as a discourse articulated by bodies.[1]

The body of the fiction is thus the *locus* where fiction gives body to unconscious desire and discovers from it the corporeal fate of the poetic text.[2] Writing transcribes the drives of the body, the choreographics of desire that make fantasies speak through intertextual models that function as the backdrop to psychic *récits,* narratives in which the figural representation of the self is both the repression and transformation of knowledge.[3]

In the ronsardian text, writing is the dominant subject of the quest for self-knowledge – the questions of gender and sexual identity – to which the body provides a frame. The body of fiction in Ronsard serves not only to invent fictions of the body but also to assure the implicit representation of that which is apparently unknowable. The body is therefore seized as an epistemological object thanks to the speculative project that the fictional system of representation brings to it. Eros and love are mirrored in the text through the body, poetic figures that mediate the representation of masculine desire and map out the contours of its heuristic structure; the rhetoric of the body transcribes the speculative parameters of the textual unconscious since it becomes the *locus* of the body of the fiction.

I have chosen to analyze the *topos* of the body in Ronsard's love sonnets of 1552 because they project fictions of masculine desire that are essentially ambiguous. In order to elucidate this process it is necessary to delineate the relationships maintained between the desiring subject and the body of desire, as well as between the figure of the poet and the symbolic body of the other.[4] The field of the corporeal metaphor thus emanates from perceptible object relations which translate a very primitive bond between the desiring subject and the other. The transference of libido into language, through the kinetic drive which motivates the scriptural act, reveals that the figuration of the body functions as a reservoir of rhetorical fantasies. It is an object of intertextual recall from which emanate the representations of the loved self; the rhythms of the writing transcribe and formalize what the body unconsciously dictates. This self brings to the inscription of the bodily figure the symbolic value of the idea which makes way for a fiction of optical desire paradoxically

114

considered "real"; it incarnates as it celebrates the birth of the body, and is the wellspring for new narratives whose purpose is dis-covery.

> Telle qu'elle est, dedans ma souvenance
> Je la sen peinte, & sa bouche, & ses yeus . . .
> J'ai son portrait, que je suis plus aimant
> Que mon cœur mesme. O sainte portraiture . . .[5] (p. 131)

The visceral force of the imaginary thus enables one to decipher the script of desire as it is constituted through the pirouettes of an intertextual memory. In effect, the body is not simply thematized in Ronsard's text, but becomes instead the matter of the text, the flesh and bones of poetic creation which, as the text claims, enable the writing subject to "conçevoir les enfans par escrit" (p. 443).

In the sonnet "Ces liens d'or, ceste bouche vermeille," the sight of Cassandre's body functions as the generative and symbolic substance of the text. The rhythm of the desiring subject articulates through a song-like litany a whole series of synecdochical details, figures of fragmentation that take the form of a catalogue that inventories the features of ideal female beauty. By imitating the Petrarchan intertext and by following the tradition of the *blasonneurs,* the sonnet represents the female body as a scattered object, a fragmented body constituted by a fetishistic masculine desire.[6] If the female figure is represented here, it is reduced to the image of a detotalized body which paradoxically gives birth to amorous sentiment and forms its substance – the *corpus* of the body – by a beauty constituted through a list of details. The text unveils the desire to perfect nature and to create an aesthetic ideal assembled from fragments that inevitably suggest its antithetic corollary: integration through a rhetoric of proliferation.

> Ces liens d'or, ceste bouche vermeille . . .
> Ces mains, ce col, ce front & ceste oreille,
>> Et de ce sein les boutons verdeletz
>> Et de ces yeulx les astres jumeletz,
>> Qui font trembler les ames de merveille:
> Feirent nicher Amour dedans mon sein,

Qui gros de germe avoit le ventre plein,
D'oeufz non formez & de glaires nouvelles.
Et luy couvant (qui de mon cuœur jouit
Neuf mois entiers) en un jour m'eclouit
Mille amoureaux chargez de traits & d'aisles. (VI, p. 7)

What is striking from the very beginning of this sonnet is that the figure of the desiring subject submits itself to the enigma of femininity. The amorous text is supported by a *topos* borrowed from the pseudo-Anacreon of *The Greek Anthology* in which the myth of engendering is represented.[7] The allegorical figure of Love in the intertext is described as a force capable of building a nest of eggs within the bosom of the lover; the function of the breast is to hatch little metaphorical chicks:

You come, dear Swallow, with each Spring,
And build and stay awhile;
Each autumn sends you on the wing
To Memphis or the Nile
But Love, alas! within my breast
Hath got an ever-building nest;
And one chick's well-nigh fledged, and one
Unhatched, another's callow grown,
And gaping younglings ne'er give o'er
Their chirping infant cries, and more,
The lesser by the great are fed,
. . . What can I do? I can't away
With Love in multitudes.

The rewriting of this *topos* in Ronsard's text takes on markedly physiological and graphic features which permit the amorous subject to appropriate the feminine characteristics of engendering and fecundity. The mythological figure of Love in Ronsard's poem who penetrates man with "d'oeufz non formez et de glaires nouvelles" translates the erotic image of a subject sprinkled with the liquidity of the other, a phantasmatic form of reproduction that is realized in the paradoxical absence of woman. The insemination of the masculine body by the introjected figure of Love ("feirent nicher Amour dedans mon sein") engenders the feminine in man since the incorporation of an object (Love), born from the fragmented representation of the woman, creates an

116

imaginary identification between the subject and the desired object, the symbolic other; the imagined maternal body becomes the *locus* and the object correlative of a desire "qui de mon cuœur jouit neuf moins entiers." The awakening of amorous feelings is translated through the paradisal rhetoric of the transfigured body and astonishingly gives birth to the desire to be seduced.

By a curious metamorphosis the male body lends itself to the mythology of reproduction.[8] Impregnated with Love, the figure of the male is transformed into the generative machine of "mille amoureux chargez de traits et d'ailes" and thus becomes the welcoming procreative mother functioning in the service of fertility. The process of hatching makes possible the realization of an androgynous sexuality, half-animal, half-human, and already marked by the passive glee of an equivocal subject. If woman permits man to become acquainted with the pleasures of love through the power of her radiant beauty, it is indeed this same perverse power that feminizes man and robs him of his capacity to be an active subject. In this context the "I" becomes the privileged target of reproduction, a subject sustained by the warmth of Love ("Et luy couvant . . . m'eclouit"). The text reinvests male sexuality and submits it to the pleasures of the female body; this phenomenon is inscribed in the text through the figuration of an inexhaustible cycle of engendering which renders the desiring self a subject who has been penetrated in the name of the other (Love). If man runs the inevitable risk of being feminized, as Roland Barthes suggests in *Fragments d'un discours amoureux*, it is not because he is an invert, but rather because he is a victim of love and "tremble de merveille."[9]

On another level, however, the birth of the amorous text is realized through a fiction of reproduction, a sexual fantasy that is also a creative fantasy in which the amorous subject is represented both as a passive receiver and a metamorphic agent. The myth represented here displaces the phallic inseminative power of masculine desire and substitutes for it a desire of a different kind, characterized by the metaphorical proliferation of childbirths within the text. In this perspective, the Renaissance defini-

117

tion of the word "sein," *locus* of penetration in Ronsard's poem, is particularly noteworthy. In *A Dictionnaire of the French and English Tongues of 1611,* Randle Cotgrave defines it as "mind or internal thought."[10] Accordingly, the allegorical discourse of physical procreation in this text is augmented as the mind becomes increasingly infatuated with the idea of love. The text situates this "phantasmatic fornication" within the boundaries of a mind enclosed in a space mediated by the image of the textual body; the poet attaches to the figure of the self the still yet indeterminate seeds of thought and language which give an enveloping resonance to the body through the infinity of its own desire. "Il me faut donc aimer pour avoir bon esprit/Afin de concevoir des enfans par escrit/Pour allonger mon nom au depens de ma peine" (p. 443). To write, then, in the imaginary position of the procreative woman is scripturally to hatch the symbolic eggs of Love.[11] The representation of the corporeal figure transforms the intertextual *corpus* into the *locus* of birth through the process of writing, since every creation is indeed a hatching, a parturition, an engendering that mimetically reproduces the myth of birth. The images of reproduction in this poem – "nicher . . . dedans mon sein," "glaires nouvelles" (source of protein, thus a force of energy), "couver," and "faire eclore" – all refer to the generative force of writing, to the scriptural birth of metaphor, and to the possibilities of creation by a subject fertilized by the power of a lover's discourse that he shelters within his breast. The body of the fiction thus invents a fiction of the body which makes love proliferate through the jubilation associated with the writerly act.

The sonnet "Ces flotz jumeaultz de laict bien espoissi," allegorizes the mental swaying associated with desire and love; the poem constitutes a textual configuration that transcribes the erotic movement of the beautiful breast. Owing to its mediative function, this *topos* communicates the euphoric workings of the imaginary and its particular attachment to the idea of beauty through the representation of a landscape that can be anthropomorphized or feminized. Within this text the desired object, the female figure, surges forth and is reduced to the anatomical

118

features of a breast in nature whose "arabesques" trace out a libidinal ballet of desire. The sensuous bosom thus detaches itself from the female body and becomes the *locus* of nurturance emanating from a venerated object.

> Ces flots jumeaulx de laict bien espoissi,
> Vont & revont par leur blanche valée,
> Comme à son bord la marine salée
> Qui lente va, lente revient aussi.
> Une distance entre eulx se fait, ainsi:
> Qu'entre deux montz une sente esgalée,
> En toutz endroitz de neige devalée,
> Soubz un hyver doulcement adoulci. (CLXXXVII, p. 118)

If this poem transcribes the sensuality of movement and pleni-tude as I. D. McFarlane affirms, it is indeed because the staging of this corporeal landscape reproduces a rocking movement associated with dream and pleasure, realized through the ondu-lating rhythms of the text.[12] The figure of the breast furnishes the necessary sensations to generate the imaginary, the required stimulus to set the image into motion and transform it into a fantasy machine that blurs the line of demarcation between the landscape and the body; it also stimulates the erotic appetite of the desiring subject since this synedochical representation of the female body exists not to stifle libidinal energy but rather to arouse it. The discovery of this metaphorical sea within the parameters of the imaginary – "qui lente va, lente revient" – makes dormant fantasies melt (the "neige devalée and the "hyver doucement adoulci") and thus opens the text to the unfolding of desire. This expansive movement eventually slows down and demonstrates how sexuality produces fantasies whose rhythms caress the contours of the textual body by figures of doubling ("ces flots jumeaulx") and refrain ("vont . . . revont/va . . . revient"). The metamorphosis of the corporeal landscape thus emanates from the process of poetic movement and is realized in the "springtime of the imaginary" when the poet has embarked adrift with his fantasies, "quand en Hyver le vent s'est adouci" (1578).

The aquatic metaphors of waves and fluctuations ("ces flotz

jumeaulx") in the first two quatrains of the poem change direction in the last tercet and become those of spiritual elevation which ultimately suppress the body of the woman (the physical) and replace it by the body of the idea (the mental), a curious phenomenon which causes the text to undergo a process of purification and symbolically realize a fiction of the ideal. The anaphors which follow translate the movement of the elucidation of thought and at the same time strip the body of the fictions engendered by its ornaments of femininity. The power of this movement is such that it figuratively transcends earthly beauty and projects an idea depicted in the image of two mountains which, according to a variant of Ronsard's poem, represents and shelters the essence of perfection, the roundness from which all its other forms abound: "en la forme ronde gist la perfection qui toute en soy abonde."

> Là tout honneur, là toute grace abonde:
> Et la beaulté, si quelque'une est au monde,
> Vile au sejour de ce paradis.

The flight described in the last verse of the poem, and referred to by Henri Weber, leads the fiction of the body towards the realm of platonism, a visionary act whose goal is to wash away the sexual desire alluded to at the beginning of the poem by sublimating it in the beauty of the Idea.[13] The transcendence of desire gives birth to a more abstract form of beauty which turns away from the beauty that the fiction of the body produced. To be sure, the fading away of the eroticized women at the end of the poem may only be the result of the figural representation of a quest in which desire is capricious and finally submits itself to the force of platonic love.

In fact, the female body is lost in a performative incantation, a vast movement of affect that spiritualizes the corporeal fantasies first alluded to but which ultimately resists the representation of flesh by the verb. Woman is thus desexualized as the text becomes increasingly detached from the erotic in favor of more purely abstract and elusive images of female beauty. This unquestionable disappearance of material beauty and its flight towards spiritual elevation projects masculine desire onto the framework of a redefined notion of beauty. The scriptural act thus constitutes for the masculine subject both an asceticism and a sterilization of desire, a purifying aesthetics in quest of a truth that disintegrates the material form of the desired object. The figure of the poet frees itself from an eroticized body and substitutes for it an epistemological penetration that raises the writing subject to the level of transcendental knowledge.

In another sonnet which treats the *topos* of the beautiful female breast, "Ha seigneur, dieu, que de graces ecloses," the text derives from the transformation of two passages taken from Ariosto that constitute Alcina's portrait: "White snow is the lovely neck, and milk the breast, two unripened apples, green yet ivory, move to and fro like a wave."[14] The corporeal metaphor of "due pome acerbe" [two unripened apples] is inscribed within the descriptive system of the beautiful garden and becomes "deux gazons de lait," *locus amoenus* that assimilates the richness of the garden to that of the "sein verdelet." The figure of the breast "vert de lait" fecundates the desiring subject with the power of metamorphosis, a phenomenon which engenders an imaginary repetition of the constitution of the self and suggests that the appetite for pleasure is associated with a self-distancing.[15] In order to authenticate its desire the male subject therefore seeks identification through a fiction of otherness.

> Ha, seigneur dieu, que de graces écloses,
>   Dans le jardin de ce sein verdelet,
>   Enflent le rond de deus gazons de lait,
>   Où des Amours les fléches sont encloses!
> Je me transforme en cent metamorfoses,
>   Quand je te voi, petit mon jumelet.   (XLI, p. 27)

Ronsard's text enacts here a myth of seduction related to the ontological stripping away of the desiring subject. If the fiction of seduction permits Jupiter to be transformed into a bull in order to steal away with Europa, that of the poet, inspired by the neo-Latin and petrarchan traditions, reduces the masculine figure to the role of a flea in order that the object of desire – the breast – be riveted to, sucked, indeed bitten by the child–flea.[16]

S'Europe avoit l'estomac aussi beau
De t'estre fait, Jupiter, un toreau,
Je te pardonne. Hé, que ne sui-je puce!
La baisotant, tous les jours je mordroi
Ses beaus tétins, mais la nuit je voudroi
Que rechanger en homme je me pusse.

This attempt to diminish oneself by the metamorphosis of the flea into a disguised phallic power translates one of the paradoxes of amorous conquest. This insect signifies not only a figure of erotic titillation by its reference to an intertextual tradition (Virgil's *Culex*), but the parasitic relationship in question permits the desiring subject to nourish himself from the desired female object while veiling his masculinity. Male sexuality thus submits itself to a game of deceit, a masquerade that indulges in the freedom of metaphorization, a phenomenon animated by means of symbolic proxy.

In fact, this text thematizes the ambivalent relationship between man and the figure of femininity. The body of the woman is symbolically divided by the masculine perspective since man seeks to find the other in this body by transforming the mother into a whore; the object of nurturance must be disassociated from the object of pleasure. In daylight, the masculine figure disguised as a flea takes advantage of substantial forepleasure [*préjouissance*], an erotic child's play derived from libidinal attachment to the maternal object; the entire effort is in anticipation of a sought-after nocturnal masculine ecstasy. If the child–flea aims at becoming a man again at night, it is because the desire for woman situates him within a phantasmatic process of exchange that transforms the sought-after object into an object of pleasure while the self is represented as the captured other, indeed the veritable image of a divided lover. The expression "to become once again a man" ["rechanger en homme"] thus implies the attempt to attribute to oneself the image of an ideal masculine self which separates the subject from a more primitive self-image. If the amorous conquest is realized through dissimulation, male sexuality displays itself here fundamentally as a kind of ruse; the desire to seduce represented in the poem can only be

122

realized through the enactment of a fiction which may be recognized as the process of desire's inevitable displacement.

The mythology of amorous conquest is the subject of the sonnet "Je vouldroy bien richement jaunissant," where desire is transcribed through a spectacular contemplation envisioned by a self attached to the persona of Jupiter. The amorous subject does not pursue a person but rather an image invested with the generative power of metamorphosis. The text records an invisible transformation, an assimilation between the desiring subject and the female body. This phenomenon is translated by mytho-poetic metaphors belonging to three classical legends which define the desiring subject in this text in terms of continuously changing self-representations. Caught in the *trompe-l'œil* of writing, Jupiter is transformed into a shower of gold in order to seduce Danaë; he undergoes metamorphosis into a bull so that he may steal off with Europa who is described as innocently gathering flowers; and he would like to become a Narcissus who drowns himself in a fountain.[17]

From the beginning of the poem, the figure represented by Jupiter is that of the apparent conqueror of the female body. The contemplation evoked here is already an imaginary realization, a provisionary seduction before it becomes an established reality. The speech act "Je vouldroy" is a speculative device, a libidinal utterance that is the optative guarantee of an imaginary relationship that absorbs the self in the other through the threshold of the beautiful breast.

> Je vouldroy bien richement jaunissant
>   En pluye d'or goute à goute descendre
>   Dans le beau sein de ma belle Cassandre
>   Lorsqu'en ses yeulx le somme va glissant
> Je voudroy bien en toreau blandissant
>   Me transformer pour finement la prendre,
>   Quand elle va par l'herbe la plus tendre
>   Seule à l'escart mille fleurs ravissant.   (xx, p. 15)

Deprived of a perceptible form, the figure of the poet undergoes bodily effacement; it loses itself in the fluid movement of the masculine seed ["jaunissant"], a phenomenon which relays what

André Gendre describes as "the female-like suppleness of liquid."[18] In effect, this liquidity represents the paradoxical desire for possession of the loved female object since the need that the figure of the poet enacts for her demands a dispossession of the desiring body: the poet becomes another presence, an internalized shower of gold fecundating the woman, and one who disappears, fusing with her through the erotic sliding of the inseminative act. The figure of the poet flows like gold in a movement that adapts itself to the contours of desire.

If the masculine figure referred to in the first quatrain does not possess density of substance in its act of seduction, the one in the second quatrain demonstrates a paradoxical seductive force since the mythological bull in question conquers through warm caressing ["blandissant"]. The abduction of Europa by Jupiter draws attention to a persona whose "softness" is inviting; indeed seduction is not represented as an unmitigated conquest, but rather as a ludic act of possession through which the figure of the poet can take her by means of of a ruse.

In adopting the legend of Narcissus in the last tercets of the poem, the ronsardian sonnet modifies the intertext. Instead of drowning in the reflection of his self-image in a fountain, the figure of the poet is placed in a phantasmatic scenario which translates the desire for a child-like regression into a quasi-maternal *locus*. Tortured by his pain, the desiring subject plunges into a fountain which has become Cassandre, the symbolic object of pleasure; the poet substitutes the dream of a fulfilled wish for a yet unmet demand. The writing subject would like to maintain the need for love and thus envisions a situation permanently capable of satisfying the appetite for the desire of the loved woman.

> Je vouldroy bien afin d'aiser ma peine
> Estre un Narcisse, & elle une fontaine
> Pour m'y plonger une nuict à sejour:
> Et vouldroy bien ceste nuict encore
> Durast tousjours sans que jamais l'Aurore
> D'un front nouveau nous r'allumast le jour.

The amorous subject seeks to situate himself in an atemporal and indistinct future where he would be immersed in idle activity. This proposed bliss emanates from the image of a self fatally tied to its loved object. The fusion with the body of the woman represents an attempt to attain the stability of rest; he wishes to "aiser ma peine" [ease my pain] by means of an imaginary symbiosis in the liquidity of a prenatal world in which a more primitive pleasure is rediscovered.

The amorous encounter that the text describes is enacted in a kind of hypothetical future ("Je vouldroy") where the atemporality of love ("sans que jamais l'Aurore . . . nous r'allumast le jour") fulfills the desire of the amorous subject and leaves him irredeemably frozen in the place of the other.[19] The self is thus defined by petrification in the image of the other from which the anxiety of separation is erased through a signifier that tries to be one with a signified. The assimilation in question here is a defense against loss ("ceste nuict encore/Durast tousjours"), the emptiness produced by the tragic separation from maternal plenitude. The pleasure principle is indeed operative here through the figuration of a permanent amorous embrace, the desire for absorption in the course of submersion in the shadows of an eternal night of non-being; indeed suffering and anguish, the archetypal symptoms of Petrarchan love, can only be alleviated in a sexual union free from the paralyzing presence of phallic hegemony. The final image which the text evokes projects a dream which refutes the "irritation" of desire; at the same time it represents the triumph over desire by attempting to abolish the movement associated with temporality so that the amorous subject may recapture the originary bliss with the mother ["pour m'y plonger . . ./Durast tousjours"] who is reified as the *Mater* of an ideal order.[20]

This scriptural gesture – the transcription of the desire to lose oneself in the other – is both an erotic and mortal experience. The fountain in which the desiring subject submerges himself is that of a nurturing corporeal source in which water is dormant in the eternal night of his dreams. In the end there is perhaps only a single form of escape from the threat of amorous conquest: the desired immobilization of the amorous subject realizes a metaphorical death – "sans que jamais l'Aurore . . . nous r'allumast le jour" – through a certain stability or equilibrium of the self, indeed a strange phenomenon which paradoxically re-covers a man incapable of engaging with the dangers of an active female sexuality.[21]

The metamorphosis of the poet–Narcissus in this text is that of the transformation of amorous sentiment into a poetic corpus in which the *locus* of love becomes the space, the *mater* or the matter, of writing. By adapting the fiction of bodily assimilation, the poet constitutes himself as the body of a fiction transposed in the folds of the logos. From the metaphorical death of this desiring body surge forth the flowers of rhetoric. They represent the figuration of an exemplary passivity, the scriptural eulogy for a sexuality whose death instinct reduces the perilous vicissitudes of desire to zero.

In a last sonnet "Soit que son or se crespe lentement," the *blason* of beautiful hair, overdetermined by intertexts of Petrarch and Ariosto, is represented by a quasi-voluptuous movement in which the figure of the woman is reduced to the indefinable ambiguity of a stirring coiffure; Cassandre's hair is immediately apprehended as movement.[22] The desired object is identified here through the image of a female swimmer caught in the swaying of a capillary sea, that assimilates the flow of waves to that of the hair. The gentle movement of physical oscillation at the heart of this sensual description functions as another fiction of the body ready to serve the phantasmatic dynamics of textual production through metaphors evoking the mobility associated with sexual desire.

> Soit que son or se crespe lentement
> > Ou soit qu'il vague en deux glissantes ondes,
> > Qui cà qui là par le sein vagabondes,
> > Et sur le col, nagent follastrement
> Ou soit qu'un noud diapré tortement
> > De maintz rubiz, & maintes perles rondes
> > Serre les flotz de ses deux tresses blondes,
> > Je me contente en mon contentement.   (xc, p. 56)

The syntax of the ondulating rhythms ("Soit que . . . ou soit que

... ou soit que"), as discussed by I. D. McFarlane, projects an essentially unstable image (the play on the word "vague") onto the imaginary sea of the text. The aquatic metaphor is raised to the level of the visceral; the amorous subject is attracted to a detachable part of the female body, a fetishized object, that is displaced according to the contours of desire.

In the tercets of the poem, the loss of sexual identity is outlined in the form of a spectacle of otherness, a mimesis of the instability that the fiction of the body translates. The female figure who had already surfaced on the scene of writing dissipates in the fading of the textual project. By a paradoxical reversal, the figure of the woman drowns in the "fog of writing." To be sure, the ronsardian text follows a path in which the libido is withdrawn from the desired female object (the head of hair) and transposed onto the fantasized image of a boy–woman. Initially attracted by the female body, the poet sees in it an ambiguous sexuality, a symbolic representation that takes the form of an adonized head, born from the sea of writing.

> Quel plaisir est-ce, ainçoys quelle merveille
>   Quand ses cheveux troussez dessus l'oreille
>   D'une Venus imitent la façon?
> Quand d'un bonet son chef elle adonize
>   Et qu'on ne sçait (tant bien elle disguise
>   Son chez doubteux) s'elle est fille ou garçon? (xc, lines 9–14)

By its appearance here, the indeterminate figure of Venus, sprung forth from the imaginary wave of writing in a transient vision, makes itself a source of ambiguity through a metonymic confusion of gender that unites femininity with an effeminized masculinity. Moreover, the text further projects an essentially uncertain atmosphere through the use of the indefinite article ("une Venus") and the perlocutionary force of the interrogative phrase that constitutes the first tercet. Far from being an *encomium* of female beauty, this desired object presents itself in the form of an elusive and blurred image because in itself it is already double, a figure that reveals a bitextuality or traces of the masculine inscribed onto the image of the female body. Each gender is at the same time the dividing force and the support of

127

the other, simply an androgynous composite that constitutes a cross-dressing and perhaps also an aesthetic ideal.

The rewriting of the intertextual myth reveals the contours of masculine desire in the form of an equivocal sexuality that creates a kind of vertigo in terms of gender identity; the nature of poetic representation here suffices to transform the desiring subject into a devirilized man. The undecidability of the identity of the represented object – the hair – permits the articulation of the coming of pleasure until then unknown ("Quel plaisir est-ce, ainçoys quelle merveille").

Now according to the Athenian version of the myth, Adonis, progeny of his father's incest with his sister Myrra, is neither a husband nor a virile being for the Greeks; he is nothing other than a lover and an effeminate whose faithful followers, according to Plutarch, are enlisted amongst women and the androgynous.[23] But in another context, the ronsardian intertext refers back to Horace's *Odes* (Book ii, Ode 5) in which a young man is infatuated with a girl who has not as yet reached sexual maturity. In order to evoke her potential beauty in a time yet to come, the Horatian text compares her to the figure of Gygès: "Better loved than Gyges, a boy/So beautiful that, set in a crowd/Of girls, he'd puzzle the wisest stranger,/His hair so flowing, his face gorgeously ambiguous."[24] Whereas the addressee of the Horatian ode is described as having an interest in boys as well as girls, the desiring subject in Ronsard's text manifests an eroticized appetite for an androgynous figure (that of the adonized woman). The disjunctive synthesis figured in this text breaks down the essentialized categories of the masculine and feminine. Ronsard's poem constructs here a subject who is defined by the fantasy and the taste for disguise that he projects; the instability of the other is a way of opening up to one's one sexual difference. The text enacts a veritable climax of indecision: since the Athenian intertext describes Adonis' object of desire as an androgynous being, the Ronsardian subject permits itself, through metonymic displacement, to identify with the object of contemplation (the figure of Venus–Adonis); he identifies with it and is absorbed by it.[25] The desiring subject therefore finds himself engaged in a

double fantasy, a phenomenon according to which the representation of the body functions as a narcissistic mirror reflecting the
subject's relation to the other: "Je me contente en mon contentement." Thus the sexuality of the two figures inscribed in the text
are destabilized since the "reverie" that constitutes the scenario
of sexual desire puts into question the identity of both subject
and object.

On another level, however, the transfiguration of Venus,
goddess of love and fecundity, into Adonis, inverse figure of
marriage and sexual union, is in fact very revealing.[26] Deprived
of offspring and destined to fall into a garden of stone, Adonis'
seed will never be transformed into a root as a fertile object. The
desiring subject delivers Adonis from Venus, a symbolic gesture
engendering an image which theatricalizes the textual unconscious. The sterility in question here suggests the infertility associated with the equivocal love of a man for a woman and problematizes masculine desire through the enactment of a fantasy.
In the end, the representation of the female body gives birth to
the figure of a young man – Adonis – incapable of the generative power of procreation, perhaps a fantasy of impotency that
emblematizes the consequences of the active presence of the
feminine in man.

The figuration of the female body in Ronsard's 1552 sonnets
permits the male subject to display the vicissitudes of his desire
on the body of the fiction. And from this fact, the fiction of the
body invents an ambiguous and complex game from which the
sexuality of man is both affirmed and interrogated. Instead of
establishing the identity of the desiring subject, the ronsardian
text problematizes it in a writing-body ["une écriture-corps"]
which incarnates the image of an ambivalent desire living off its
own fantasies. If the desiring subject in Ronsard escapes a reified
image of male gender identity, it is because the allegorical representation of desire destabilizes the binary imprisonment of
sexuality, a phenomenon without which a lover's discourse
would never be possible. "Any thought, any feeling, any interest
aroused in the amorous subject," claims Barthes, "is in fact
instigated by the figure of the loved body."[27]

B. THE TEXT AS BODY

8

MY BODY, MY TEXT:
MONTAIGNE AND THE
RHETORIC OF
SELF-PORTRAITURE

Freud has more in common with Proust and Montaigne than with
biological scientists, because his interpretations of life and death are
always mediated by texts, first by literary texts of others, and then by his
own earlier texts, until at last the Sublime mediation of otherness begins
to be performed by his text-in-process. In the *Essays* of Montaigne or
Proust's vast novel, this ongoing mediation is clearer than it is in Freud's
almost perpetual self-revelation.
Harold Bloom, "Freud and the Poetic Sublime: A Catastrophe Theory
of Creativity"

I

Montaigne's essay "Sur des vers de Virgile" (III, 5) promotes an
anatomical discourse in which a metaphorical equivalence is
established between text and body.[1] The essayist seeks self-
knowledge and displaces the self onto the figure of the body, a
linguistic representation that mediates the intrapsychic dynamics
of an author who is to be observed and analyzed. The study of the
nature of artifice termed text inscribes within the essay a mirror
which reflects the movement of the writer. Like Plato's *Phaed-
rus,* Montaigne's essay explores the problems of both love and
rhetoric.[2] However, Montaigne's chapter presumes a highly
abstract concept of text and creates a figurative reversibility
between sexuality and language, the anatomical representation
of self as erotic other. In fact, what Montaigne terms "l'action
genitale" functions, in part, as a metaphor for the generative act
of writing: the project of writing about sexuality is most closely

associated with self-representation and the lack which constitutes desire.[3] The signifier of writing (sexuality) and the text (the
body) portrays its image before the reflection of the scriptural
mirror: the sign of creation transmits an index of its textuality.
Each theme (body : text/sexuality : writing) defines itself through
its relationship to the other, and is subject to multiple transform-
ations which compel the text to fragment and travel over numerous *topoi*. Montaigne's essay therefore disseminates its meaning
obliquely since signs play on multiple levels at once; the figures of
Montaigne's discourse represent erotic codings revealing the
traces of concealed desire.

II

In response to the onset of old age and sexual decline, Montaigne
transforms his text into a surrogate object of pleasure mediated
by an interplay between the fragments of classical writing and the
rhythm of a subject in search of self-knowledge. The project of
desire is to recapture the lost object (sexuality) through writing,
a need that is ultimately impossible to fulfill, since nature cannot
be retrieved by art. Yet words alone, as best they can, solve the
problem of the absent object; language bridges a gap between
old age and youth since it becomes a playground for thinking and
manifesting the traces of physical reference. What Montaigne
terms the "foible luicte de l'art contre la nature" (p. 819) reveals
the latent desires of a subject in search of regeneration through
the pleasures of the text.[4]

Jusques aux moindres occasions de plaisir que je puis rencontrer, je les
empoigne ... Puisque c'est le privilege de l'esprit de se r'avoir de la
vieillesse, je luy conseille, autant que je puis, de le faire; qu'il verdisse,
qu'il fleurisse ce pendant, s'il peut, comme le guy sur un arbre mort.
(pp. 819, 821)

If the desire for sexual pleasure declines in old age, it is textual
exploration which enables the essayist to sustain the pleasures of
youth through the materiality of language itself. Sexuality, in
particular copulation, is regarded as a center, an ideality whose

plenitude eliminates tension and dissipates desire. "Tout le mouvement du monde se resoult et rend à cet accouplage: c'est une matiere infuse par tout, c'est un centre où toutes choses regardent" (p. 835). Consequently, given this lack, the writer finds himself obliged to seek an object of cathexis to satisfy his need for wholeness and plenitude, and thus immobilize desire. The fantasies of the mind struggle against the division between body and soul which old age makes apparent by creating a self-portrait capable of achieving consubstantiality between writer and text; the anticipation of a unified self becomes the source of an ontological and epistemological idealization.

The essays are composed in an interval of waiting, in the gap between the disappearance of the other (perhaps La Boétie) and the goal of consubstantiality, the narcissistic identification with the self-portrait.[5] The barred relationship between subject and desired object therefore motivates the writer to "empoigner" that which is elusive and to regain impossible unity. Montaigne's vaunted self-awareness through the exploration of loving and knowing becomes a screen that shields him from desire. The essayist's apprenticeship, mediated through the materiality of the script, reveals the necessity of conjoining mind and language in the region where one ostensibly locates the act of creation.

The need to animate one's text, and identify with it, illuminates the writer's latent desire for eros to triumph over thanatos. When evoking the therapeutic function of writing, Montaigne claims: "Je l'estime salubre, propre, à desgourdir un esprit et un corps poisant" (p. 870). For Montaigne, the essay functions as a regenerative pleasure-giving substitute which reproduces that which is absent and transforms the observable self into a textual other. The pleasure principle is indeed operative here as exemplified by the essaying process which "binds psychic energies and sustains the narrative through multiple detours" that give new life to art and ultimately create the illusion of a deferred ending.[6] The genre of the essay is always in the process of *becoming*; its true essence lies in the reality that it is incapable of completing itself or of establishing a conclusion. To be sure, not only may the act of writing be identified as the drive of desire toward the restoration of an earlier plenitude and the need to attain that end; it is also a perpetual swerving away from repression which reduces all libidinal energy. To write of sexuality and love, Montaigne therefore claims:

(b) me divertiroit de mille pensées ennuyeuses, (c) de mille chagrins melancholiques, (b) que l'oisiveté nous charge en tel aage (c) et le mauvais estat de nostre santé; (b) reschauferoit au moins en songe, ce sang que nature abandonne; soustiendroit le menton et allongeroit un peu les nerfs (c) et la vigueur et allegresse de l'ame (b) à ce pauvre homme qui s'en va le grand train vers sa ruine. (p. 872)

The resistance of the subject to decay and death reveals the essayist's continual attempt actively to assert control over his destiny through a kind of imaginative mastery.

The transference of energy from the lugubrious to the pleasurable operates an awakening in the text, the birth of the essayist's unequivocal intention to opt for the recovery of a lost pleasure.[7] In order to defend his own project, Montaigne criticizes those who fixate on negativity or displeasure:

(b) Je hay un esprit hargneux et triste qui glisse par dessus les plaisirs de sa vie et s'empoigne et paist aux malheurs; comme les mouches, qui ne peuvent tenir contre un corps bien poly et bien lissé, et s'attachent et reposent aux lieux scabreux et raboteux; et comme les vantouses qui ne hument et appetent que le mauvais sang. (p. 822)

These lines suggest – through a kind of rhetorical negativity – the physical experience that appears to be the central motif of the text. The verbs *empoigner, tenir contre un corps poly,* and *humer,* used here in a negative context, signal full immersion in erotic imagery. The Janus-like figure's effort to resist being vanquished by time produces a form of self-gratification through a rhetoric of confession, manifesting the erotic relationship in its parasitic aspect. Through the corrective lens of writing, the symbiotic rapport between the self and the object of displeasure must eventually be renounced; it must permit itself to be replaced by a narcissistic self-reflexivity. The audaciously volitive declaration "Je me suis ordonné d'oser dire tout ce que j'ose faire" (p. 822) clearly places the analytical experience under the

136

aegis of a self-contained specularity and focuses the expenditure of desire on the enterprise of displaying the writer before the mirror of his own writing. Indeed the fetishistic object of desire reflects back on the desiring subject.

The problems of mimesis and self-representation permeate the essay. The text sets up an indeterminate play between rhetoric and sexuality at the same time that it expresses the wish for a rhetorical potency that would capture and authentically represent the energies figured in the self-portrait. The "clothed body" *topos* elucidated by both Thibaudet and Gray suggests the fundamental doubts and uncertainties which the writer confronts in the transformation of thought into script.[8] To be sure, the essayist wants to resist the external form's possible dissimulation of the internal, and he therefore extends his moral imperative to those who "envoyent leur conscience au bordel et tiennent leur contenance en regle" (p. 824). Montaigne does not wish to divorce language from the reality he purports to describe; he opts, instead, to overcome the difficulty of giving body to his thought by advocating the clarity and transparency of his ontological speculation; that is, the presumed isomorphism between the writing subject and the image represented in the texture of the essay: "moy ... qui me voy et qui me recherche jusques aux entrailles, qui sçay bien ce qui m'appartient" (p. 824).

That the incompatibility between inner states of consciousness and the act of writing is a thematic concern of "Sur des vers de Virgile" is clear from those sections of the essay which treat the word/thought *topos* and its relationship to sexuality. In the wake of the passage where Montaigne openly criticizes those who deny their humanity by refusing to discuss sexuality, the conflict is openly stated: repression dissimulates thought, and sexuality ultimately resides in the vacant locus where meaning fails to be articulated:

(b) Qu'a faict l'action genitale aux hommes, si naturelle, si necessaire et si juste, pour n'en oser parler sans vergongne et pour l'exclurre des propos serieux et reglez? Nous prononçons hardiment: tuer, desrober, trahir; et cela, nous n'oserions qu'entre les dents? Est-ce à dire que moins nous en exhalons en parole, d'autant nous avons loy d'en grossir la pensée? (c) Car il est bon que les mots qui sont le moins en usage, moins escrits et mieus teus, sont les mieux sceus et plus generalement connus. (p. 825)

The consciousness of the repression of thought inscribes within the text an essential tension in which the self is experienced through a complex interplay between the desire to articulate thought and the awareness of the inability to realize those desires. The trajectory of Montaigne's scriptural quest seems to depict a portrait capable of rejecting the language of artifice which could potentially disguise thought; the writer's impetus to give as complete a coverage of himself as possible. ("Je suis affamé de me faire connoistre," p. 824) aims at the realization of an ideality, an illusory representation of text as living body of "chair et os" which would incarnate the vigor of the mind's activity and function as a "metaphoric supplement of physicality."[9] Therefore the writer's goal paradoxically becomes one of depicting nature through art; we might almost say that the essay represents the struggle of artifice against the erosive power of temporality. "(c) Si j'estois du mestier, je naturaliserois l'art autant comme ils artialisent la nature" (p. 852). Yet, however unrestrained and pure Montaigne attempts to render his portrait, he ostensibly finds himself subjected to regarding rhetorical potency as an illusion based on the nostalgia for a forgotten physicality.

III

Montaigne's point of departure for his discussion of rhetoric and sexuality is a text quoted from Virgil's *Aeneid* (VIII, 387–92; 404–6) which focuses on the relationship between nature and art.[10] Although embedded within the essay, Virgil's text constitutes a kind of illusory narrative center – a point of origin essentially unmediated – that initially frames the essay and creates an internal cleft. The problem that the virgilian text provokes Montaigne to investigate concerns whether or not poetic language is capable of transmitting experience and representing it in art.

Montaigne's critique seems to question the possibility of reaching any truth, essence or origin through a representational mode.

The reality depicted in poetry measures a considerable distance between textual expression and the referential foundation of the object under study. The passage from Virgil not only misrepresents love in the literary work but illustrates, above all, how artistic expression cuts us off from a nature to which we cannot have access: "Venus n'est pas si belle toute nue, et vive, et haletante, comme elle est icy chez Virgile" (p. 826).[11] Virgil's poetic description, as Terence Cave points out, acquires rhetorical potency through the process of *enargeia*.[12] Instead of having a direct relation to a presumed nature, the writing process is the cause of imaginary fabulations which, through rhetorical counterfeiting, render thoughts more visible than real. And yet, as Montaigne reminds us, in transposing the art/nature *topos* onto that of virtue/nobility, visual perception may become arbitrary and consequently obfuscate the parameters of the object under scrutiny. Just as Virgil's description of passionate love in marriage is misrepresented ("il la peinct un peu bien esmeu pour une Venus maritale," p. 827), so too the a priori connection between virtue and nobility may become implausible:

Ceux qui pensent faire honneur au mariage pour y joindre l'amour, font, ce me semble, de mesme ceux qui, pour faire faveur à la vertu, tiennent que la noblesse n'est autre chose que vertu ... [La noblesse] c'est une vertu, si ce l'est, artificiele et visible; dependant du temps et de la fortune.   (pp. 827–8)

The analogy that Montaigne wishes to establish between the essayist and the poet indicates that there is no more continuity for a writer spatially and temporally cut off from past satisfaction than there is referential veracity in the poetic description of the nature of love. Through a rhetorical displacement, the text indirectly manifests its own inadequacies as well as the inability of writing truly to incarnate nature in an unequivocal fashion:

(b) Que je me chatouille, je ne puis tantost plus arracher un pauvre rire de ce meschant corps. Je ne m'esgaye qu'en fantasie et en songe, pour

139

destourner par ruse le chagrin de la vieillesse. Mais certes il y faudroit
autre remede qu'en songe; foible luicte de l'art contre la nature.

(p. 819)

Montaigne's questioning points to the fear of the inadequacy of
the textual body's reproductive faculties and the possibility of
inseminating the narrative space with a fertile language capable
of giving birth to authentic self-representation.

The writer's project takes shape during the moment at which
he textualizes the goals of his scriptural praxis through a discussion of the physical nature of love. When addressing himself to
the artifical restraints imposed upon feminine desire, Montaigne
recalls an earlier moment in the essay when he refused to restrain
the direction of the self-portrait. "C'est donc folie d'essayer à
brider aux femmes un desir qui leur est (c) si cuysant et si (b)
naturel ... Je suis fort serviteur de la nayfveté et de la liberté"
(pp. 844–5). The attainment of that goal – the liquidation of
desire through a parasitic relationship with the other – would
eliminate further need for plenitude, be it sexual or textual. In
physical love as in writing, aroused desire opens the possibility
for both mastery and self-expenditure and brings into play the
delights of ecstasy and prerogatives of the will.

The desire to give body to one's thought is further examined in
a passage that Montaigne abstracts from Lucretius in which the
sexual passion described between Venus and Mars conveys a
more appropriate representation of what it is supposed to portray.[13] Montaigne's project of *descriptio* is derived from Lucretius, whose text expresses corporeal effects through erotic
images which function as an ego ideal ("a model text") and serve
as a springboard for the desire to write. The image of the ideal
discourse motivates the writer to emulate the Lucretian intertext
so that the essay would acquire the characteristics of a vital living
organism caught in a seductive anatomical pose:

Leur langage est tout plein et gros d'une vigueur naturelle et constante;
ils sont tout epigramme, non la queuë seulement, mais la teste, l'estomac et les pieds ... Ce n'est pas une eloquence molle et seulement sans
offence: elle est nerveuse et solide, qui ne plaict pas tant comme elle
remplit et ravit; et ravit le plus les plus forts espris.   (p. 850)

Vigorous and potent writing translates both movement and stimulation, and displaces the overflow of this psychic energy from
text to reader; the libidinal flow of *descriptio* catches the reader's
attention and renders him victim of the ravishing force of language. Furthermore, the semantic elements in the text are
suggestive of the incantatory power of poetic language to sweep
the reader into a state of immobility through the unquestionable
authority of subject matter to incarnate the body it generates:
"C'est la gaillardise de l'imagination qui esleve et enfle les
parolles . . . le sens esclaire et produict les parolles; non plus de
vent, ains de chair et d'os. Elles signifient plus qu'elles ne disent"
(p. 851). Presumably, we are to accept here language as real life,
"plaines conceptions," which represent, through lexical expansiveness, the erective virtues of a phallically potent discourse. An
ideal linguistic act constitutes the substance that it serves to
describe and validates the premise that rhetoric is more than
mere words: "Quand je voy ces braves formes de s'expliquer, si
vifves, si profondes, je ne dicts pas que c'est bien dire, je dicts,
que c'est bien penser" (p. 850).

Through Montaigne's reading of Lucretius he fertilizes his
own text: he makes a concerted effort to adopt the modalities of
the metatext as well as to delineate the principles of an *ars
poetica*. Montaigne wishes to copy a role, and by metonomy an
art, through the metamorphosis of interpretation into essay. To
be sure, he praises the so-called naturalness and vigor that he
perceives in Latin literature at the same time that he denigrates
the "miserable affectation d'estrangeté" of French. Artificial
language fetters the transubstantiation of self into text and fis-
sures the fragile liaisons connecting thought and meaning. Thus,
the essayist opts for the projection of a textual density capable of
transmitting the utopian illusion of presence and fullness. "Il ne
s'y voit qu'une miserable affectation d'estrangeté, des déguisements froids et absurdes qui, au lieu d'eslever, abbattent la
matiere" (p. 851). The wish to elevate the substance of language
places Montaigne within a configuration brought about by
images representing writing, erotic desire, and self-knowledge.
There are multiple elements in the text symbolic of hunger and

thirst which point, more importantly, to the need for "fulfill-ment" and the elaboration of that wish. Montaigne's quest for rhetorical power is modeled after his Latin predecessors and their ability to embody language and energize it. "Le maniement et emploite des beaux espris donne pris à la langue, non pas l'innovant tant comme la remplissant de plus vigoreux et divers services, l'estirant et ployant" (p. 851). Montaigne's text appears to advocate a narrative exuberance, a polyvalent language that is an integral part of the body from which it is born.

The drama of the birth of self as textual body emanates from the writer's desire to abstract the textual psyche from an intertex-tual framework, enabling the essayist to escape the contamina-tion of foreign discourses whose raw material barred the body's presence unto itself. In other words, the movement is away from the discourse of the other as beloved object towards the illusory presence of the self-image, Montaigne's spatially incarnated textual representation. "Quand j'escris, je me passe bien de la compaignie et souvenance des livres, de peur qu'ils n'interrom-pent ma forme . . . il me vient aussi à propos d'escrire chez moi, en pays sauvage, où personne ne m'ayde ni me releve" (pp. 852–3). We have here an allegory of a reader becoming a writer, abandoning the security of the father–text, communicating in his own voice rather than through the authoritative voice of the other. "Je l'eusse faict meilleur ailleurs, mais l'ouvrage eust esté moins mien, et sa fin principale et perfection, c'est d'estre exacte-ment mien" (p. 853).

The montaignian literary enterprise thus finds its strength in its resistance to domination and in an unmitigated violation of convention; it is a self-generating, autoerogenous writing project that enables the essayist to account for himself. Words become for Montaigne physical entities – sexually charged generative bodies – which mediate the Imaginary and relegate writing to an erotic activity enacted through the coupling dynamics of derived associations.[14] As I have attempted to demonstrate elsewhere, every subject in the montaignian essay is a point of entry into a new narrative threshold; it carries within itself the memory of its own origin.[15] The dynamism of text as living body is self-perpetuating; each *topos* generates an open-ended play of displacements that attest to the fertility of the peripatetic mind. "Tout argument m'est egallement fertille. Je les prens sur une mouche" (p. 854). Of course images are caught in a pattern of intragenerative signs that produce an endless flow of subjects. "Que je commence par celle qu'il me plaira car les matieres se tiennent toutes enchesnées les unes aux autres" (p. 854). The text's "cogitations informes" manifest a free association whereby each object under study refers to an element other than itself and thus breaks free of any possible textual closure. Montaigne's exercise of judgment through the writing process is therefore an attempt to submit knowledge to a discourse without a center. The text provides a space in which the illusion of the essay can be played out; it generates a structure whose specificity consists of a perpetual process of expansion.

IV

Throughout most of "Sur des vers de Virgile," Montaigne expresses the desire for absolute frankness in both sexuality and rhetoric.[16] In Montaigne's discussion the thematics of sexuality which stress the physical, unconstrained aspects of love are quite literally displaced and transposed into an unmitigated critique of repressive writing. Clearly, the nudity and transparency made operative through the essaying process require an external projection of the internal: "Je m'y fusse très-volontiers peint tout entier, et tout nud" (p. 9). The desire and appetite for the undissimulated self reveal a text ideally conceived of as the transgression of the law of repression; the goals of transparency and freedom of movement assert themselves by rejecting an artificially veiled discourse that would levy upon the inventions of language an immediate denial of itself: "Je me suis ordonné de dire tout ce que j'ose faire . . . je me confesse en publiq" (pp. 822, 824). And it is therefore of little surprise that Montaigne criticizes Pope Paul IV's suppression of the natural and the physical through the castration of the artistically represented male member: "(b) Ce bon homme, qui en ma jeunesse, chastra tant

143

de belles et antiques statues en sa grande ville pour ne corrompre la veue" (p. 837). Castration potentially eliminates the untempered subjectivity of the world of fantasy and creation.

However, despite the incessant refusal to adopt an artificial rhetoric, Montaigne's text capsizes its very own theoretical presuppositions and conveys an intentionality which undermines its stated goals; artifice, then, is paradoxically valorized, and the writer appears to accept a partially repressed and veiled discourse. The refusal of absolute transparency expresses certain reservations about the poetic idealism first expressed, and suggests that a text can produce meaning through its censorship or repression; desire is stimulated due to the breakdown or interruption in the signifying process:

Les vers de ces deux poetes, traitant ainsi reservéement et discrettement de la lasciveté comme ils font, me semblent la descouvrir et esclairer de plus près. Les dames couvrent leur sein d'un reseu, les prestres plusieures choses sacrées; les peintres ombragent leur ouvrage, pour luy donner plus de lustre; et dict-on que le coup du Soleil et du vent est plus poisant par reflexion qu'à droit fil.   (p. 858)

In the imagery he uses here, Montaigne makes the text become, through the cumulative layering of meaning, a point of convergence relevant to both sexual and rhetorical *topoi*; sexuality and textuality reflect a kind of reversibility indicating that desire becomes more potent within a state of absence or lack. What is striking here is the power of the imagination to sublimate sexual drive – both in writing and through the observation of the body – into the realm of fantasy. Partial inaccessibility to both body and text maintains the tension inherent in desire, and ultimately permits the observer to sustain pleasure through the power of fantasy to discharge psychic energy:

Qui n'a jouyssance qu'en la jouyssance, qui ne gaigne que du haut poinct, qui n'aime la chasse qu'en la prinse, il ne luy appartient pas de se mesler à nostre escole. Plus il y a de marches et degrez, plus il y a de hauteur et d'honneur au dernier siege. Nous nous devrions plaire d'y estre conduicts . . . sans esperance et sans desir, nous n'allons plus qui vaille.   (p. 859)

144

Montaigne's text therefore glorifies the pleasures of frustration and incompletion; it represents an infinite appetite for desire, an ever-unsatisfied yearning for an absent pleasure. When describing the masculine need to captivate women, Montaigne boldly declares that an unsatisfied quest is infinitely more appealing than the attainment of the goal: "soudain qu'elles sont à nous, nous ne sommes plus à elles" (p. 859). Pleasure is enhanced by difficulty and risk, since it "cherche à s'irriter par la douleur" (p. 596). Lack thus motivates desire and makes the writing of the essay possible.[17]

Montaigne's discussion of the realignment of values concerning the problematics of representation demonstrates how sexuality and rhetoric are interchangeable.[18] In commenting on a quotation from Ovid, Montaigne indirectly focuses the discussion to reflect back upon himself, to perpetuate his own narcissistic speculation; he reveals how writing about rhetoric exposes his own sexuality. The essayist's remark "Oyez cettuy-là [Ovid] plus ouvert,/Et nudam pressi corpus adúsque meum,/il me semble qu'il me chapone" (p. 858) suggests more than meets the eye. The castration anxiety that is expressed here evokes the writer's belief that the denial of fantasy at the expense of authenticity would eliminate the only pleasure left to him.[19] The essayist therefore seeks solace in the theatricality of poetic fantasy which symbolically recreates sexuality through writing and portrays what Lacan terms a veritable delusion of being (*leurre de l'être*):

nous avons besoing d'estre sollicitez et chatouillez par quelque agitation mordicante ... un corps abattu, comme un estomac prosterné, il est excusable de le rechauffer et soustenir par art, et, par l'entremise de la fantasie, luy faire revenir l'appetit et l'allegresse.[20]   (pp. 870, 871)

The power of the text emanates from the power of the imagination which temporarily enables the writer to avert "death"; a life without "plot" or desire would fetter the quest for lost pleasure. For Montaigne, conflict may be attributed to the necessity of having to choose either fantasy and movement or reality and stability. The dissipation of fantasy openly threatens the essayist's desiring energies, since imagination – the ability to "transferer la pensée des choses fascheuses aux plaisantes" (p. 809) – constitutes the only outlet for sexual decline and inactivity.

Montaigne's reaction to the Ovidian quotation narrates yet another story: the suppression of the artificial enactment of what is no longer naturally possible affirms inadequacy and eliminates the pleasure that can only be symbolically fulfilled through the re-productive energy of the essaying process. To write about castration, then, suggests the fear of being unable to create, the anxiety concerning the mind's possible sterility, and its subsequent inability to fertilize the text and "plot desire."[21] Paradoxically, repression becomes an object substitute as well as a rhetorical stance, with fantasy the mental corollary of desire.

The fluidity and movement associated with the release of tension emanating from the explosive force of desire is enacted through the *topoi* concerning both sexuality and writing. In his discussion of love, Montaigne describes the centrifugal movement of desire and the pleasure derived from the instinctual discharge of psychic energy: "l'amour n'est autre chose que la soif de cette jouyssance (c) en un subject desiré, ny Venus autre chose que le plaisir à descharger ses vases" (p. 855). In both cases, pleasure is regarded as a lowering of tension through a process of "emptying out"; a soul of the common sort "s'affole d'estre trop continuellement bandée" (p. 818). However, owing to its artificiality – that is to say, the sublimation of sexual drive into scriptural artifact – writing can never produce an authentically effective discharge; the search for significance is offered through an erotic textual practice which figurally reproduces the repressed libidinal impulses of the writer. Pleasure ultimately becomes a simulacrum of the original, an experience mediated through the choreographics of an elusively present textual representation which is condemned to be deflated without having the potency to infuse new energy. The artificiality of the quest further undermines the already problematic nature of the text and obliges it to lay bare its ontological illusions. The basic phenomenological underpinning of Montaigne's text suggests that the essayist's narrative is unable to attain the same gratification that sexuality can, and that unresolved, the inexhaustible "flow of babble" fails to transcend the scene of writing. Montaigne's text remains fragmentary and incomplete; it forces the writer into a labyrinth from which he is henceforth unable to attain the ecstasy of desired pleasure: "Qui ne voit que j'ay pris une route par laquelle, sans cesse et sans travail, j'iray autant qu'il y aura d'encre et de papier au monde?" (p. 922).

Part III

ALLEGORIES OF REPRESSION

9

SCÈVE: THE RHETORIC OF DREAM AND THE LANGUAGE OF LOVE

In Scève's world of love the use of the dream *topos* permits the elaboration of a fictive space where desire is played out. Within that *locus* the quest for Délie as supreme object of knowledge engenders a being whose reality cannot be separated from the very conditions under which that knowledge is produced. Délie becomes the point of reference of poetic invention, the desired object who overwhelms soul and sense and generates the possibilities of love within the framework of the dream. "Ma liberté lui a toute asseruie" (D. 6).[1] The text depicts the poet's journey into an unknown world by representing the desiring mind's engagement in an aesthetically sublimated form of intersubjectivity that is essentially self-consuming. Against the figural backdrop of the mind's private "eye," the subject enters into a relationship with the other, not as a real being, but rather as a mental object reflecting the anxieties of love. The dream narrative thus enacts a discursive fable that catalyzes the poet's energy towards the unthinkable, a domain to which he is drawn but from which he must ironically flee. Accordingly, this paradoxical situation is represented in the text by the specular relationship established between the desiring subject and the projection of an elusive feminine presence that gives substance to that desire and yet intermittently blocks its emergence. "Ie le vouluz, & ne l'osay vouloir" (D. 76).

The rhetoric of dream in the *Délie* makes the writing subject conscious of the apparently contradictory drives emanating from the conflict between the sensual and spiritual orders; it represents the effects of sexuality and the tensions it creates for the desiring subject through a figural enactment of the unconscious. The amorous subject submits itself to a series of imaginary representations tied to the dialectics of lucidity and blindness, a phenomenon that manifests a tension between an erotic narrative struggling to surface and the forces of chastity striving to repress it. Within the parameters of the dream narrative, Scève's discourse projects a voice whose poetic incantations transcribe what ostensibly cannot be realized: the desire to be loved and possessed and the delight of self-completion through an amorous relationship with the "idol of his life." Desire is thus sketched out in the rhetorical fantasy of dream where one transcends "life," where the poet's unrealized intensity of passion makes the delusion of the lover the effect of an ontological idealism. "Me contentant d'estre par moi deceu,/Pour non m'oster du plaisir, ou ie suis" (D. 341). Subjectivity is therefore the consequence of a figural staging in which the dreamer engages in a form of voyeurism and becomes the subject and object of a penetrating gaze.

Throughout the *Délie,* memory becomes a source of figuration, a generative agent more powerful than reason which compensates for the absence of the beloved; it provides the narrative framework necessary for representation to take shape and constitutes a fantasy machine that activates the return of the beloved at the expense of a certain loss of self.[2] "Me contraingnit a m'oblier moymesmes/Pour mieulx pouoir d'aultruy me souuenir" (D. 289). In effect, Scève's narrative ascribes to the dream work the invention of sexuality. Pleasure is therefore revealed as the delight resulting from the fantasy of an attempt to metaphorically draw life out of the Petrarchan passion associated with death.

> Car tu y vis & mes nuictz & mes iours,
> Voyre exemptez des moindres fascheries;
> Et ie m'y meurs en telles resueries,
> Que ie m'en sens haultement contente,
> Et si ne puis refrener les furies
> De ceste mienne ardente voulenté.   (D. 216)

More than just a mere intellectual curiosity, the act of dreaming produces intense affect; it satisfies the need to prolong desire and fatally trap the mind within the labyrinth of memory. "Ce grand desir de mon bien oblyé,/Comme l'Aultour de ma mort immortelle,/Ronge l'esprit par vne fureur telle,/Que consommé d'un si ardent poursuyure" (D. 77). If, as Speroni implies, love is perfected by the separation of the two lovers, it is the contemplative activity of memory that painfully keeps Délie alive and yet paradoxically endows her with a kind of immortality that is the result of her absence.[3] "Car, si en rien ie ne m'en souuenois,/Ie ne pourrois sentir douleur parfaicte" (D. 404).

Sporadically the image of the beloved in the *Délie* is presented as a nameless object, one that is momentarily present but is nevertheless capable of engaging the desiring subject in the euphoric state of narcissistic timelessness.

> En diuers temps, plusieurs iours, maintes heures,
> D'heure en moment, de moment a tousiours
> Dedans mon Ame, ô Dame, tu demeures,
> Toute occupée en contraires seiours.   (D. 216)

To be sure, Délie comes to represent the emptiness of a need that must be fulfilled; she becomes an abstract agent that causes the dream work to be perceived as a quest for self-delusion. In essence, emptiness is a symptom of the malaise the mind wishes to purge through the creation of a fantasy that thwarts this feeling of nothingness.

> Quasi moins vraye alors ie l'apperçoy,
> Que la pensée a mes yeulx la presente.
> Si plaisamment ainsi ie me deçoy,
> Comme si elle estoit au vray presente:
> Bien que par foys aulcunement ie sente
> Estre tout vain ce, que i'ay apperceu.   (D. 341)

The act of dreaming conceals the fiction underlying the perception of the desired object. But if the illusion of the dream is challenged by the poet's recognition of the "fantasy" of the constructed image, it is because it is more important to aspire to the pleasures of fabulation than to engage in the labor of phenomenological adequation. To dream is therefore to mark the

intrusion of a phantasmatic but elusive other that no consciousness can ever really control or be completely in possession of.

> Mais le matin (trop hastif) m'à priué,
> De telz plaisirs, ausquelz, comme vent vistes,
> I'estoys par vous, traistres yeulx, arriué,
> Qui cloz mon bien, et ouuertz mon mal vytes.   (D. 340)

In diametrical opposition to the dream narrative in which the
desiring subject attempts to gain access to the figure of Délie,
stands a discourse of repression characterized by silences, sighs,
stammerings, and physiological disorders producing a disturbance of reference. The language of repression performs at the
border of discourse and articulates a relation of language to the
body.[4] The raging fire of the lover's internal soliloquy escapes
only in a residual form of inexpression, best described metaphorically as the smoke ("la fumée") of a fire that once burned out of
control.

> Comme au Faulxbourg les fumantes fornaises
> Rendent obscurs les circonuoysins lieux,
> Le feu ardent de mes si grandz mesaises
> Par mes souspirs obtenebre les Cieulx.   (D. 178)

The "furnace" representing the poet's inner self reduces the
explosive energy of passion attacking the very core of his being
and transforms it into the willful repression of violent rage. Self-
mastery, as it is represented here, is little more than a negatively
conceived exorcism that stresses the fundamental division of the
desiring subject. Scève's text rewrites the Petrarchan *topos* of the
agony of expression and transcribes it as a linguistic anxiety
revealing the inability of language to signify itself properly:
"L'Esprit vouloit, mais la bouche ne peut" (D. 364). Erotic
tension is maintained because the libidinal energy of desire
remains buried beneath the surface of language.

In effect, the malady of repressed drives reaches its highest
level of intensity in a speechlessness that temporarily obliterates
the referent of desire through the creation of an epistemological
rift between word and thing. What Pascal Quignard refers to as

"l'impossibilité de la nomination" demonstrates the repressed subject's failed efforts at verbalizing "mes silentes clameurs."[5] Silence represents the voice outside discourse that confronts the amorous subject with the inability to speak the missing word and to designate the *locus* from which love emanates: "Que tel se taist & de langue, & de voix,/De qui le cœur se plaint incessament" (D. 359).[6]

If silence can abolish the possibility of nomination, it is also capable of yielding to a resurgence of affect through an elliptical and intermittently fragmented syntax characterized by hesitations and lacunae. Quite clearly, the amorous subject never reaches a state of verbal plenitude because the enactment of poetic discourse veils the object of his desire through the overwhelming power of his aphasic disorder. "Ie parle aumoins. Ce n'est que phrenesie" (D. 71). These verbal disturbances, communicated by periodically fragmented speech patterns, produce a discursive uncertainty predicated on the contradictory imperatives emanating from the desire to speak and the need to remain silent. "Et si m'en plaings, & bien m'en vouldrois taire" (D. 314).

In a sense, then, the impossibility of mastering desire – "dont, comme neige au Soleil, ie me fondz" (D. 118) – leads to a narrative deployment of that impossibility in the rhetoric of the dream where the inner drama of psychic forces are transmuted into aesthetic forms. Scève chooses the allegorical mode to represent the self in dream narrative. He thereby transforms the figural representation of the mind into an arena in which the forces contending for mastery – "ces deux uterins freres" (D. 318) – engage in an inner struggle between opposing "vices" and "virtues." Focusing on the hesitations and contradictions associated with the Petrarchan tradition, Scève's text portrays the amorous subject through a succession of desiring personages whose suffering, dispersed in time and space, is acted out by agents of doubt, hope, desire, and fear.

> Ie voys, & viens aux vents de la tempeste
> De ma pensée incessament troublée . . .
> De *doubte*[,] espoir, desir & ialousie,

155

Me fouldroyantz tels flots la fantasie
Abandonnée & d'aydes et d'appuys.   (D.393)

In translating the intricacies of human passion, Scève's allegorical narration splits the desiring subject into a number of aspects that populate the imaginary landscape of the dream and are fatally drawn to worship a female figure radiating the magical power of a primitive God, "constituée Idole de ma vie" (D. 1).

What Scève characterizes as the "sainct obiect de mon affection" (D. 361), functions as a divine force accounting for the libidinal drives from which allegorical representation poses the question of the ambivalence of love or the poet's complex relation to a figure constituting both intense sensuality and deep spirituality. "Que presque mort, sa Deité m'esvueille/En la clarté de mes desirs funebres" (D. 7). Thus one could conceivably argue, as in the case of Angus Fletcher, that "anxiety . . . is the most fertile ground from which allegorical abstractions grow."[7] In studying "the psychoanalytic analogues" of allegorical writing, Fletcher associates compulsive and obsessional behavior with narratives of purification which usually transmit an ethical imperative. Fletcher draws upon Freud's *Totem and Taboo* and relates these psychoanalytic concepts – "compulsion and obsession" – to the notion of ambivalence reflected in the dialectical relationship with a tabooed object that is sacred and yet forbidden. In this context Scève attributes magical power to the figure of Délie – "percant corps, cœur & raison despourveue" – who, although she metaphorically penetrates the body and fatally submits it to the imperatives of desire, also makes herself forbidden; the amorous subject wishes to come into contact with the desired object and yet fears proximity to it.

The cleavage in the representation of the desiring subject thus corresponds to the more primitive aspects of the self and enables the poet to enter into an allegorical contract in which identity is mediated by a series of discrete voices depicting the power of inner conflicts. Here the amorous subject enters into an internal struggle between the delightful threats of pleasure associated with physical appetite and the imperatives of a more spiritual order. The lover's self-reflexivity results in a loss of personal identity that is effectively depicted by a mixture of antagonistic elements.

> Le hault penser de mes frailes desirs
> Me chatouilloit a plus haulte entreprise,
> Me desrobant moymesme a mes plaisirs,
> Pour destourner la memoire surprise
> Du bien, auquel l'Ame demoura prise.   (D. 118)

If the *frailes desirs* of the amorous subject work to disengage memory from the spiritual figure of goodness (*bien*) to which his soul (*ame*) was drawn, it is because the identity of the self is fatally entangled in the eternal cycle of amorous dialogue. Ultimately, the dizain transcribes the image of a lover victimized by the tragedy of self-dissolution and the fall into oblivion: "Je m'abysme aux oblieuses rives." The energy and stability of the self is undermined by the conflicting postulates that the allegorical figures represent, and in that process forecloses on the possibility of establishing a guiding principle. "Dont maulgré moy, trop vouluntairement/Ie me meurs pris es rhetz, que i'ai tendu" (D. 411).

Many of Scève's dream poems begin by evoking the nocturnal anxiety experienced during the lover's awakened state. In D. 100, for example, the *topos* of insomnia derived from the Latin poets Tibullus and Propertius is juxtaposed with the Petrarchan *topoi* of extravagant comfort and laziness. By shifting emphasis away from the ethics associated with greed, the scèvian text transforms the *locus* of sensual enjoyment – the soft feathered bed – into one of uncontrollable torment and physical displeasure.

> L'oysiueté des delicates plumes,
> Lict coustumier, non point de mon repos,
> Mais du trauail, ou mon feu tu allumes,
> Souuentefois, oultre heure, & sans propos
> Entre ses drapz me detient indispos,
> Tant elle m'à pour son foible ennemy.

The amorous subject depicts himself as a weak and vulnerable being whose physical intensity renders him symbolically "worn out".

What is important here is not just the war-like image of the woman that makes its "destructiveness" so literally an effect of the desiring body, but the challenge to the subject's virility by a reference to an excess of sensual delight. In this context, as Dorothy Coleman suggests, Leon Hébreu's 1551 gloss on the word "delicates" as "quelques voluptés superflues, et non digne d'un homme robuste et ferme" is revealing.[8] In essence, what escapes the amorous subject is the sense of being capable of mastering desire. The tactile perception of the desiring body represents the masculine subject as attached to a negative *locus* within the phallic system; the sexuality of the devirilized male is therefore articulated as an enunciative act translating a passive acquiescence to the object of desire. This drive crosses the threshold of sensuality – "l'oysiueté des delicates plumes" – a phenomenon that reveals more than simple pleasure, but which eventually silences itself and subsequently produces the paralytic effect of being *indispos* (or what Cotgrave terms a state of "sickliness").

As soon as the scèvian subject crosses the threshold of dream in the final quatrain of the poem we witness a shift to a more abstract tone in which the drama of acceding to a higher form of love is allegorized by the figures of the mind and the body. The subject undergoes a symbolic split in the discourse of the dream. Not only does the text represent the unbridged distance that divides "I" in terms of mind versus body, it also portrays an ontological break underscoring the radical discontinuity between the "I" as so-called "subject of existence" and the "I" as the discursive subject of the fantasy.

> Là mon esprit son corps laisse endormy,
> Tout transformé en image de Mort,
> Pour te monstrer que lors homme a demy,
> Vers toy suis vif & vers moy ie suis mort. (D. 100)

The dream narrative enacts the symbolic murder of the desiring body by transforming it into a lifeless corpse. Physical desire therefore takes on negative connotations because of its power to extinguish desire itself; it must be abandoned to engender a rebirth that can only be realized by a spirit engaging in a fiction of metaphysical object-cathexis.

But the survival of mind over body in Scève's dream narrative unquestionably involves a loss of self in other, a phenomenon accompanied by the belief in the omnipotent woman who ensures the desiring subject's life. The dreamer's lack of being can only be fulfilled by this object of nurturance; the rhetorical movement that makes possible the poet's focalization on Délie as unique object of desire is metonymy, the contiguity or the presence of the two lovers. It is therefore the symbolic m-other – "Vers toy suis vif, & vers moy is suis mort " – who recreates him through a spirituality that enables the poet to live in his mistress and to accept that fantasy as real. "En toy ie vis, ou que tu sois absente" (D. 144). As in the case of Leone Ebero's *Dialoghi d'amore,* love is not based on pursuit and possession, but rather on the spiritual symbiosis of the two lovers living in harmony.

Scève's narrative recounting death-in-life thus undergoes a chiasmatic reversal in the dream, and this life-in-death enables the amorous subject to gain access to the desired object, to embody himself in her, and yet transcend the frustrating excesses of corporeal desire. The quest for the desired object can only be realized within the antiseptic constraints of the dream where sexuality is transformed into a maternal tenderness that keeps desire alive but extinguishes the anxiety associated with sexual difference. The object in question guarantees the veritable being of the amorous subject for he can only find his place outside himself in the body and soul of his mistress. Surely it is no coincidence that the amorous subject as mediated by the figural abandonment of body for soul finds its self-definition ("lors homme à demi") in the figure of a woman who is conspicuously desexualized. This metamorphosis of the desiring subject into a composite figure realizes the dream of a platonic re-naissance and perhaps accounts for the incapacity for meeting "real" erotic demands.

Dizain 101 represents a dream narrative in which the amorous subject's quest for recognition is thwarted. As he sleeps, the figure of the poet invents the composite figure of Délie–Venus who is depicted in an idealized relationship in which the conjunction of images produces a simulacrum of harmony.

> Sur le matin songeant profondement,
> Ie vy ma Dame auec Venus la blonde.
> Elles auoient vn mesme vestement,
> Pareille voix, & semblable faconde:
> Les yeulx riantz en face, & texte ronde
> Auec maintient, qui le tout compassoit.

If seeing, as it is evoked here, is surveying with the eyes of the unconscious, it enables a veritable con-fusion of being.

In due course, Scève's text revises the initial image of symmetry and reveals the amorous subject's perception of Délie as more rebellious and less pitiful than that of Venus. The poet's desire to be the desire of the other – to be recognized as desirable by the other – allows him to enter into an amorous relationship in which the quest for pity is acted out; it is indeed the rejection by the object of the poet's love, and the relation of the subject to that rejection, that figures a break in the composite image.

> Mais vn regret mon cœur entrelassoit,
> Apperceuant ma Maistresse plus belle.
> Car Cytarée en pitié surpassoit
> Là, ou Delie est tousiours plus rebelle.

In surrendering to the demand for pity in the dream narrative, the subject realizes the need to remain a subject or what Lacan terms a "being in want" (*manque à être*); it simply evokes the "want-to-be loved" by the desired object.

This representation of psychic life reflects its own sense of violence: the poet implicates himself in a sadistic relationship derived from the rebellious chastity of the desired object. Even if the sought-after object of libidinal pleasure is lacking in the other, it nevertheless functions as an imaginary *locus* where the subject grounds its hopeless desire. The rejected lover's need for recognition ostensibly implies that desire must be conserved until it is recognized. In this context, Scève's dream narrative thus depicts the amorous relationship as a "model of frustration" in which the object of desire has been inscribed as the effect of the other's unwillingness to reply to its demand. This fantasy of domination leaves the amorous subject faced with isolation as the only possible alternative to the reciprocity of love.

If D. 101 reinforces the sense of unfulfilled desire, then D. 126 offers a contrary result that is ironically only achieved through a kind of inner blindness. In the first part of the dizain the text enacts the Petrarchan quest for the nocturnal; it personifies the figure of the Dream – Somnus, the Roman god of sleep – who slowly overcomes the amorous subject's mind at nightfall and endows it with the freedom to transcend the repressiveness of daily anguish.

> A l'embrunir des heures tenebreuses,
> Que Somnus lent pacifie la Terre[,]
> Enseuely soubz Cortines vmbreuses,
> Songe a moy vient, qui mon esprit desserre,
> Et tout aupres de celle là le serre,
> Qu'il reueroit pour son royal maintien.

As initially represented in the text, the relationship between the poet and Délie is mediated by the abstract figure of the mind; it worships the desired object as a kind of deity whose *royal maintien* creates a symbolic distance between himself and the desiring subject.[9] Quite clearly, Scève's text empowers the female figure with the authority to be recognized, and yet at the same time it demystifies the illusion of the possible reciprocation of love. The scèvian text renders intimate contact with this royal figure beyond the realm of social *bienséance*; it portrays a need essentially unsatisfiable in everyday life because its object – cold, isolated, and inaccessible – cannot ever be authentically apprehended.

However, it is in the rhetoric of the nocturnal dream that the scèvian text represents the illusion of pleasure by releasing the amorous subject from the fear of proximity to the desired object and the dangers of erotic attachment. The lover's discourse enacts the phantasmatic omnipotence that the desiring subject confers upon the woman; the desire for submission is realized within the parameters of an "imperialistic" embrace that attracts his spirit so as to make it hers. If it is the woman who exerts influence and power, it is because it is she who dispossesses man of his strength and dramatizes his state of helplessness.

> Mais par son doulx, & priué entretien
> L'attraict tant sien, que puis sans craincte aulcune
> Il m'est aduis, certes, que ie la tien,
> Mais ainsi, comme Endimion la Lune.　　　　　(D. 126)

In a sense, not only does Délie become more accessible in the world of dream due to her "doulx & priué entretien" but this also links her, as Dorothy Coleman suggests, "to the occasions when reciprocation of love in some physical sense is implied."[10] The dream-work therefore transforms the prohibition associated with the law of *bienséance* into its opposite and demonstrates that sexual enjoyment can only be realized in an unconscious state.

But the distance between the lovers previously alluded to in line 6 resurfaces in the clausal analogy established between Luna's possession of Endymion and the Moon-goddess Delia's imaginary seduction of the poet. According to the composite model of the classical legend that Scève's text draws upon – Cicero and Apollonius – Endymion fell in love with Hera and Zeus punished him for the crime of having desired his wife by putting his victim to eternal sleep on Mount Latmus.[11] As a result, Luna fell in love with Endymion and unconsciously made him the father of fifty daughters. Endymion thus comes to represent a passive object of seduction with whom the scèvian subject wishes to identify; the fulfillment of desire that is figured in the dream requires its recognition to remain essentially unrecognizable. Paradoxically, he longs for a desire that does not know its object; at the same time he confers upon it those aspects of Délie – possession through seduction – which the poet is apparently reluctant consciously to acknowledge.

In essence, Endymion becomes an alienated subject within the dream's mental topography. Through the creation of a dream which celebrates the joys of ignorance, the discourse of love

162

allegorizes the poet's fantasy to counteract the dangers of libidinal energy. Even in the unconscious state of the dream, the dreamer transmits knowledge that he wishes to extricate himself from. Yet at the same time he silently pursues in a fearless manner (*sans craincte aulcune*) the quest for that magical moment that holds the desiring subject motionless, in eternal sleep, and transforms him into the passive victim of female seduction. The Endymion metaphor thus depicts the ego's imaginary identification with a figure who wishes to situate himself in the prelapsarian bliss of erotic attachment, a phenomenon that can only be realized if the desiring subject does not know the *truth* of his own desire. The subject who is profoundly marked by passivity can temporarily engage in a more active sexuality.

In dizain 143, the memory generated by the dream arouses a forbidden desire, one that must ultimately be purged. From the start, memory generates thought and becomes the *locus* of a fiction-making process dependent on the illusion of the experience of seeing.[12] Scève's text represents memory as the repressed content that seduces the desiring subject and nurtures him with the specular illusion of a "sweet lie"; its very substance thoroughly permeates his thought and ravishes it beyond reason.

> Le souuenir, ame de ma pensée
> Me rauit tant en son illusif songe
> Que n'en estant la memoire offensée,
> Ie me nourris de si doulce mensonge.

Entry into the world of dream puts the mind to rest and sets the stage for an allegorical struggle between a slumbering mind and an intensity of passion that threatens the integrity of the amorous subject.

> Or quand l'ardeur qui pour elle me ronge,
> Contre l'esprit sommeillant se hazarde,
> Soubdainement qu'il s'en peult donner garde,
> Ou qu'il se sent de ses flammes greué.

The memory of Délie thus penetrates the mind's body and oppresses it with a terrifying specter of force that the dreamer prefers not to acknowledge. The disruption and internal conflict

163

caused by this excess of energy reveals what the writing subject can only articulate within the parameters of dream narrative. Desire's belligerency activates the subject's abandonment of mastery in the libidinal struggle, a phenomenon transcribed in poetic fantasy as a challenge to the imperatives of the contemplative order. In order to extricate himself from the world of dream, the figure of the poet must describe an appropriate way of regulating his now ungovernable imaginative activity.

In the last two lines of this dizain a more "authentic" image of Délie emerges through a striking comparison with the figure of the serpent raised up *in deserto*. This image suppresses the illusions of lustful dreams and replaces them with the closest thing possible to absolute sight, a glimpse at a purely visual abstraction.

> En mon penser soubdain il te regarde,
> Comme au desert son Serpent esleué.

Here Scève draws upon a biblical intertext (*Numbers,* xxi, verses 6–9) in which "Jehovah, in anger, sent a plague of venomous serpents upon the Israelites to punish them for blasphemy."[13] That same narrative reveals, according to Ian McFarlane, "that Moses had intervened on behalf of the rebellious Israelites; he created a bronze serpent, hoisted it upon a pole," and empowered it with the ability to cure those who had been bitten by poisonous snakes through the mere act of gazing upon it.[14] As in the case of the venomous serpents, the wounds of love implicitly alluded to here can only be healed by the paradoxical presence of the beloved; the poison is also the cure. A spiritual rebirth is enacted through reference to the Brazen Serpent, which in Renaissance iconography symbolized the resurrection of Christ, and is used in this context to maintain the illusion of transcendence.

In using this biblical reference as narrative frame, Scève's text re-vises the image of Délie, and in that process crosses a threshold of differentiation between what stands for the "real" and the representation of its image in dream. The dizain activates a figure of psychic transformation that bridges the gaps between the discourse of desire and the zone of restraint. Once he gazes on the erect idol-like image Délie now represents in his mind's eye, the poet is able to replace the disturbance of memory with the figure of a self-contained being whose function is to cleanse and repress through affective distancing. Délie's state of omnipotence, with its absence of tension, gives birth to a fantasy of domination. In a way, this sudden metamorphosis makes the sight of Délie function as a sign out of which the symbolic order may be constructed; it wards off the terrifying excess of desire which the blasphemous activity of memory has afflicted upon him. The conscious mind therefore discovers within itself the image of Délie which, unlike the one in the dream, now has a curative effect, a purely intellectual re-vision that counters the initial passion and offers the desiring subject a phallic persona who is irresistible.[15] Like the mule woodcut further along in the *Délie,* this image is meant to portray both the sterility and the attitude of dominance which characterizes the goddess.[16]

If the figure of the poet flees carnal relations it is to submit itself to the image of a mistress become master; the law of the father becomes that of a mother commanding the sacrifice of pleasure for a new order represented by the image of a divine figure in its purest and most abstract form ("en mon penser soubdain"). Clearly, Scève's text attributes ontological priority to the woman as cult object. She represents spiritual omnipotence through the visual association with the serpent erect and idol-like on the staff. The enactment of the phallic woman's sterile imperialism entombs the power of desire within the confines of a phantasmatic discourse (that of dream) and inflicts the amorous subject with the silence and anonymity of a repentant lover. Paradoxically, the only "real" contact with Délie can be realized through a figural ground within which desire is engulfed by the image of a woman who insures the integrity of the lover's self-image.

The archetypal image of the serpent often resurfaces in the *Délie* and reveals the moral dualism attributed to the female subject (the ability to both generate and repress desire) as well as the psychological ambivalence of the lover. The goddess-like figure's visual penetration of the lover in D. 1, for example, establishes what might be described as an "erotic trauma" in which the amorous subject, although sensually agitated, does not succeed in taking possession of the woman's body. Because the power of desire is so strong, the poet must invent imaginary defenses to remain in control before the aimless meandering or the *jeunes erreurs* preceding his entry into the sacred sphere of divine love. In fact, the sight of Délie – referred to by Scève as an *idole* or, translated in sixteenth-century language as *fantasme,* image, decree, ordinance or act – ironically produces a self-consciousness that transforms the possibility of phallic enjoyment into a kind of moral defeat.[17] The youthful inconstancy associated with the rhythm of petrarchan temporality yields to a transcendent force that purifies desire and subjugates it to a higher value.

> L'Oeil trop ardent en mes ieunes erreurs
> Girouettoit, mal cault, à l'impourueue:
> Voicy (ô paour d'agreables terreurs)
> Mon Basilisque auec sa poingnant' veue
> Percant Corps, Cœur & Raison despourueue,
> Vint penetrer en l'Ame de mon Ame.
>   Grant fut le coup, qui sans tranchante lame
> Fait, que viuant le Corps, l'Esprit deuie,
> Piteuse hostie au conspect de toy, Dame,
> Constituée Idole de ma vie.

If the excessive instability (or "errors") of the desiring subject is put to rest here it is because the lethal power of "mon Basilique," another serpentine figure, yields to the phantasmatic demands of a causative agent, a false image, invented to facilitate the quelling of desire. In a way, like the pool in which Narcissus views his reflection, this phenomenon enables the poet at first to see what he takes to be the object of desire, and then to see himself as it is decreed in the realm of fantasy.[18] The ego thus becomes the reflection of a narcissistic urge grounded in the return of the lover's image to itself through the rewriting of the Ovidian intertext of self-recognition.[19] Accordingly, Scève–Narcissus becomes the victim of a projected image, one to which he is hopelessly susceptible as the victim of a paradoxical female figure who tells him what he wishes to know. "Car mon desir par ta parolle ouyt,/Qu'en te donnant a moy, tu m'estois Dame" (D. 133). The visual perception of the other is but an encounter with the other imprinted within himself. Ironically, Scève's text attributes the power of the gaze to the man, however vulnerable he may appear to be. Going far beyond Délie as an object to be contemplated, this dizain makes way for a male subject to be observed as a spectacle in himself.

But the reenactment of a similar rhetorical situation in D. 143, through the allegorical figure of the *serpent élevé au desert,* realizes a form of closure that is thoroughly phallocentric in nature. The desexualization of Délie in a field of vision external to that of dream paradoxically projects the sacralization of her image in a phallic performance that is devoid of sensuality. It appears, then, that the scèvian subject can only transcend the trauma of sexuality when the relation between the sexes fails. The impetus to reinscribe the *topos* of the phallic woman here bears witness to the amorous subject's demand to be overtaken by a curious abstinence creating a stable, reborn self, fashioned by the threatening gaze of the other. With the female figure as phallus we are all, as Kristeva puts it, *"arrêtés* (stopped, arrested) by this fabulous truth."[20] The writing subject's figurative redemption from the ravages of passionate desire displays how poetic language does justice to the affect of fear and to the mechanisms of its mitigation.

Perhaps more than any other poem using the dream *topos,* dizain 159 evokes the fatality that all love relationships must endure in spite of attempts at mastery. While in a state of deep sleep, the desiring subject imagines being touched by the beloved's hand which is both the object of desire from which sexual attraction emanates and the catalyst for its extinction. The libidinal delight associated with the power of touch – however slight it may be – awakens the lover's unconscious thoughts and extricates him from the symbolic death called repression. The self-reflexivity generated here figurally transcribes the tragic passion that burns within the soul.

Si de sa main ma fatale ennemye,
Et neantmoins delices de mon Ame,
Me touche vn rien, ma pensée endormye
Plus que le mort soubz sa pesante lame,
Tressaulte en moi, comme si d'ardent flamme
Lon me touchait, dormant profondement.

The mind allows passion to violate it to such an extent that desire takes on the character of a life force whose energy is insatiable and whose very process of becoming constitutes its excess and ultimate ruin. In essence, the rebirth of the lover's unconscious thought gives sight to blindness. Yet overwhelmed as he is by an intensity of passion for the figure of the beloved, the desiring subject's newly awakened lucidity must remain outside his control.

The final four verses of this dizain reveal that Scève's dream of love is little more than the tragedy of its ultimate failure. In essence, the desire that Délie incarnates is the cause of his death. The more the amorous subject flees desire the more deadly it becomes. The text effectively evokes quiescence through the paradox of stimulation. Battling against the exigencies of a more profane love, the spirit finally succumbs to the force of the death instinct as the only possible release from the anguish of excitation.

Adonc l'esprit poulsant hors roidement,
La veut fuyr, & moy son plus affin,
En en ce poinct (a parler rondement)
Fuyant ma mort, i'accelere ma fin.

Here Scève's text draws upon the emblem of the wounded stag that introduces the group of poems to which D. 159 belongs. Based on a tradition that runs from Virgil's *Aeneid* (IV, 69–74) to Petrarch's "I dolci colli," the image of the wounded stag is not only a symbol of carnal passion but also translates the dilemma that the lovesick subject finds himself in: the flight to save his life ironically intensifies the pain that he must endure and precipitates his encounter with death. The stag's instinct of self-preservation enables it to follow the path to its own ruin by maintaining the hunter and the hunted in a power structure based on the myth of absolutism.

What distinguishes Scève's rewriting of this *topos* in the dream narrative is the way in which he juxtaposes sexual and intellectual modes of desire into an allegorical representation of the death instinct as self-chosen act. If death becomes the object that the subject strives for, it is because it signifies a form of desire that is beyond itself. The negativity to be overcome here ("ma mort") paradoxically transforms the object of life into a form of non-being ("ma fin"). The attempt at exorcism is therefore doomed to failure. "Fuyant ma mort, i'haste ma fin." The energy of the desiring subject produces a mode of thought which, in attempting to evade desire, turns murderously upon the love and accelerates the death of thought itself.

Thus the nature of desire, as represented in the figurative language of Scève's dream narratives, is to create a situation in which it cannot ever be authentically fulfilled. "Ce mien trauail iamais ne cessera" (D. 167). What is at stake here is nothing less than the amorous subject's quest for self-recognition in a struggle between eros and the intellect. And yet, throughout, the lover cannot grasp the truth of his sexuality but only its effects emanating from the figure of an omnipotent female whom he both worships and fears. Indeed the enigma (and perhaps the pleasure) of the anxious male subject is maintained by reducing woman to the status of censoring object through which an insatiable appetite may be tamed; desire is found in the tension towards, rather than through the attainment of, the object of love. Scève's dream of love is derived from a scenario in which sexual difference is the result of an interdiction that valorizes the asymmetry of gender roles and consequently the masculinity attributed, in this particular case, to the female object. If the lover's discourse uncovers the repressed wish to be possessed, it also demonstrates the impossibility of that possession through an allegorical rhetoric that reveals that the thought of erotic love is essentially disturbing and that its realization is ultimately unattainable. "O Dieux, ô Cieux, oyez mes douleances" (D. 70).

10

SEXUALITY AND THE POLITICAL UNCONSCIOUS IN RABELAIS' *QUART LIVRE:* THREE CASE STUDIES

Pro-logos: excess and the golden mean

By the time Rabelais was ready to compose the *Quart Livre*, the need to defend his book against the blasphemous attacks of his detractors became increasingly critical. Condemned by the Sorbonne after the appearance of the *Tiers Livre* in 1546, and subsequently censored by the Sorbonagre de Puy-Herbault in 1549 and Jean Calvin in 1550, Rabelais, victimized by the most extreme mechanisms of psychic and social repression, found it necessary to repress his wildest impulses and obey a law conceived in the name of the other.[1] To be sure, the text is the obedient and servile offspring, the scriptural representation – that glorifies the edicts of paternal law while at the same time unconsciously trangressing it. Although Rabelais proposes moderation – the golden mean – as an ideal, his text puts this notion into question through an ever-surfacing fear of excess and uncontrollable appetite. In other words, moderation is posited as an ideal while in fact the text reveals its antithetical correlates. The rabelaisian novel must therefore be read as an artifact in which the text's unconscious counterplot reveals, through its language, that any knowledge of self or other remains purely elusive. The signs of the text are symptoms, never directly interpretable in themselves, but only in terms of an imaginary "sub-text" which lies within the symbolic order of language. The reader must penetrate the archaeological strata and illuminate the latent forces entrapped there by elucidating the book's psychotextual structures which constitute the way in which the text

171

unveils its dissimulated self-preoccupations; if the Rabelaisian unconscious is evoked, it is only within the context of the material form of discourse. The narrative thus provides a passageway to subjectivity through the re-inscription of obsessive *topoi* which function as a mimesis of the production of meaning. Rabelais externalizes the internal; he establishes within the text a relationship in which the narrative subject is portrayed through the figurative choreographics of the script.

The signature to the prologue of the *Quart Livre* – "François Rabelais docteur en medicine" – implicitly points to Rabelais' chosen therapeutic role: the physician whose profession is to cure the suffering body, to restore health (the divinely ordained condition of man) and harmony to the world by the purgation of that which is excessive.[2] At the outset, the author–narrator's sense of self is structured in another's discourse. Rabelais' textual presence is mediated through the alterity of scripture and secular history. In the first case, the writer indicates that he relies on the will of God as evidenced in Luke IV where the physician who neglects his own health is criticized and told: "Medicin, o, gueriz toymesmes" (p. 12); this reference indirectly evokes the writer's perception that he is the victim of the menacing gaze of the other.[3] The biblical text(s) returns the writer's self-portrait to the introjected earliness, an identification of poet with exemplary physician. The second reference, taken from Claudius Galen, reveals the writer's fear of exposing himself to satirical jibes as well as the consciousness of the precariousness of his public role; the physician who himself is not healthy cannot claim an authoritative function.[4] "Cl. Gal. non pour telle reverence en santé soy maintenoit, quoy que quelque sentiment il eust des sacres Bibles et eust congneu et frequenté les saincts Christians de son temps . . . mais par craincte de tomber en ceste vulgaire et satyrique mocquerie" (p. 12). To be sure, Rabelais aims at repressing his own uncanny instincts so that he may substitute evenness and health for the excesses of *Antiphysie*. Rabelais' appropriation of these introjected narrative voices reveals a latent paranoia, a fear of being judged which yields itself to complete personification. And so Lacan is correct when he writes that "l'inconscient est discours de l'Autre" because the other constitutes an inescapable mediation, a third term, which always falls between the ego and the object of desire.[5] The so-called authoritative and omni-present *je* self-effaces under the veil of borrowed voices; it uses various forms of exemplary fictions to defend the writer's rhetorical praxis as well as the autonomy of the imaginary self. Rabelais lures us to accept a fictional narrative stance which uses structure to re-present a displaced, textually mediated psyche. Hence the rabelaisian discourse is not only a message addressed to the other, but is also a discourse whose source is located elsewhere.

Immediately following this introduction to the prologue, Rabelais presents a text in which he equates health with one's right to claim back lost private property. Health becomes inextricably associated with the financial metaphor, particularly with private property and the right to inherit what one is bequeathed. In this context, the legal axion *le mort saisist le vif* is striking.[6] On the literal level it signifies that the dead shall "seize the quick" or cling onto life. Figuratively this expression belongs to the language of legal discourse and indicates that before dying the testator exercises his will and confers properties on his inheritors.

Si, par quelque desastre, s'est santé de vos seigneuries emancipée, quelque part ... avecques l'ayde du benoist Servateur rencontrer! En bonne heure de vous rencontrée, sus l'instant soit par vous asserée, soit par vous vendiquée, soit par vous saisie et mancipée. Les loigs vous le permettent, le Roy l'entend, je le vous conseille. Ne plus ne moins que les legislateurs antiques authorisoient le seigneur vendiquer son serf fugitif, la part qu'il seroit trouvé. Ly bon Dieu et ly bons homs! n'est il escript et practiqué, par les anciennes coustumes de ce tant noble ... royaulme de France que *le mort saisist le vif?*   (p. 13)

In the context of Renaissance writing, the partaking of the *hereditas* is related to the dynamics of imitation and invention. As a Renaissance writer, Rabelais does not create *ex-nihilo*; he fills his narrative space with inherited property whereby the intricacies of the writer's thoughts are mediated through the wealth of literary sources to which he gives new form. The writer returns to the scene of the origin of narrative from which he appropriates various subjects; inheritance involves the appropriation and re-naming of property legally under the banner of textual imperialism. The realm of intertextuality implicitly evoked in the financial metaphor places the *je* in the position of an "interchange," where the bequeathed material is the pre-text to be sorted out and re-presented within a new textual web. The dead man breathes new life into the writer who also writes for posterity. The association of health with the transference of private property seems to valorize – however indirect it may be – the legal appropriation of the discourse of the other as a commodified product or an abstract form of value.

But the allegorical reading of the text must leave its unresolved riddles in place; the reader's process of understanding is soon arrested when Rabelais re-inscribes the judicial adage within a medical perspective evoking the health of both body and mind. "Sans santé n'est la vie que langueur; le vie n'est que simulachre de mort. Ainsi doncques vous, estants de santé privez, c'est à dire mors, saisissez vous du vif, saisissez vous de vie, c'est santé" (p. 14). The text thus becomes the successive and cumulative experience of these tangles of meaning and figuration. The refusal of death not only points to Rabelais' endless quest for health (through the Platonic theme of *bios abiōtos*), but implicitly signals an instinctual process which effectively opposes ends (death, quiescence, non-narratibility) to beginnings. To seize life is to seize the narrative thread of existence, the masterplot of endless desire. Yet the drive for a salvific cure does not lie in the power of man alone since it is to God that Rabelais ultimately directs us to address humble prayers made in firm faith: "J'ay cestuy espoir en Dieu qu'il oyra nos prieres, veue la ferme foy en laquelle nous les faisons; et accomplira cestuy nostre soubhayt, attendu qu'il est mediocre" (p. 14). God – the archetypal father – becomes the legislator who dictates the author's course of action and makes it possible for the law to be erected and for prayers to be answered. And the book's moral imperative is made explicit in the *aurea mediocritas topos*; the ideality of the other (Horace, *Odes,* ii, 10) ultimately gains entry into the text of the subject:

174

"Mediocrité a esté par les saiges anciens dicte aurée, c'est à dire precieuse, de tous louée, en tous endroictz agréable" (p. 14). The gold motif, as it is used here, figuratively denotes an abstract form of inward value associated with sanity and health.[7]

The main part of the prologue is built around a series of embedded tales and anecdotes, some of which relate to the loss of a *coingnée* (hatchet, phallus). Rabelais' adaptation of the Aesopic fable of the woodsman who loses his axe and the Lucianic council of the Gods into which it is integrated, takes up a major portion of the prologue, and functions as an exemplary restatement of the moral correlatives previously considered: moderation of desire, diligent work, and submission to God's authority. Through his appropriation of this tale, Rabelais reinscribes the ethical maxim within a socio-economic context. The tale recounts the trials and tribulations of Couillatris who is chopping wood when suddenly his hatchet – his sole source of survival – is lost.

> car de sa coingnée dependoit son bien et sa vie . . .
> sans coingnée mouroit de faim. La mort six jours
> après, le rencontrant sans coingnée, avecques son
> dail l'eust fauché et cerclé de ce monde. (p. 16)

Jupiter, upon hearing Couillatris' plea for restitution of the lost hatchet, responds and sends his messenger Mercury, god of thieves, who presents the woodchopper with three axes to choose from: iron, silver, gold. Since he chooses his own – and behaves within the boundary of the mean – he is rewarded with all three. Couillatris thus functions as a kind of ego ideal for Rabelais, the ultimate ground on which he may build all of the ideological concerns of the *Quart Livre*. However, the abstract form of value associated with the ethical *topos* concerning moderation is transposed here so that the riches acquired by Couillatris take a concrete "literal" form that is paradoxically enumerated in the excessive style of the *copia verborum*:

> En Chinon il change sa coingnée d'argent en beaulx
> testons et aultre monnoye blanche; sa coingée d'or
> en beaulx salutz, beaulx moutons à la grande laine,

175

belles riddes, beaulx royaulx, beaulx escutz au
Soleil. Il en achapte force mestairies, force granges,
force censes, force mas, forces bordes et bordieux,
force cassines, prez, vignes, boys, terres labourables.   (p. 25)

Couillatris' wealth leads to the re-establishment of plenitude as well as to the satisfaction of desire whereby the self is reassured of its integrity as a result of its unselfconscious spontaneity. The Couillatris model therefore serves as the representation of an ideal self in which the principle of tempered desire enables productivity to flourish. The exchange of the gold and silver hatchets yields profits which permit Couillatris to buy material to sow the land and thereby return to a more "primitive" economy.

Rabelais' exemplary fable has yet a negative counterpart – what we might call a dialectical inversion – that surfaces in the second half of the story and displays the many nefarious effects of excess. Learning of Couillatris' reward, his neighbors decide to become "perdeurs de coingnée" in order to get rich quick. They exchange their swords for *coingnées* and thus purposely lose them, a self-nihilating act that induces a void to be continually compensated for.

Adoncques tous perdirent leurs coingnées. Au diable l'un à qui demoura coingnée! Il n'estoit filz de bonne mere qui ne perdist sa coingnée. Plus n'estoit abbatu, plus n'estoit fendu boys on pays, en ce default de coingnées.   (p. 26)

When asked to choose the hatchet they rightfully own, these men select those made of gold, and the price they pay for their dishonesty and lack of restraint is decapitation. Now this self-inflicted loss represents the desire for wholeness, both an increment and a substitute to replace an original sense of lack. Yet the symbolic loss of the hatchet, instead of supplementing the psychological void at the center of the ego, makes the subject suffer further detachment and fragmentation. The investment, based on wild speculation and motivated by an uncontrollable appetite, ends in bankruptcy; the attempted theft of the gold *coingnée* ultimately leads to the non-restitution of the original loss and the robbers' precipitous death. The uncontrollable – perhaps even perverse – quest for plenitude ultimately produces the dissolution of nature and the thieves' irreparably unsatisfied desire. Material greed therefore reduces the neighbors' libidinal energy to a state of impotence, forbidding them to regain their self-presence and humanity.

Rabelais' inversion of the lost hatchet story seems fairly straightforward until one realizes that the fable can be read figuratively as a psycho-sexual allegory of writing.[8] The psycho-dynamics evoked here make reference to more than just an internal conflict; they are concerned with representing the affective structure of the fable, what we might call the textual unconscious in which displaced psychic signs play out the author's repressed fear in the form of sexual metaphors whose choreographics bring the text out of self-imposed silence by creating a new narrative. Writing thus becomes an instrument of repression which supplements the author's voice; it takes the place of what it purports to signify and becomes the voice of the dissimulated other.

At a meeting of Jupiter's council, Priapus plays on the semantic ambiguity of the word *coingnée* and thereby directly introduces the sexual metaphor into the framework of the prologue. When Mercury informs Jupiter of Couillatris' outrageous prayers, the textual system undergoes a tropological substitution whereby the shift from literal to figurative level signals the specular inversion between the metaphors of economic and sexual desire. Priapus' witty homophonic equivocation of the word *coingnée* leads to a discussion of the scatological meaning of the word:

Roy Juppiter, on temps que, par vostre ordonnance et particulier benefice, j'estois guardian des jardins en terre, je notay que ceste diction, *coingnée,* est equivocque à plusieurs choses. Elle signifie un certain instrument par le service duquel est fendu et couppé boys. Signifie aussi . . . la femelle bien à poinct et souvent gimbretiletolletée. Et veidz que tout bon compagnon appelloit sa guarse fille de joye: ma coingnée. Car, avecques cestuy ferrement (cela disoit exhibant son coingnouoir dodrental) ilz leurs coingnent si fierement d'audace leurs emmanchouoirs qu'elles restes exemptes d'une paour epide miale entre le sexe feminin: c'est que du bas ventre ilz leurs tombassent sur les talons, par default de telles agraphes. (pp. 21–2)

The figure of sexual conjunction serves as a paragon of ideal beauty which portrays the sexual harmony of opposing elements – the ultimate desire of the appetitive soul – as the liquidation of emptiness and absence; the inversion of the hatchet into the helve – "coingnée est emanchée" (IV, ix) – relates the synecdochical make-up of the composite ideal, an androgynous entity through which one has access to wholeness and the universal harmony of love.[9] It is therefore not surprising that Rabelais chose Priapus, the phallic deity ("roydde dieu des jardins"), the god of horticulture and potency, to relate the manner in which to arrest fear and achieve plenitude. The tropological substitution at work here is grounded in a consistent system of thought, announced at the beginning of the prologue and developed throughout. Couillatris, whose name evokes the male genitals, announces the themes of generativity and potency; through the tempered use of the *coingnée* (hatchet, phallus, or metonymically a "well-swived woman"), plenitude and abundance are achieved. The "perdeurs de coingnées" fall victim to the misfortunes of sterility and are punished by a simulacre of castration that results in the loss of productivity; their heads are severed because of their excessive desire for gain. Relayed by the trope of sexuality, the hatchet becomes a figure of generativity and potency whose misuse proves the unmitigated value of modesty and restraint.

It could be argued that the mimesis assumed here thematizes a self-reflexive metaphor for the act of writing. The homophonic equivocation produced through Priapus' solecism (the play on words *mens* [esprit] and *mentula* [member]) equates the mind with the irresistible drive of desire for the wholeness and plenitude from which the book is born; an intertextual memory – the locus of *inventio* – functions as the generative force of the book.[10] "J'ay mentule, voire diz je memoire bien belle, et grande assez pour emplir un pot beurrier" (p. 22). The specular structure between economy and sexuality and sexuality and thought is interiorized in a text in which the author's presence is mediated through the figurative power of language whose thematic axis hinges upon reflections on desire, wealth, and creativity; the free-floating play of substitutions and repetitions masks the subject's all too powerful libidinal thrust which itself is ultimately fictional, a misnaming which reconstructs what the name of the lost object might signify. The association of the mind and phallus established here – through metonymic displacement: *coingnée*-→ hatchet (earning power)→ phallus (source of fertility, reproduction, creativity)→ mind→ memory – furnishes the textual evidence for the assumption that the fear of dismemberment (the punishment for the misuse of the *coingnée* or the *memoire* as used by the *mentula*) and amputation that appears throughout the *Quart Livre* is a figure of Rabelais' near-obsessive concern with the mutilation of the poetic self (the mind as thinking agent). The seizure of the phallic metasignifier – the very locus of plenitude and potency – creates a void symbolizing the lack that is constitutive of desire. The play on words thus functions as the pretext and pre-text for the refusal of a transparent representational thought.[11] The arbitrary power-play of the signifier operates through an immeasurable paranoiac machine that functions metaphorically as the text's reading of the writer's fear of punishment for excessive self-expression.

Freud's later interpretation of the castration complex has brought our attention to its inextricable relationship to the Oedipal crisis and the subject's phobic formation centering on the father's real role as castrator. The fear of castration threatens the ego's integrity; it is a true "external danger" that motivates anxiety.[12] If the penis remains on the body it has no general symbolic value; it is only in castration, that is by threatening a constituted whole, that the body symbolically becomes the figure of absence and incompletion. At the base of the castration complex is the anxiety of being accused of theft, the fear of punishment by a patriarchal authority for having usurped parental authority, for transgressing the law of the father and desiring that which is *forbidden*. The fantasmatic theatricalization of the

179

consequences of immoderate desire – as evidenced in the "per-deurs de coingnées" sequence – entails a ruse of writing in which the author's obsessional neurosis surfaces; those who engage in ostentatious behavior and transgress the "rule" of law – "pour soy gourgaiser à la monstre" – are destined for misfortune. The rational way must purge the poisonous effects of the uncontroll-able appetite from which "ne vous ne advient que le tac et la clavelée, en bourse pas maille." Disease and poverty thematize emptiness and absence.

Rabelais' exemplary fable prefigures many of the appetitive crises that constitute the plot of the *Quart Livre*. Amongst them is the chapter concerning how the devil was fooled by an old woman of Popefigeland. Rabelais once again re-inscribes the metaphors of economy and desire within the text. On this island populated by those who have fallen on hard times, the devil attempts to illegally appropriate part of an innocent farmer's land so that he may share in the profits. The devil, believing that he was twice fooled by the farmer, requests the scheduling of a scratching match, the loser of which shall forfeit his share of the field. The old woman deceives the devil and falsely claims that the farmer had practiced scratching her and tore a huge hole between her legs. The devil's desire for excessive gain and self-aggrandizement is thwarted by fear of punishment for his satanic appetite. The vaginal abyss functions as the metaphorical inver-sion of the search for abundance, the fear of the consequences of phallic dismemberment. The vacant cavity that haunts the devil – "enorme solution de continuité en toutes directions" – evokes in him an emptiness, a body "seemingly" without reproductive organs, the price he would conceivably have to pay for the mode of excess and for stealing that which does not belong to him. It is therefore due to anxiety that the devil is obliged to renounce his aggressive activity; the objective correlative of his fear is a vacant *locus* wherein the subject is obliged to recognize the potential consequences for his assault against "rationality," normality, and good behavior. "Le Diable ... s'escria; 'Mahon, Demiour-gon, Megere, Alecto, Persephone! Il ne me tient pas! Je m'en voys bel erre. Cela! Je luy quitte le champ" (p. 178). The playing out in his mind of the imaginary castration translates the fear of chastisement and oppression, the inevitable consequences of the castration scenario, which subjugates desire and functions as a remedy to uncontrollable greed.[13] The language of dismemberment symbolically portrays the irrational impulses that motivate an untempered need for self-aggrandizement.

The prologue problematizes the role and function of repression and its relationship to the impasses of controversy, fate, and self-expression. Rabelais' defense strategy is emblematized in the mechanical remedy imposed on the pernicious bickering of those who are in conflict. At the meeting at Jupiter's council we learn of his difficulties in resolving the dispute raging between Ramus and Galland, two dialectical philosophers of the period who argue over principles of Aristotelian and Platonic philosophy. As Jupiter emphatically declares, each philosopher is what he is destined to be, the victim of a "partial" insight, an egotistical personage irreconcilably different from the other. "L'un est un fin et cauld renard; l'autre mesesdisant, mescrivant et abayant contre les antiques Philosophes et Orateurs, comme un chien" (p. 18). The comparison of Ramus to a fox and Galland to a dog creates a chain of metaphorical substitutions which – through the relay of the theme of "destiny" – evokes discord and factionalism, the antithesis of health and harmony. "Le chien, par son destin fatal doibvoit prendre le renard; le renard, par son destin ne doibvoit estre prins" (p. 18). Suddenly Priapus intervenes in the conversation and advises Jupiter to settle the Ramus–Galland matter the same way he once handled the quarreling fox and dog: turn them both to stone. However, Priapus' problem finds its ultimate solution in the semantic isomorphism established between the predicative (the verb "petrifier") and nominal forms (the name "Pierre") and the anti-logic of the Limousine proverb; the characters' names arbitrarily determine the "judicious" solution of their fate.

La metamorphose n'est incongnue. Tous deux portent nom de Pierre. Et parce que, scelon le proverbe des Limosins, à faire la gueule d'un four sont trois pierres necessaires, vous les associerez à maistre Pierre du Coingnet, par vous jadis pour mesmes causez petrifié. Et seront, en figure trigone equilaterale, on grand temple de Paris, ou on mylieu de pervis, posées ces trois pierres mortes, en office de extaindre avecques le nez ... lesquelles, vivantes, allumoient couillonniquement le feu de faction, simulte, sectes couillonniques, et partialté entre les ocieux escholiers. A perpetuele memoire que ces petites philauties couillonniformes plus tost devant vous contempnées feurent que condamnées.

(pp. 19–20)

Excess appears to be liquidated through petrification which, in effect, suppresses the kinetic energy of the libido. Priapus inauthentically attentuates the conflict through the immobilization and reification of movement; he represents the moment when the text sublimates its self-knowledge, which seems to involve an artificial reduction of tension to zero. Petrification is therefore the return to an inauthentic order, the harmony created "en figure equilaterale" which, in fact, liquidates the need for ideological victory and dissimulates anxiety through a projection into a homeostatic syncretism.[14]

The reference to Pierre du Cugnières, a medieval jurisconsult who defended the monarchy of Phillipe VI against a church that attempted to draw money illegally out of France in the name of the "holy" Decretals, ostensibly links this narrative digression to the *coingnée* motif of the fable.[15] Not only is this association established by phonological contiguity, but the name itself, through its indirect reference to the phallus (Cugnières → Coignet → coingnée), functions as the signifying agent of "repressed" desire. In order to avenge themselves of the Gallican activities of Pierre du Coignet, the church fathers placed a stone statue (*pierre*) in a corner (*coin*) of Notre Dame (thus a "Pierre du Coignet") where candles were meant to be extinguished. This attempt to transform "coignet" into "Pierre" reveals allegorically the fundamentally homogenizing process of repression. The discourse on desire in this sequence does not promote the phallus (the ultimate signifier of appetite) to a central role in stimulating and releasing quanta of energy, but rather suppresses it. *Coingnée,* the foregrounded signifier, proliferates throughout the prologue as a poly-referential linguistic entity whose semantic core is never made explicit but which is nevertheless always present. The name Pierre de Cugnières is no longer what it was in the so-called reality of the pretext; the play of mimesis is but a fabrication of signs which introduces the anxiety of repression (the petrification of the phallus) into the text. Rabelais reintroduces the phallus (the signifier of desire) into a discourse which denies it so that he may opt for the reductive philosophical coherence of moderation and the golden mean in a society which prohibited the creation of a language capable of articulating irreconcilable controversies.

The fact that petrification serves as a reminder that "ces petites philauties couillonniformes" (p. 20) were scorned rather than condemned seems to indicate that although factionalism is regarded as inappropriate behavior it is indeed not considered worthy of censorship. Those who quarrel and disturb the tranquility of life, as Jupiter points out, paradoxically have their "delirium" attenuated through the creation of a tomb that immortalizes them and sets them apart: "Car, veu que tant ilz couvoitent perpetuer leur nom et memoire, ce seroit bien leur meilleur estre ainsi après leur vie en pierres dures et marbrines convertiz que retourner en terre et pourriture" (p. 20). And as Jupiter reminds Priapus: *Et habet tua mentula mentem* (p. 18). The identification of Priapus with *Nous (mens)* suggests that the mind's need for a stabilizing order – the silence "under fire" – becomes the regulatory principle of harmony through which one escapes "destiny" and attains moderation. The commentary that is therefore generated by Jupiter applies synecdochically to the totality of the *Quart Livre*: the appetite for self-expression is silenced; it remains mute, discrete, and effaced. The process of petrification paradoxically becomes a symbol of fear and repression (Jupiter, himself the castrated god, performs the act of petrification during *l'année des couilles molles* [p. 19]) as well as one of permanence which *defers* controversies through the creation of a syncretic figure of harmony and perfection.[16] Rabelais indeed plays on the polysemic meaning of the word *pierre* (to turn to stone, to fear); the factionalism described in the book (the petrified immortal object) expresses the author's fear of choosing, of refusing to yield the clarity one expects of him. The writer is indeed left in the realm of suspended judgment, cornered like Pierre de Coignet (the phallus turned to stone) between ideological extremes, the unfortunate victim of repression. The textual scenario evoked here functions as an emblem of Rabelais' rhetorical practice, and as such defines itself as a kind of metadiscourse, a narrativized subject that is inevitably projected beyond itself.

The motif of indecision – the expanse of blankness that Rabelais presents – situates him therefore in the framework of a static ideal and not of temporal praxis. It is therefore not surprising that the narrator's guarded behavior is mediated by theological considerations; he requests that the reader submit himself to the will of God, avoid perversion of appetite, and accept God's power to determine man's fate: "s'il plaist au bon Dieu, vous obtiendrez santé, veu que rien plus que santé pour le present ne demandez. Attendez encors un peu avecques demie once de patience" (p. 28). We have here the ultimate deflection of the movement inherent in desire; although Rabelais appears to espouse the doctrine of a fully autonomous will, it is God alone, the guarantor of good health, who shall ameliorate man's condition. This use of the word "patience" appears to have connotations which may be related to many other themes in the prologue: moderation, restraint, adherence to the paternal law. On the one hand, the reader is requested to exercise control; on the other, he is implicitly asked to be courageous and endure the adversities of life (the word *patience* is, of course, derived from the latin *patientia*; its root *pati* signifies endurance). In other words, unsatisfied desire requires patience; the attempt to control fate – to function as its sole origin and source – ends in catastrophe.

Throughout the prologue, the impetus toward temperance is thus motivated by the fear of transgressing the law of God the father. The anecdote which serves as rhetorical coda to the prologue is almost a repetition of the dislocating gesture of the Couillatris fable; it recounts the story of the Genoese who gather in their offices every morning and decide from whom "ilz pourront tirer denares" (p. 28). Having decided who is to be cheated, they go on to the Exchange and greet one another with the expression "sanità e guadagno." And the narrator concludes by warning us that "ilz ne se contentent de santé, d'abondant ils soubhaytent gaing, voire les escuz de Guadaigne" (p. 29). Rabelais' use of the expression "sanità e guadagno" sets these two terms in diametrical opposition and thereby ironically undermines the cliché's stability; the harmony associated with health contrasts strikingly with the dysphoria brought about through the desire for excess. This oxymoronic rhetorical figure functions as a kind of mirror of the Couillatris fable since it reiterates the tale's thematic inversion – a reflexive reinscription – that synthesizes contrasting elements. The play on words between *guadagno* (gain) and *Guadaigne* (the name of the Florentine banker residing in Lyon) deliberately undermines the "seriousness" of the expression "sanità e guadagno" by setting up an ironic equivalence whereby the negative connotation attributed to the word *guadagno* is contained in the dishonesty associated with the proper name; it points to the fact that property acquired through usurpation ends in disaster. The quest for gain is the element of libido, of anarchic and potentially destructive freedom. Rabelais' prologue displays a warning indicating that the need to place economic well-being and self-aggrandizement (gain) over that of health nullifies both since the seizure of paternal law – the usurpation of God's power to determine man's fate – ultimately ends in illness and bankruptcy.

Rabelais' call for moderation appears to be obsessive; the word *mediocrité* occurs in the prologue at least ten times alone. It could conceivably be argued that the true meaning of the text is unarticulated, and finally, that it signifies *ex-contraris*.[17] The prologue continually invites a reading according to the *topos aurea mediocritas*, and then suddenly the text undermines the law constituted by the Aesopic fable; the narrative persona alternates between the "ego ideal" and the dissimulated *je* who wishes to define itself figurally within the scene of writing. Rabelais attempts to restrain his psychic impulses; he opts to accept the law of repression.[18] The questions of excess and legality emerge incessantly; the re-inscription of these obsessive *topoi* reveals what has been repressed. Through repetition, Rabelais' discourse embodies the fear of punishment for untempered behavior. The repression of anxiety is portrayed through the ideological indecision displayed in Rabelais' text, an anxiety which ostensibly accounts for the numerous philosophical inconsistencies in the *Quart Livre*. The writer's self-imposed silence is mediated through counterfeit currency – the intertextual references which he legally inherits – that authorizes rather than reveals value. Yet the ambiguity that is derived from the translation of the Aesopic fable into French (the sexualization of the economic metaphor due to the tropological inversion of *coingnée*) and the reference to Pierre de Cugnières, belies Rabelais' fear of loss of identity as well as the unconscious necessity of unveiling latent tension. The referentially free exchange among words has as its goal the disappearance of self-imposed silence through homophonous terms that form the shield of the intertextual entity. The loss and/or petrification of the *coingnée–Coignet* introduces a figural dimension into the prologue that establishes the metaphor of the text as entropic body. Within the prologue that Rabelais narrates is the story of the dissimulated nature of his textual posture, an interpretation of its interprete. That Rabelais' very self-conception is bound up with the fiction he read and *translated* indicates that the self is situated within a symbolic order, in the realm of fictional relations.

Rabelais exploited his sources by the merging of reality and fantasy, a phenomenon that implies the elocutionary disappearance of the writer who loses his sovereignty in favor of the other who is now regarded as absolute. The rabelaisian ego is therefore always mediated and subsumed by other texts whose critical posture is one of a moral imperative: Aesop, Erasmus, Lucian, Luke, Claudius Galen, and Horace. The ego is indeed established as a construct, the result of an imaginary identification that declares itself to be the law. Under the auspices of invention, the libido appropriates "inherited" textual fragments that are "monied" and transposed into an inclusive whole that eventually annuls direct self-expression; we may therefore perceive the

186

prologue as an act of remembrance which undermines itself by the self-displacements of a subject who is in fact victim of a cultural malaise. The origins of self are therefore in otherness; the self, impelled by an inner lack, turns for acceptance to an other, teaching us to acknowledge it as fundamentally estranged. The question that thus arises is where imitation ends and where invention begins, the point of breakage between the quest for neutrality and the impetus toward self-expression. The plenitude that Rabelais strives for is, by its very nature, empty; self-expression is *supplemented* by a fictional presence that disperses itself in a rhetorical labyrinth. The *mens/mentula/memoire* matrix is paradoxically the sign of both plenitude and emptiness; Rabelais' text fertilizes dead language and consequently valorizes the book as a commodified product which dislocates the original story from its referent. The tropological and phonological acrobatics of the prologue indirectly make commentaries on a text whose center is missing, but which inevitably functions as an allegory of repression, the unconscious discursive avowal of the fear of punishment. Rabelais' unconscious instincts manipulate the fable and exploit it to his own ends through a process of de-sedimentation which undermines the perlocutionary force of the multiple *explà*. The counterfeit currency – through the non-centered floating of an unanchored signifier – becomes a negative sign of misplaced desire; the excessive appropriation of the *mediocritas topos* proclaims a bankrupt economy of desire, which proves that a text may be saying something quite different from what it purports to say.

Rabelais' comedy of cruelty: the Chiquanous episode

The *topoi* of slander and censorship emerge in the *Quart Livre,* and in no other episode are they more relevant than in the Chiquanous chapters where the rabelaisian text repudiates power relationships that unjustly repress. As early as the publication of the 1548 prologue, Rabelais reveals an aggressively bitter sense of contempt for the authority and calumnious accu-

sations of theologians whose intemperate attacks against innocent victims such as himself cause needless pain and suffering:

> Si par ces termes entendez les calumniateurs de mes escripts, plus
> aptement les pourrez vous nommer diables. Car, en grec, calumnie est
> dicte diabole. Voyez combien detestable est devant Dieu et les anges ce
> vice dict calumnie (c'est quand on impugne le bien faict, quand on
> mesdit des choses bonnes) que par iceluy, non par autre, quoy que
> plusieurs sembleroient plus enormes, sont les diables d'enfer nommez et
> appellez. Ceulx cy ne sont (proprement parlant) diables d'enfer, ilz en
> sont appariteurs et ministres. Je les nomme diables noirs, blancs, diables
> privez, diables domesticques. Et ce que ont faict envers mes livres, ilz
> feront (si on les laisse faire) envers tous aultres. Mais ce n'est de leur
> invention. Je le dy à fin que tant desormais ne se glorifient au surnom du
> vieux Caton le censorin. (pp. 574–5)

Traditionally, historical critics of the *Quart Livre* have convincingly demonstrated, through the uncovering of the so-called
"realism" underlying the text, how Rabelais' aggressive instincts
dominated his fictional production.[19] While it is undoubtedly
true that from a historical perspective social allegories "surface
in polemical situations when for political or ideological reasons
something cannot be articulated," it is also quite clear that this
kind of narrative cannot be simply reduced to a form of positivist
literary history.[20] Rather than assuming a mode of direct self-
expression, the rabelaisian subject transcribes the "real" world
allegorically through a rhetorical "counterfeiting" in which the
texts point to the social circumstances and power relationships
that both shape and inhibit the politics of representation. To be
sure, the theatrically motivated fictions in the Chiquanous episode convey an ideological effect (the resentment against provocative figures of censorship) through the rabelaisian storyteller's
imaginary subjection to the incorrigible fictions of power. Rabelais' narrative unequivocally enacts a "symbolic unconscious,"
staged fictions of sublimated desire emanating from a tension
between the need to satirize legalistic abuses and the exigencies
of personal recognition.[21] It therefore becomes imperative to
unravel the "symbolic unconscious" of the text, a narrativized
staging of repressed fantasies that plot the need for revenge.

The view of Rabelais as curative physician whose functional narratives prescribe purely comic treatment for the ills that trouble the world has been studied much of late.[22] This claim is based on the assumption that logotherapy (*pharmakon*) can be truly beneficial for the comic purgation of social ills.[23] In the *Quart Livre* this notion is, of course, emphasized in the epistle to Odet de Chastillon in which the Rabelaisian text is defended for its curative effect as a medicine destined to cure the sick: "Seulement avois esguard et intention par escript donner ce peu de soulaigement que povois es affligez et malades absens, lequel voluntiers, quand besoing est, je fays es presens qui soy aident de mon art et service" (p. 3). Yet, not only is comedy to be regarded as a civilized and civilizing generic mode because of its therapeutic social function (*castigat mores ridendo*), it is also, as Freud would put it, a psychic symptom that expresses a repressed wish or unconscious desire.[24] In this perspective, if indeed the form of the comic work assimilates and situates certain perceived aspects of the socio-cultural world, it never merely reifies empirical reality or enacts a neutral transformation of the "social intertext." What transpires in the enactment of comic allegory is a process that reinscribes social material into ostensibly new images of the world which, like the dream work itself, "represents a wish or desire that determines its progress" (Fineman, p. 26). In other words, the perceived power relationships that comprise the socio-cultural intertext serve as a backdrop which enables the writer to turn unconscious desire into latently aggressive social impulses that take the form of agonistic fictional scenarios. These narratives transcribe the hostility underlying dissipated desire and thereby become the generative force of narrative production. Accordingly, the Chiquanous episode is built on the unequivocal destruction of an established and oppressive social order; its aims are to mediate repression through the dissimulative practice of *staged fantasies* which challenge the so-called mastery of a perceived figure of authority by allowing fiction to become something other than it claims to be. Rabelais assumes the narrative role of repressed satirist whose comedy of cruelty in this episode grants a privileged status to

189

"theatricality," the projection of an illusion, a displaced invest-ment of desire that can never precisely articulate its name but is nevertheless omnipresent. The comedy of cruelty protects and promotes the pleasures of play through the screen of theatrica-lity, and yet at the same time maintains its unequivocally tenden-tious manner.

On the island of Procuration, the Pantagruelists encounter, in the course of their journey in quest of the Dive Bouteille, the Chiquanous, legal officials, who earn their living ("naïfves mois-sons") by serving slanderous summonses on innocent victims whom they insult. Accordingly, these insinuations provoke physical attack upon the Chiquanous who are subsequently able to profit financially by taking legal action for "assault and bat-tery" against the angry defendants who beat them up. The Chiquanous or the "quibbling sargeants at law" are automatons who engage in a verbal game of chicanery – through the use of subterfuge and legal trickery – and commit themselves to a double profitmaking scheme in which the servility of their trans-gressions circumvents the sovereignty of the law. Rabelais' text acquaints us with the anarchy that undermines the so-called legal world and reminds us that the Greek *nomos,* law, which may be traced to "division or sharing," is anything but a "sedentary structure of representation."[25] The technology of law serves a capricious power structure that legislates corruption, deception, and theft in the name of hedonistic earthly pleasure: "Cela faict, voylà Chiquanous riche pour quatre moys. Comme si coups de baston feussent ses naïfves moissons. Car il aura du moine, de l'usurier, ou advocat, salaire bien bon, et reparation du gentil-homme, aulcunefois si grande et excessive que le gentilhomme y perdra tout son avoir, avecques dangier de mise rablement pour-rir en prison, comme s'il eust frappé le Roy" (pp. 70–1). Yet, not only does the rabelaisian text present a satire of a legal system that sanctions profit through the harassment of an innocent other, it also clarifies the Chiquanous' excessive greed and desire for economic gain: "Qui veut guaingner vingt escuz d'or pour estre battu en Diable? – Io, io, io, respondirent tous. Vous nous

190

affollerez de coups, monsieur, cela est sceur. Mais il y beau guaing" (p. 86).

The corrective measures against the excesses of the Chiquanous are narrated in the tale of how the Lord of Basché punished these blasphemous summoners who enjoyed being beaten to death. In the episode itself the Chiquanous are invited to a wedding reception arranged by the Lord of Basché. There they are to be punished for having inflicted pain and suffering on others through a game of deceit. When the Chiquanous arrive at Basché's to serve slanderous summonses (commissioned ironically but not surprisingly by a figure of the church, the Fat Prior) the members of Basché's household disguise themselves as false personages (*les personnaiges de la farce*) and prepare to "jou[er] bien ceste tragicque farce" (p. 77) so that they may "legally" attack the Chiquanous by following the custom according to which young men give one another memorable "punches" at weddings.[26] This "staged" wedding which reenacts the "coustume observée en touts fiansailles" (p. 72) legitimizes what is traditionally considered abusive and inadmissible behavior (flogging): "N'ayez paour d'en estre reprins en justice," affirms Basché, "Je seray guarant pour tous. Telz coups seront donnez en riant, scelon la coustume" (p. 72). The theatrical staging of Basché's "punition exemplaire" of the bumbailiffs thus locates the agonistic encounter within a narrative drama itself; the "play" within the fiction allegorizes the revenge against a repressive force and serves the crucial narrative function of a metaphorical façade which maintains public decorum. This masquerade permits the Basché clan to "play out" a form of symbolic satisfaction and lower the tension towards an object worthy of attack, the Chiquanous. In essence, the fiction-making process legitimizes the impulse to destroy and suggests the appetite for revenge elaborated by the public travesty out of which the comedy of cruelty takes shape.

By appropriating the Senecan tradition of the Saturnalia and the popular custom of young men giving one another memorable thrashings at weddings, the rabelaisian text symbolically stages a carnival rite to punish those who unjustly accuse and torture others.[27] Rabelais' text activates what Bakhtin has so aptly termed the "carnivalesque–masquerade" *topos* which not only provides an alternative world order, but also makes possible an escape from the coercive forces of repression, thanks to the anonymity of cultural mythologies. The freedom sanctified by the nuptual ritual (people beating one another up) permits deceit (the staged wedding) to win out over deceit itself (the behavior of the slanderous Chiquanous). The legal imposters are foiled by other characters who adapt a strategy of duplicity and thereby defeat the hypocritical Chiquanous at their own game. Instead of having the theatrical stage of cultural mythology represent the "real" world, the so-called "real" world becomes a stage upon which the distinction between truth and illusion is blurred in ingenious interlacements freed from the empirical constraints imposed by "reality." In effect, fiction-making is punished through the enactment of another fiction. And Rabelais' text has as its ostensible aim the dynamic dramatization of conflict through fictional alterity or a fiction within a fiction. The fradulent performance functions as a powerfully subversive comic device whose playful mimicry imposes an artificial resolution on conflict and social disorder while it undeniably takes on an exemplary status:

"Des nopces, disoient ilz, des nopces, des nopces, vous en soubvieine!" Il feut si bien acoustré que le sang luy sortoit par la bouche, par le nez, par les aureilles, par les œilz ... Croyez qu'en Avignon, on temps de Carneval, les bacheliers, oncques ne jouerent à la raphe plus melodieusement que feut joué sus Chiquanous. (p. 80)

Thus, the "acting out" of the Basché clan becomes an ambiguous form of social behavior since it invokes the power to generate and quell disorder simultaneously; it dramatizes a projected fantasy in which the repressive other is destroyed through the narrative transactions carried out in this fiction within a fiction: "Depuis n'en feut parlé" (p. 80).[28]

The resolution of conflict through masquerade and theatrical behavior appears to be a compensation for the unresolvable anxieties of reality. To "act out" is to project an illusion, a dramatized image enmeshed in the unequivocal investment of self in the other. The enactment of this travesty indeed protects one from an exclusively annihilating vision since the representation of the event is not what the event appears to be (a wedding), but rather a carnivalesque fantasy that projects a didactic undermining of hypocrisy and corruption. "Jouer la Tragicque comedie" (p. 72) underscores the oxymoronic nature of Basché's theatrical presentation: the comic strategy of feigning points to the anger and dissimulation associated with the foolish antics that constitute Rabelais' rhetorical praxis. The staged wedding is but a form of trickery that has the potential to punish the perpetrators of disorder (the aggression carried out by the Chiquanous) at the same time that it attacks the aggressors. The theater metaphor therefore functions as a trope that destabilizes infelicitous power structures and makes the tragic discovery that "reality" is nothing more than an illusion based on the fictions of power.

One could conceivably argue that the generative force of this episode emanates from a free-floating comic cruelty that shifts from one representational level to another and reveals conflicting accounts of the source of pleasure; for every mode of satisfaction that the text puts forward it also argues for its opposite. The Chiquanous become a *locus* of narrative ambiguity: they receive gratification and economic gain for the violation of the law and for the affliction of unjust accusations on others. Yet, their most authentic source of pleasure is derived from the *consequences* of the violation of that law, the punishment for intemperate control and irresponsible manipulation of power. To beat the masochistic Chiquanous is in fact an act of kindness that equates the pain derived from punishment with erotic pleasure. Through the processes of inversion and transference the object of Basché's aggression (the Chiquanous) is converted into desiring subjects who receive gratification from the punitive effects inflicted upon them for having violated the contract of law. The pleasure acquired through the need to dominate and inflict slanderous accusations thus undergoes a radical transformation so that pleasure is not achieved solely by internalizing the suffering of dis-

193

pleasure of the other (those on whom summonses are served). To be sure, Rabelais' text articulates throughout the Chiquanous episode a paradoxical tension between a rigorously rendered drive for mastery and the masochistic delight experienced from the profit-making pleasure derived from subjugation and punishment:

Reverend pere en Diable, Monsieur, si m'avez trouvé bonne robbe et vous plaist encores en me battant vous esbatre, je me contenteray de la moitié, de juste pris. Ne m'espargnez, je vous en prie. Je suys tout et trestout à vous, Monsieur le Diable: teste, poulmon, boyaulx et tout. Je le vous diz à bonne chere! (p. 87)

The dual role of aggressor and aggressee projects a perverse power relationship articulating an amorphous form of desire that can never be isolated since it is always "extended toward the desire of something else"; each function engenders both a force of attraction and a force of repulsion.[29]

If indeed the rabelaisian text blurs the potential identity of the Chiquanous by the to-and-fro movement of mirrored opposites, it does so through the reinscription of the fundamental forces that structure the play of *logos* and the moral and legal consequences that it entails. The "game" which assists man's play within the social "play" of the world delineates the degree to which the forces of repression and punishment threaten the slightest possible transgression. On the one hand, the Chiquanous repress; they are guilty not only because of their slanderous accusations against others but, above all, for their unconscionable theft. The illegal acquisition of wealth by those whose uncontrollable appetite and passion dominate their being brings about damnation and demands punishment. Accordingly, the money they unjustly earn is inevitably destined to acquire the oxymoronic character of a bankrupt economy in which abundance is transfigured into financial loss;[30] "l'argent de Basché plus estoit aux Chiquanous et records pestilent, mortel et pernicieux que n'estoit jadis l'or de Tholose, et le cheval Sejan à ceulx qui le possederent" (p. 84).[31] But, on the other hand, within the same episode the Chiquanous are also innocently repressed; they

194

become "victims" and are implicated in an exaggerated fantasy of transgression in which deceitful and powerful men are manipulated and punished by those who are even more deceitful and powerful. In short, the other's drive for mastery becomes a decisive factor in guaranteeing one's own subjugation. If at one point in the episode the Chiquanous were portrayed as the mediators of ecclesiastical repression (serving summonses at the command of the Fat Prior), they now become the very object of that same repression which victimizes through a somewhat capricious and severe legal system.

At the end of the Basché story we learn of the Pantagruelists' encounter with two old She-Bailiffs who reveal that two Chiquanous have just been hanged for having "desrobé les ferremens de la messe, et les avoient mussez soubs le manche de la paroece" (p. 88). Here the Chiquanous have indeed been victimized for having committed a benign misdemeanor. The interpretation of these "playful" antics is transcribed figuratively so that its ironic perspective represents a fantasy of transgression and unjust punishment. The essentially comic register of the judgment, as Rabelais' *Briefve Declaration* reveals, transcends its trivialized status and does little more than enact a hyperbolic fiction in which the literal is dissimulated in a figural and abstract language: "*Les ferremens de la messe,* disent les Poictevins villageoys ce que nous disons ornemens, et le manche de la paroece ce que nous disons le clochier, par metaphore assez lourde" (p. 253). Thus, paradoxically enough, it is mystification that is demystified here. Epistemon's exegetical retort to the interpretation of the Chiquanous' supposedly "playful" crime ("Voilà ... parlé en terrible allegorie," p. 88), implicitly obviates the slightest possible temptation to accept the illusion that the pillaged material constitutes the *real* cause of punishment. To steal church ornaments is, in effect, regarded as a sacrilegious and heretical act, a simple prank that is interpreted as an usurpation of power because of ecclesiastical law's will to impose a punishment that far exceeds the *crime.* In effect, the She-Bailiffs' narration reveals – through the figural inversion of the literal – how legal hermeneutics can potentially transform innocent playfulness into crime and thereby permit political oppression to reveal its undiscriminating motives; it describes how metaphoric language wilfully perverts the law and leads to the death of the innocent (*la stragne degli innocenti*). As in the case of Rabelais' own work, the ludic play of the text has serious consequences that raise questions regarding the interpretation process governing the law and the reference to empirical reality that it implies; Rabelais ascribes to his writing the same natural and "ethical" innocence of a "transparent" language that is sensible to the law of the divine:

Mais le calumnie de certains Canibales, misantropes, agelastes, avoit tant contre moy esté atroce et desraisonnée qu'elle avoit vaincu ma patience, et plus n'estois deliberé en escrire un iota. Car l'une des moindres contumelies dont ilz usoient estoit que telz livres tous estoient farciz d'heresies diverses . . . de folastries joyeuses . . . (c'est le subject et theme unicque d'iceulx livres); d'heresies poinct, sinon pervesement et contre tout usaige de raison et de languaige commun, interpretans ce que, à poine de mille fois mourir, si autant possible estoit, ne vouldrois avoir pensé. (pp. 6–7)

But yet, throughout the Chiquanous episode, the text implicitly directs our attention toward the relationship between potency and censorship, the equivocal pleasure derived from the punishment for transgression. As Peter Brooks so aptly puts it, "deviance is the very condition for life to be narratable."[32] In this perspective, the production of meaning within the rabelaisian text is founded on an allegorical system of signs controlled by a libidinal energy which animates the narrative process through the enactment of repressed desire. And in spite of his claim that "hors toute intimidation, je mectz la plume au vent" (p. 8), it is perhaps the veritable risk of punishment for transgression that leads us to think about how Rabelais' very own writing economy demonstrates that an increase in tension can be both pleasurable and productive.

Within the *Quart Livre* there are numerous references to the myth of Orpheus which functions as an emblem of displaced desire. This myth envisions poetic inspiration as a sacrificial agony in which the gentle but comfortless artist falls victim to

196

flaying and dismemberment as a result of the punishment for this act of transgression against nature. Characterized in part by the need for atonement, the Orphic fable of bodily dismemberment and suffering is played out in Rabelais' narrative, particularly the need to transcend it through the power of regeneration. And in no other episode is the life-generating force more striking than in that of the perverse Chiquanous who, claims Panurge, earn their living by being eaten up and are like those who "ne peuvent le nerf caverneux vers le cercle equateur dresser, s'ilz ne sont très bien fouettez" (p. 70).

The equivalence of the infliction of pain with pleasure epitomizes the paradoxical imperatives of desire represented metaphorically in the mysterious tension that structures Rabelais' textual unconscious.[33] To be sure, this is an episode that transcribes the dynamics of "erotogenic masochism," the origin of the narcissistic delight of displeasure. The sensations of pain and suffering produce a simulacrum of ecstasy that is regarded as crucial to the phallic potency underlying the generative act; the phallus can only become erect from the stress of displeasure when pain is celebrated. And it is here that the importance of the sexual metaphor within the context of this episode is particularly revealing. The expression "battre son tabourin" ("to beat the drum") not only signals the beginning of the gauntlet wedding, but also surreptitiously generates a fantasy of revenge that masquerades as a fertility rite:[34] "Tabourins à nopces sont ordinairement buttuz; tabourineurs bien festoyez, battuz jamais" (p. 82). Most certainly, this expression has erotic connotations that are associated with sexual conjunction; the beating of the drum by the "baston de mariage" or the phallus symbolizes potency, reproduction, and generation through an act of aggression. If, in fact, one reads this episode as a phantasmatic representation of the paradoxical logic generating the writing act, one might conceivably regard the fictional "playing out" of repressed violent instincts as the desire to be punished masquerading as the desire to attack the other: "Appellez vous cela jeu de jeunesse? Par Dieu, *jeu n'est-ce*" (p. 83). The plotting of Rabelais' narrative, then, is overdetermined by the binding force of a desiring subject

197

who "pleurante rioyt, riante pleuroit" (p. 83) and is figured in the text by a split between the need for revenge and the pleasures of repression.

Accordingly, the instinct to destroy and be destroyed simultaneously realizes the libidinal delight of the figure of a writing subject whose descriptive prose transcribes a narrative intensity that mimetically reproduces the aggression figured in Basché's theatrical spectacle.[35] In essence, the anatomical disarticulation of the injured bodies produces a kind of lyrical euphoria which allows Rabelais' writing to reach epic proportions:

Adoncques feirent gaunteletz leur exploict, si que à Chiquanous fut rompue la teste en neuf endroictz: à un des records feut le bras droict defaucillé, à l'aultre fut demanchée la mandibule superieure, de mode qu'elle luy couvroit le menton à demy, avecques denudation de la luette et perte insigne des dens molares, masticatoires et canines. (p. 82)

The bacchic atmosphere is imaged typographically in the form of lexical expansiveness that corresponds to the conversion of "scoptophilia' (*Schautrieb,* desire or lust) into anxiety and vice versa. The comedy of cruelty thus mediates a violent, albeit sublimated, desire in the form of re-membered lexical fragments which emblematize the linguistic shattering of the human subject:

Estes vous des Frappins, des Frappeurs, ou des Frappars? Ne vous suffisoit nous avoir ainsi morcrocassebezassevezassegrigueliguoscopa-popondrillé tous les membres superieurs à grands coups de bobelins, sans nous donner telz morderegrippipiotabirofreluchamburelurecoque-lurintimpanemens sus les grefves à belles poinctes de houzeaulz?

(p. 83)

Rabelais' comic allegory proves that masochism indeed generates life and is transcribed in the text by an endless series of verbal ejaculations whose path of energy is catalyzed by a generative force that transfers sublimated desire into a self-extending discourse.

Within the Basché narrative one finds a digressive text in which the *topoi* of desire and exchange interact with one another and stage another drama of vindictive pleasure against a menacing object of interdiction. The enigmatic figures of the repressive

198

and the repressed surge forth once again in the story of Villon's vengeful but exemplary trick against the local sacristan Tappecoue, who refuses to lend the robes ("une chappe et estolle," p. 75) necessary to play the role of God the Father in the passion play that the poet and his troupe of actors wish to perform: "Tappecoue ... alleguant que, par leurs statutz provinciaulx, estoit rigoureusement defendu rien bailler ou prester pour les jouans" (p. 75). Unquestionably, Tappecoue represents an obstacle, a figure of the church who refuses to grant credence to the realm of fantasy and fiction; he rigorously serves an authoritarian imperative that forbids the celebration of a staged theatrical representation. Rabelais' text once again thematizes the tension associated with the potential abuse of the law, a phenomenon that emanates from the possibility of its multiple interpretations and which enables the status quo to imbue legal signs with didactic ethical values. Villon's attempt to clarify the immoderate reading of this interdiction projects the juridical meaning of the law as having been derived from historical experience and effaced by the imposition of limits and boundaries: "Villon replicquoit que le statut seulement concernoit farces, mommeries et jeuz dissoluz, et qu'ainsi l'avoit veu practiquer à Bruxelles et ailleurs" (p. 75). The Villon story is thus destined to follow the internal logic of the Chiquanous episode and destabilize the established inequalities imposed by the social order. Tappecoue must be punished for his suppression of freedom and the infelicitous act of censorship. Rabelais therefore assigns this embedded narrative a positive exemplary force, a speculative elaboration of the comedy of cruelty that has already unfolded in the Basché episode. One masquerade engenders and amplifies another: Villon's actor-friends, disguised as devils, cross the footlights (there is no barrier between stage and street in the *diablerie*) and use kitchen utensils to frighten Tappecoue and precipitate his demise.[36] The masquerade functions as a necessary catalyst to attack the debilitating vices of the status quo. Justice becomes, in Orphic hands, vengeance against the forces of evil through the celebration of a theatrical nihilism that represents a gratifying fantasy of retribution and takes the form of a charivari.

199

From the perspective of the "actor-devils," Tappecoue becomes a negative target of attack, the object of their rage and frustration against whom "Dieu feroit vengence et punition exemplaire bien toust" (p. 75). The clergy's power to invoke the rule of law is called into question through a carnivalesque rite that results in an intemperate realization of vindictive pleasure. And the unmitigated authority of the dismemberment metaphor is once again brought into focus when Villon's cohorts prepare squibs and firebrands and throw them unexpectedly at Tappecoue, whose horse "de luy ne portoit que le pied droict et soulier entortillé" (p. 77). Desire is generated here by the imperatives of an excessively negative energy that is intended to unsettle authoritarian values and to have a cathartic effect through the paradoxical foregrounding of the so-called "reality" factor underlying the narrative fiction: "O que vous jourrez bien! . . . O que vous jourrez bien!" (p. 77).

As a reaction to the stifling exigencies of empirical reality, the fictional "playing out" of vengeance not only creates what Bakhtin has termed "an alternative social world," but also one in which the need for mastery can only be defined in terms of the theater metaphor, which is ostensibly a desire for otherness, an object substitute, a play of all that masquerades and yet remains *real*. The "legalized" transfer of acting from stage to street permits the projection of a fictional self which has been constituted in relation to the exigencies of the social order. This is particularly interesting in the context of Lacanian psychoanalysis in which the subject is regarded as an effect of the signifier; and the veiling of the self through the theatrical "illusion" that we witness in this episode situates the notion of the "barring of the subject" within the realm of socially acceptable behavior.[37] But in the end, theatricality, or the fiction within the fiction, functions as an inauthentic means of catharsis; it mediates a release of conflict by dissimulating the real violence for which it is ostensibly a metaphor.

The refusal to circulate property freely which is thematized in the Villon narrative suppresses any possible means for peaceful interaction and exchange. Tappecoue aggressively incarnates the critical *doxa* of medieval Christian ideology because of his adherence to provincial statutes according to which the clergy "estoit rigoureusement defendu rien bailler ou prester pour les jouans" (p. 75). This failure to license a theatrical representation will be confronted by an apparently "realistic" travesty, one which shows cognizance of its own metaphoricity as an instrument for subverting the system which refuses to sanction the realm of the imaginary. The repression of desire unequivocally precipitates sublimation acted out in the form of aggression which, for Rabelais, can be defined as the repetition of satisfaction through the enactment of multiple fictions of revenge.

The Chiquanous episode reveals the way in which the rabelaisian text uncovers its dissimulated preoccupations. Accordingly, the narrative focuses on the modalities and conditions of *violation*, socially sanctioned revolt through the ubiquitous force of displacement and condensation. Wish fulfillment is attained through deceit and masquerade is realized within the realm of fictional relations. The theatricality represented in this episode reminds us that deception and fiction-making are operative at all levels of the narrative encounter. The ostensible objects of revenge in the Chiquanous thrashing (the Fat Prior) and in the savage dismemberment of Tappecoue (ecclesiastical law) are figured in the text as targets of a fictional execution energized by a highly mobile desire. In both cases, what is at stake is power and the usurpation of power; and in both narratives the punitive measures are presented as an act of revolt against the excesses of repression. The rabelaisian text thus transcribes a sadistic tendency to destroy an aggressor through the enactment of a comic allegory in which latent hostility is sublimated and yet unconsciously adheres to the ideological imperatives that dictate the power of repression.

Rabelais in Papimania: power and the rule of law

Rabelais' vicious attack on the political and economic abuses of the Vatican against the interests of the Gallican church are strikingly revealed in the *Papimanes* episode of the *Quart Livre*. Fiction-making did indeed become a dangerous enterprise for Rabelais precisely because it meant unmasking reality in order to reveal the scandalous behavior of the papal curia and papalist lawyers. The object of Rabelais' attack in this episode is not religion as such; it is rather papal ideology, the "ex-cathedra infallibility" of Papal administration and law that are questioned as outrageously aggressive activities threatening peace and security.[38] Rabelais' text satirizes those Catholic idolaters – the *Papimanes* – who worship the reigning Pope *quasi Deus in terris* and ascribe to him, through their sacrilegious behavior, the herculean task of the *imitatio dei*; the Pope serves as plenipotentiary substitute for a divine presence, precipitating the same sacrosanct worship ordinarily reserved for God the Father. Accusing the arbitrariness of an omnipotent authority, the episode undermines the papal authoritarianism which royalist Gallicans abhorred. Rabelais' text propels itself forward through a process that stresses the symbolic force of the writing act so completely as to reify its social ground. The text thus enacts a form of theatricality whose efforts at representation phantasmatically reflect an inert social given: the unequivocally repressive policies of the Papal order. Fiction in Rabelais' world compels us to be pensive and consider the substance of "scriptural" perversion and the unjustifiable abuses of ecclesiastical law.

Rabelais' bitter satire is inextricably linked to the 1551–2 Gallican crisis in France where the Holy See was attacked because of the power of decretaline law to subtly draw gold out of France and direct it to the papal coffers in Rome.[39] What is at stake here is the insatiable appetite of the Roman Catholic Church and its unjustifiable intervention in France's internal affairs. Rabelais' text mobilizes itself against the autocratic power of the Pope and the sacred Decretals, books of papal ordinances responding to questions directed to the Vatican in Rome. Not only does the rabelaisian text attack the elimination of the salvific cooperation between men as evidenced in the legal enactment of *canons* and *decrets*, it also censures the reversal of certain theological norms whereby evangelical and divine law are

202

translated into purely material concerns.[40] The gross hypocrisy of the papacy in its unscrupulous quest for material gain undermines whatever possible "moral" precepts might be found in the Decretals, and paradoxically transforms them into an object of ridicule. Law – in its etymological sense of that which is laid down or fixed – takes on a negative connotation within the context of the Papimanes episode by becoming *decret-ales* (decrees taking on wings) that which alludes the boundaries of legality. The decretaline fantasies are never more than just another stage in the supplemental movement of a legal process whose endless proliferation of the word "faict et journellement augmente en abondance de tous biens temporelz, corporelz et spirituelz le fameux et celebre patrimoine de sainct Pierre" (p. 199).

The Papimanes episode constitutes a text whose specificity lies in a relation of variance with a socio-theological code. To be sure, Rabelais' text destroys the integrity of God's words to Moses at the burning bush – *Ego sum qui sum* (Exodus, III) – by putting them into the mouths of the Papimanes who sacrilegiously refer to the Pope as "L'Unique" (p. 179), a fictional character whose function is to live up to his so-called "referential" implication. The biblical utterance becomes ridiculous through a shockingly comic subversion of the biblical intertext, demonstrating the rabelaisian inability to separate literal reference from figural connotation.

– Seigneurs, dist Epistemon, nous ne entendons telz termes. Mais exposez nous, s'il vous plaist, de qui entendez, et nous vous en dirons la vérité sans dissimultation.
– C'est, dirent ilz, celluy qui est. L'avez vous jamais veu? (pp. 179–80)

The transformation here is quite conspicuous in its transparency, the text's willful manipulation unmistakable because it disfigures the primacy of the biblical reference and feigns belief in the verisimilitude of its own referential foundation. This re-inscription of the biblical text makes Rabelais' text remark, and in remarking mock and deprive the biblical of the epistemological delusion of its transcendental status. In an attempt to revive the meaning and power of propaganda, the rabelaisian narrative draws the reader's attention back to the aggressive creative energy at the source of fictional invention. The *deus absconditus* is substituted by a temporal "visible" God whose unquestionable degree of humanity transforms the narrative into a "literalized fiction," a story that instates the visible as condition of symbolic functioning, with the male organ the standard of visibility required. "De sorte qu'en subtile philosophie Decretaline ceste consequence est necessaire: il est Pape, il a doncques couilles. Et quand couilles faudroient on monde, le monde plus Pape n'auroit" (pp. 180–1). The obsessive references to both the visible and the material undermine the divine qualities traditionally associated with a heavenly God who becomes, as Pantagruel suggests, the very antithesis of what he is supposed to represent. "Oncques certes ne le veismes, et n'est visible à œilz corporelz" (p. 180). The Papimanes, exemplars of the naive reader, fall victim to "optomania," a condition which forces them to dream the dream of presence and blindly accept as "real" what, in fact, they have actually perceived in an essentially metaphorical way.[41]

The rabelaisian text adopts the procedures and customs of the Roman Catholic liturgy only in order to violate their structure and content in a radical way. The scene of religious celebration passes from the confines of the cathedral to the expansive sensuality associated with the dinner table ("la repaissaille feut copieuse et les beuvettes numereuses" [p. 189]); abstinence and humility are replaced by fullness, gluttony, and *jouissance*: "O dives Decretales! tant par vous est le vin bon bon trouvé!" (p. 190). Rabelais' text ironically parodies – through the blatant transgression of the Christian intertext – the miracle according to which Christ transforms water into wine. The parodic exercise performs an implicitly sacrilegious act based on the coexistence and crossover of codes (spirituality/sensuality) which allows the text to suggest the Papimanes' material lust and tendency towards perversity. Rabelais' narrative thus calls into question the authority of scriptural norms through an analogically deceptive play.

The traditional view of satire as purely moralistic literature may be questioned within the context of this episode. Quite clearly Rabelais is writing both a satire and an attack on the nefarious effects of contemporary institutions and institutionalized ways of thinking by showing us just how destructive these fictions of authority are. The celebration of papal laws and codes forcibly imposes an ideal state emanating from an individual who acts with the same arbitrariness as a God. Homenaz, leader of Papimania, functions as a crude receptacle of language whose untempered authority licenses him to articulate the paradise myth through the hyperbolic praise of the Decretals. In essence, the Decretals evoke the vision of a Golden Age in which laws have a salvific status in a conflict-free world.

O seraphicque *Sixiesme!* dist Homenaz . . . tant ous estes necessaire au saulvement des paouvres humains! O cherubicques *Clementines!* comment en vous est proprement contenue et descripte la perfaicte institution du vray Christian! O *Extravaguantes* angelicques comment sans vous periroient les paouvres ames, les quelles, ça bas, errent par les corps mortelz en ceste vallée de misere! (p. 190)

Yet the lyrical illusions produced through the encomiastic contemplation of this paradise-like state have a way of paradoxically generating their opposites: violence and the brutal force of oppression. Rabelais presents the Decretals as fetishized, self-focusing texts; they are destined to become an instrument of an obsessive will to power that will ensure the cultural hegemony of papal law. The decretaline fictions are regarded as absolute; they reify the whims of authority in order to make paradise and hell coalesce into a perverse form of harmony.

The island which the Papimanes inhabit is a closed, cellular community, a "prismatic world" whose government demands the repression of imagination in order to manipulate its citizens; it can be argued, however, that the ruse that institutionalizes the rule of law can only be articulated in terms of the decretaline fictions in which even the most extreme paradoxes appear quite natural. The state that fetters both freedom and the realm of the imaginary becomes a kind of earthly paradise in which the "real" embodies – largely through the power of negation – the realm of

205

fiction. The constraints of the singular – the transcendent decretaline fictions – obliterate the contradictions of the plural; the
world of difference falls prey to one of apparently absolute
transcendence in which the fiction of authority constitutes the
authority of the fiction. The radical depersonalization of the
Papimaniac voice is suggested here by the tendency of decretaline discourse to absolutize itself and forcibly impose an ideal
condition. The "reason" of papimaniac law installs an empire of
the irrational that institutes the preeminence of that law.

Vous aultres gens de bien, si voulez estre dictz et reputez vrais Christians, je vous supplie à joinctes mains ne croire aultre chose, aultre
chose ne penser, ne dire, ne entreprendre, ne faire, fors seulement ce
que contiennent nos sacres Decretales et leurs corollaires.   (p. 197)

The appropriation of knowledge for the *vray Christian* therefore
constitutes a situation in which the epistemological ground of
consciousness can no longer be self-referential; true Christian
consciousness must be mediated by the paradoxical imperatives
of a decretaline otherness that censors and signifies the suppression of an autonomous speaking subject.

The world of the Decretals is one in which charity and
exchange are abolished at the expense of submission to the
supreme and absolute power of the other. A good part of the
Papimanes episode examines the question of what constitutes
the "perfaicte institution du vray Christian." At several
instances the rabelaisian text ironically undercuts the notions of
vray Christian and *bon catholicque*. When the Pantagruelists are
preparing for departure, Homenaz and his followers present
them with a gift that they are to export to their native Touraine:
belles poyres (p. 201). The quintessential difference between the
Papimanes and the Pantagruelists is illuminated here. Through
the voice of Pantagruel, the rabelaisian text comments on the
Papimanes' perverse necessity to find presence where there is
none, to equate flatulence with spiritual reverence. By naming
his gift *poires du bon Christian* (p. 201), Pantagruel illustrates his
function as an ironic reader of signs who assumes that appearances are not essences. As Michael Screech has pointed out,

poyre in Old French meant to "break wind."[42] This commentary may be read as the rhetorical punch-line to the Papimanes episode since their actions, behavior, and the substance of their liturgical routines do little more than reflect the vacuousness of decretaline law. Homenaz follows a discursive strategy in which potential differences are domesticated by an illusion of identity which eliminates any trace of the equivocal. "Nous sommes simples gens, puys qu'il plaist à Dieu. Et appelons les figues figues, les prunes prunes, et les poires poires" (p. 201). It seems evident, then, that Homenaz's reading strategy consists in making everything conform to the status of nature, while Pantagruel's consists in uncovering a text that suppresses ambiguity and difference at the expense of a universal and absolute law. Homenaz and the Papimanes read every sign "literally" so that their readings may be consistent with the homogeneous spirit of peace, order, and authority; reading, commentary, and interpretation, on the other hand, do violence to language and treat signs as pure illusion and fantasy.

Homenaz and his followers are indeed "nominalists" who authorize their fictions to elaborate a literalized discourse about reality.[43] They are enamoured of texts which create a false and empty utopia and at the same time destroy subjectivity and difference. To be sure, the self-imposed "transparent" and arbitrary relationship between word and image that Jean Paris has described as the cornerstone of ideological authoritarianism in the Renaissance manifests itself in Homenaz's reading of the papal portrait which he interprets literally as representing the Platonic idea of a benevolent Papal essence.[44] "C'est l'idée de celluy Dieu de bien en terre, la venue duquel nous attendons devotement, et lequel esperons une foys veoir en ce pays ... celluy bon Dieu en terre, duquel voyant seulement le portraict, pleine remission guaingnons de tous nos pechez memorables" (p. 186). Idolatry, as used here, is a form of perceptioin activated when need becomes obsessive and forecloses on the self's ability to distinguish between the substance of things and the dynamics of their representational resources. The portrait of the Pope acquires magical powers based on an aesthetics of need that renders the object of representation present to the mesmerized subject. Homenaz's interpretative practice evokes a divine figure that is not described as a transparency, but rather as an allegorical representation literally read. The idolatry of the Papimanes forces them to reify the image through a quintessentially aberrant hermeneutic; it literally creates presence where there is none by permitting the image to become the represented object and thereby enable appearances to project essences. If idolatry is a means to project magical qualities onto objects or images, which in turn dissimulate vacuousness, then we have indeed entered a world of political impotence. Ultimately, the rabelaisian text uncovers the Papimanes' illusion that their illusions of mastery constitute reality.

Homenaz's encomiastic enumeration of the wonders of decretaline law demonstrates – through the fundamental humanistic techniques of rhetoric and persuasion – that the papal ordinances mythologize and project a utopian harmony capable of legitimizing a given power structure. The decretaline text dictates the principles which we must adhere to. It dramatically illustrates how writing functions as a malicious perversion that naturalizes the powers of the magical through discursive manipulation, a process enabling the fictions of authority to master the anarchy of the world and yet appear quite "real."

Qui faict en plusieurs pays le peuple rebelle et detravé, les paiges frians et mauvais, les escholiers badaulx et asniers? Leurs gouverneurs, leurs escuiers, leurs precepteurs n'estoient Deretalistes ... Qui a fondé, pillotizé, talué, qui maintient, qui substante, qui nourrit les devots religieux par les convens, monasteres et abbayes, sans les prieres diurnes, nocturnes, continuelles des quelz seroit le monde en dangier evident de retourner en son antique Cahos? Sacres Decretales.

(pp. 198–9)

Homenaz's litany constitutes an unending attempt to grasp utopian discourse as process, which Terence Cave sees as *enargeia,* enumeration, productivity.[45] The excessively repetitive allusions to the benevolent effects of the Decretals eventually results in an ironic shift in the hermeneutic practice of law from dynamic process to reified and utopian end-product, defined within a materialist conception of ideology. Rabelais' text produces an extended tautology; it is in fact an uninterrupted *copia* that depicts the *trompe l'œil* illusionism of u-topia itself, the non-place in which papal law is invented. The speaking subject seeks to dissimulate a bankrupt political ideology behind a hyperbolic discourse that transcends the limits of nature and logic. Homenaz exhausts himself in an uncontrollable verbal frenzy that underscores his isolation in the universe of discourse; he is indeed a prisoner in solitary confinement, a victim of utopian formulae.

Homenaz and the Papimanes thus set into motion a "fantasy machine" whose utopian impulses and intense desires are registered in the text through numerous references to fetishistic delight. Within such a scheme, the Papimanes' authentic source of pleasure is derived from the material: objects in the text evoke sexuality, particularly the imaginary representation of the subject's powerful relationship to a cathected object.[46] When Homenaz shows the Pantagruelists an archetype of the Pope, a visual and tactile phenomenology coincide and enable nature to become a text. The narrator intervenes and demonstrates how ecclesiastical authority consolidates power and transfers the drive of desire from the self to reified objects endowed with the power to control "[Homenaz] nous monstra une imaige paincte assez mal, scelon mon advis, y toucha un baston longuet, et nous feist à tous baiser la touche" (p. 186). And when Pantagruel is handed several pages of the Decretals, the narrator ironically informs us that "au touchement d'icelles, il sentoit un doulx prurit des ongles et desgourdissement de bras, ensemble temptation vehemente en son esprit de battre un sergent ou deux" (p. 183). This commentary seems to imply that Pantagruel's apparent quest for reason is undermined by tactile bonds of pleasure that permit entry into the fantisized world of power. The text not only stimulates and mobilizes desire, but paradoxically reduces the mesmerized subject to a state of entropy.

Fetishism producs a simulacrum of madness that transforms Homemaz into a discursive agent who thrives on the imaginary power of the Decretals; the word "fetish" thus carries its full root meaning, "made by art or skilfully contrived." The worship of the Decretals assures the passivity of the self and permits the language of the other to be inscribed in the discourse of the speaking subject. The decretaline mythology overdetermines the exigencies of society and governs the production of its culture; it dissolves individual responsibility for the enunciative function in the interests of a papal will that is essentially prescriptive in nature.

> O lors, dist Homenaz continuant, nullité de gresle, gelée, frimatz, vimeres! O lors abondance de tous biens en terre! O lors paix obstinée, infringible en l'Univers: cessation de guerres, pilleries, anguaries ... O lors joyeuseté, alaigresse, liesse, soulas, deduictz, plaisirs, delices en toute nature humaine! Mais, o grande doctrine, inestimable erudition, preceptions deificques, emmortaisées par les divins chapitres de ces eternes Decretales! (pp. 190–1)

Homenaz's lyrical fanaticism subtly evokes the parodic effect of a Christian litany whose absolute diction ascribes the author(ity) of the decretaline script to a sublimated but deific superego. The world emanates exclusively from these miraculous fictions, the prophetic exaltations of a papal author and the institution of a pseudo-divine law that systematically realizes the impossible in the utopia of the mind. The absolute ideals of decretaline will produce a simulation of "earthly" truth to be either revealed or rendered; they transport the papimaniac beyond the domain of reason to a fantasized paradise accepted as an ontological given.[47]

The fetishistic needs of the Papimanes not only give rise to idolatry but also prevent rebellion; the joyful "eroticization" of knowledge by Homenaz becomes increasingly seductive since it functions as an instrument of control to keep freedom for papal authority and yet deny it to others. To be sure, the only way that the Decretals can be read is through a shared passion that entraps the Papimanes in codified texts. The papal voice masterly enslaves an entire populace by placing itself at the service of an impotent other. "Cela [the right of Popes to wage wars] luy est non seulement permis et licite, mais commendé par les sacres Decretales, et doibt à feu incontinent Empereurs, Roys, Ducz,

Princes, Republicques, et à sang mettre, qu'ilz transgresseront un *iota* des ses mandemens" (pp. 187–8). Accordingly, this totalitarian rhetoric establishes a dictatorship in which the subject must acquiesce and is no longer free to invent his own language.

> Encores ces diables haereticques ne les [the Decretals] voulent aprendre et sçavoir. Bruslez, tenaillez, cizaillez, noyez, pendez, empallez, espaultrez, demembrez, exenterez, decouppez, fricassez, grislez, transonnez, crucifiez . . . ces meschans Hereticques Decretalifuges, Decretalicides, . . . pires que parricides, Decretalictones du Diable. (p. 197)

The ideal book for Homenaz is thus one that cannot be contaminated by the subversive exegetical strategies of a hypothetical reader so that the Papimaniac voice is destined to remain an alienated one.

Rabelais' *Quart Livre* therefore demonstrates how writing functions as an integral part of the social process of incorporation and rule; it serves power by subjugating individuals to a suprapersonal discipline or authority. Chapter fifty-two of the Papimanes episode demonstrates how the misuse of the sacred Decretals – the perverse violation of the text – is a paradigm of negativity, a prescription for punishment and failure; it regenerates the paradise myth by inversion so as to produce an archeology of sadistic fantasies. The libidinal pleasures associated with the correct use of decretaline law turns against itself here through the destructive instinct for transgression or the individual's will to power against an intemperate law. The punishment caused by the sacrilegious use of the "already" sacrilegious object produces a narrative which relates the nefarious effects of the wilfully perverse use of the Decretals: Jan Chouart's choice of decretaline leaves to beat gold produces results whereby not a single leaf comes out right; everything that the apothecary François Cornu packed in paper bags made out of the Decretals is spoiled, contaminated and rotten; Frère Jean's use of the Decretals to wipe his bum creates horrible cracks and piles; and when Rhizotome's sisters used the *Sextum* for a press all their linen became black as coal. The so-called sacrilegious use of the Decretals precipitates evil and misfortune while at the same time valorizing the sanctioned normality of the fetishist (the observance of the law) at the expense of a pseudo-abnormality (the perversion or violation of the sacred "law").

One of the anecdotes concerning the misuse of the Decretals provides a narrative ground that emblematizes Rabelais' very own scriptural enterprise. Carpalim relates the story of a tailor named Groignet who used an old Supplementary for his patterns. The result of this action is that they were "guastez et perduz" (p. 193).

> Groignet, cuydant tailler une cappe, tailloit la forme d'une braguette. En lieu d'un sayon, tailloit un chappeau à prunes succées. Sus la forme d'un cazaquin tailloit une aumusse . . . Pensant faire un manteau, faisoit un tabourin de Souisse. Tellement que le paouvre home par justice fut condemné à paver les estoffes de tous ses challans, et de present en est au saphran.[48] (p. 193)

The failure of the poetic act is, in fact, allegorized here. Representationally the text thematizes the process of poetic invention, the replaying of the same pattern in different forms. The rabelaisian text is indeed the transcription of a socio-political "texture." The cut-out patterns (the biblical and liturgical references) in the Papimanes episodes yield to a kind of rhetorical alterity from which the satire is born; the language of the episode in its turn is about other texts, codes, and cultural clichés which precede it and to which it is allegorically related. The bankruptcy *topos* (*être au saphran*) functions as a textualized *exemplum* of the fear of repudiation for everything in the text that is derived, copied or rewritten in such a way as to challenge authority.[49] The sacrilegious appropriation of intertextual forms is a gesture that is doomed to failure. The transgression of authority (both the misuse of the Decretals [the tailor's pseudo-crime] and Rabelais' abuse of the socio-cultural "text" of the Holy See) risks potential punishment for the production of "deformed" representational patterns that are inadequate to their referential mediums.

Rabelais' anecdote concerning the tailor has far-reaching consequences; it unveils the fiction-maker's latent fear of punishment for having tampered with language, and consequently having undermined the referential foundation of the socio-theological intertext. Groignet's story, through its drift in narrative register, enacts the latent defense mechanism of the textual unconscious. It translates a naive innocence concerning the myopic force of intentionality: we are told at several instances that the tailor was "cuydant" and "pensant" and that far more importantly, the "paouvre home" was condemned to suffer. The power of repression is allegorized here through the re-inscription of intertextual references in a different form which suggests a historically grounded representation of reality (the immoderate power of Papal rule). In a text threatened by the power of censorship, and in which the writer fears punishment for creating differences out of resemblances, the verbal form "duplicates what it names with a difference" since the tailor's crime becomes nothing other than a repetition of the transgression enacted by the rabelaisian text.[50] The fear of punishment is dramatized through the power of displacement which authorizes the repression which the text articulates. Rabelais' narrative transcribes an uncanny story of the tailor's punishment, a metaphorical translation of an absent yet omnipotent suprascript that enslaves and endlessly menaces. The exigencies of power overdetermine the writer's scriptural practice and inevitably subjugate his textual production to the rule of Law.

213

NOTES

Introduction

1 Perry Meisel, "Introduction," *Freud: Twentieth-Century Views* (Englewood Cliffs, New Jersey: Prentice Hall, 1981), p. 2.

2 See particularly Jean Bellemin-Noël, *Vers l'inconscient du texte* (Paris: Presses Universitaires de France, 1979); André Green, "The Unbinding Process," trans. Lionel Duisit, *New Literary History,* 12 (1980); Michael Riffaterre, "The Intertextual Unconscious," *Critical Inquiry,* 13 (1987), pp 371–85; Jean Bellemin-Noël, *Essais de Textanalyse* (Lille: Presses Universitaires de Lille, 1988).

3 Shoshana Felman, "To Open the Question," *Yale French Studies,* 55–6 (1977), p. 8.

4 Jacques Lacan, *Les Quatre concepts fondamentaux de la psychanalyse* (Paris: Seuil, 1973).

5 Naomi Schor, "Dreaming Dissymmetry: Barthes, Foucault, and Sexual Difference," in Alice Jardine and Paul Smith (eds.), *Men and Feminism* (London and New York: Methuen, 1987). Also see Elaine Showalter (ed.), *Speaking of Gender* (New York: Routledge, 1989).

1 Pernette du Guillet and a voice of one's own

1 See Gillian Jondorf, "Petrarchan Variations in Pernette du Guillet and Louise Labé," *Modern Language Notes,* 71 (1976), pp. 776–8 and Léon Hebreu, *De l'amour,* 2 vols. (Lyon: Jean de Tournes, 1551). For the purposes of this study I have consulted the standard critical edition, *Dialogues d'Amour,* translated by Pontus de Tyard (Lyon, 1551) and edited by T. Anthony Perry (Chapel Hill: University of North Carolina Press, 1974). The relationship between du Guillet's poetry and the neo-platonic tradition has been studied by

T. A. Perry, "Pernette du Guillet's Poetry of Love and Desire," *Bibliothèque d'Humanisme et Renaissance*, 35 (1973), pp 259–73.

2 Pernette du Guillet, *Rymes,* annotated edition by Victor E. Graham (Geneva: Droz, 1968). All references will be from this edition and indicated in the body of the text.

3 V.-L. Saulnier, "Etudes sur Pernette du Guillet et ses *Rymes,*" *Bibliothèque d'Humanisme et Renaissance,* 4 (1944), p. 27. Saulnier draws upon the image of teacher–dutiful schoolgirl relations in du Guillet's verse.

4 "Les *Rymes* semblent d'abord prisonnières de la parole de l'autre qui les suscite et les contrôle." Gisèle Mathieu-Castellani, "La parole chétive," *Littérature,* 73 (1989), p. 60.

5 Saulnier finds in du Guillet's ninth epigram confirmation of the idealized image of Scève as pedagogue (p. 31). "R, au dizain toute seule soubmise/M'à bon droict, en grand doubtance mise/De mal, ou bien, que par R on peult prendre/Car pour errer, R se peult comprendre/Signifiant que le loz, qu'on me preste/Soit une erreur, ou que R est riens, ou reste."

6 Mathieu-Castellani sees this issue in a somewhat other perspective: "Pernette inscrit la relation amoureuse dans la loi archäique de l'échange, dans le cycle du don et du contre-don" (p. 59).

7 The phrase "coming to writing" to characterize the specificity of woman's relation to language is found in Hélène Cixous, *La Venue à l'écriture* (Paris: Union Générale d'Editions, 1977). Colette H. Winn in "Le chant de la nouvelle née," *Poétique,* 78 (1989), p. 209, adapts the gender theory of Cixous to propose the following conclusion: "Désormais en possession du logos, Délie/Pernette s'enhardit jusqu'à récrire le scénario. 'Créature de langage,' elle se fait à présent créateur. De personnage de papier, elle se transforme en écrivain . . . Elle remet en cause l'authenticité de la Parole de son 'Créateur' et, plus encore, 'la politique du désir.'"

8 "Celebrating her love as the source of being, Pernette also conceived of it as the source of truth and knowledge, as an emancipation from 'la nuit d'ignorance.'" Robert D. Cottrell, "Pernette du Guillet's *Rymes*: An Adventure in Ideal Love," *Bibliothèque d'Humanisme et Renaissance,* 31 (1969), p. 561.

9 Cottrell takes a somewhat different stance here and suggests that "the ontological experience is expressed in terms of visual perception" (p. 562).

10 Ann Rosalind Jones in "Assimilation with a Difference: Renaissance Women Poets and Literary Influence," *Yale French Studies,* 62 (1981), pp. 135–53, concentrates on writing and the poetics of reciprocity between du Guillet and Scève.

11 Citations from *Délie* are from the edition of I. D. McFarlane (Cambridge: Cambridge University Press, 1966).

12 I discuss this issue in more detail in Part III, chapter 9, "Scève and the rhetoric of the dream."

13 In this context I have found Perry's "Dialogue and Doctrine in Leone Ebreo's *Dialoghi d'amore*," *PMLA*, 89 (1974) quite useful.

14 "In her celebrations of reciprocity, she refuses the position of all-powerful celestial lady, as she refuses any authority on the part of her spiritual mentor if it involves a lapse from the discourse of equals," Jones, p. 146.

15 Perry, "Introduction," in Hebreu, *Dialogues d'Amour*, 1974, p. 27. Perry (1973) quotes the following passage: "Sofia: . . . quel che s'ama, prima si desidera e, di poi, che la cosa desiderata s'e ottenuta, l'amore viene e manca il desiderio" (p. 260). The concept of intellect has been treated by Suzanne Damiens, *Amour et intellect chez Léon l'Hebreu* (Toulouse: Privat, 1971).

16 Saulnier's binary vision reads as follows: "Cet amour pur, elle le nomme amytié . . . pour l'opposer à l'amour, c'est-à-dire à la passion vulgaire. Son amour est savant, et l'autre est aveugle; il est éternel, et l'autre éphémère. C'est une pure et noble passion, tout *chaste* et exclusive, qui ne saurait changer d'objet ni se partager entre plusieurs" (p. 68).

17 I borrow the term "sensuous chastity" from Perry (1973), p. 268.

18 See Marcel Tetel, "Le Luth et la lyre de l'école lyonnaise," in Antonio Possenti and Giulia Mastrangelo (eds.), *Il Rinascimento a Lione* (Rome: Edizioni dell'atteneo, 1988), pp. 951–62.

19 Cixous, *La Jeune née* (in collaboration with Catherine Clément) (Paris: Union Générale d'Editions, 10/18, 1975), p. 172.

20 John Berger, *Ways of Seeing* (London and New York: Penguin, 1973).

21 Lance K. Donaldson-Evans' "The Taming of the Muse: The Female Poetic Voice in Pernette du Guillet's *Rymes*," in Jerry Nash (ed.), *Pre-Pléiade Poetry* (Lexington: French Forum, 1985), pp. 84–96, regards the poet's treatment of the Actaeon myth as an attempt "to distance herself from the female object of Scève's poetry." The metamorphosis that Donaldson-Evans describes is based on a "feeling of superiority" and her commitment to the virtues of poetic creativity.

22 For a Bachelardian approach see Paul Ardouin, *Maurice Scève, Pernette du Guillet, Louise Labé. L'Amour à Lyon au temps de la Renaissance* (Paris: Nizet, 1981).

23 Perry, 1973, pp. 265–7.

24 For the contemporary manifestations of this concept in rethinking

217

gender relations see Jessica Benjamin, *The Bonds of Love: Psycho-analysis, Feminism, and the Problem of Domination* (New York: Pantheon, 1988).

2 Rabelais and the representation of male subjectivity: the Rondibilis episode as case study

1 "Rabelais' vision is social and comparative, but he sees warfare and marriage in a metaphorical light as well as exempla of all human activity." Edward Benson, " 'Jamais vostre femme ne sera ribaulde, si la prenez issue de gens de bien': Love and War in the Tiers Livre," *Etudes Rabelaisiennes,* 15 (1980), p. 57.

2 Jean de Marconville, *De l'heur et malheur du mariage* (Paris: 1564), pp. 24–6.

3 François de Billon, *Le fort inexpugnable de l'honneur du sexe feminin* (Geneva: 1976), p. 74.

4 Henri Corneille Agrippa, *Declaration de la Noblesse et Preexcellence du sexe feminin,* trans. Martin Le Pin (Lyon: François Juste, 1537). Also see *Grandeur et suprematie des femmes,* feminist manifesto, trans. Alexis Bertrand, *Archives de l'anthropologie criminelle, de médecine légale et de psychologie normale et pathologique,* vol. xxv (Paris, 1910).

5 The conflict which is summarized here is drawn from Michael Screech, *Rabelais* (Ithaca: Cornell University Press, 1979), pp. 247–50. See also Roland Antonioli, *Rabelais et la Médecine* [*Etudes Rabelaisiennes,* vol. xii] (Geneva: Droz, 1976), pp. 244–56, and especially Françoise Charpentier's, "Notes pour le *Tiers Livre* de Rabelais," *Revue belge de philologie et d'histoire,* 54 (1976), pp. 780–96 in which she reads the Rondibilis episode along with passages of Plato's *Timaeus.* Jean Plattard's early reading of this episode is based on a purely *literal* interpretation: "Toute l'argumentation repose sur des considérations de physiologie," *L'Œuvre de Rabelais* (Paris: Champion, 1910), p. 85.

6 On this question, see Screech, *The Rabelaisian Marriage. Aspects of Rabelais' Religion, Ethics & Comic Philosophy* (London: Edward Arnold, 1958), especially chapter 6, pp. 84–103.

7 François Rabelais, *Œuvres complètes,* ed. Pierre Jourda, vol. i. All subsequent references will be indicated in the body of the text.

8 See the revelatory remarks of Ambrose Paré in *Opera Omnia* (Paris: 1585) Book ix, chapter 91: "la patiente est fort declorée et devient palle et jaunastre, ne se pouvant tenir debout, pour ce que les jambes et vertus luy defaillent; partant tombe en terre comme si elle estoit morte."

9 "Le thème du mariage se rattache à celui des dettes par un lien qu'il aura fallu quatre siècles pour découvrir: on ne sait guère que depuis Marcel Mauss quelle analogie apparente la circulation des femmes à celle des biens, comme depuis Lévi-Strauss quelle analogie les apparente toutes deux au modèle linguistique." Jean Paris, *Rabelais au futur* (Paris: Seuil, 1970), p. 185.

10 "Panurge himself takes up the argument that sexual regeneration is the mode of permanence or immortality appropriate to fallen nature." Terence Cave, *The Cornucopian Text. Problems of Writing in the French Renaissance* (Oxford: Oxford University Press, 1979), p. 189.

11 Screech, 1958, p. 95.

12 "Si Panurge veut se marier . . . c'est pour s'insérer dans la société." Daniel Ménager, *Rabelais* (Paris: Bordas, 1989), p. 88.

13 "It goes without saying . . . that castration is precisely not a reality, but a thematization of reality. A certain theorization of reality which, for Freud, is so anchored in perception that to deny castration is finally the same thing as denying the perceptional experience itself." Jean Laplanche, *Problématiques II/Castration–Symbolisations* (Paris: Presses Universitaires de France, 1980), p. 66.

14 See Sigmund Freud, "On Narcissism: An Introduction," in James Strachey (ed.), *Standard Edition of the Complete Psychological Works of Sigmund Freud* (New York: Hogarth Press, 1964), vol. XXIV and the more recent valorization of female narcissism in Sarah Kofman, *L'Enigme de la femme* (Paris: Galilée, 1981).

3 Verba erotica: Marguerite de Navarre and the rhetoric of silence

1 Luce Irigary, *Ce sexe qui n'en est pas un* (Paris: Minuit, 1977). English translation by Claudia Reeder in *New French Feminisms*, edited and with introductions by Elaine Marks and Isabelle de Courtivron (Amherst: University of Massachusetts Press, 1980), p. 99. Gayatri Spivak in "French Feminisms in an International Frame," *Yale French Studies*, 62 (1981), p. 184, suggests that there is something deviant about the clitoris. She describes a "liberated heterosexual woman . . . [who] . . . confronts, at worst, the 'shame' of admitting to the 'abnormality' of her orgasm: at best, the acceptance of such a special need." What is interesting to me in this assessment and its particular relevance to this story is the feeling that there is something abnormal about female pleasure, and its association with guilt.

2 Irigaray, *New French Feminisms*, p. 101.

3 *Ibid.*

4 Joan Kelly, "Did Women Have a Renaissance?" in *Women, History and Theory* (Chicago: University of Chicago Press, 1984). According to Ian MacLean, in most Renaissance discourses – theology, medicine, ethics, politics, and law – women are seen as inferior to men: *The Renaissance Notion of Woman* (Cambridge: Cambridge University Press, 1980). See also Madeleine Lazard, *Images de la femme à la Renaissance* (Paris: Presses Universitaires de France, 1985) and Margaret W. Ferguson, Maureen Quilligan, and Nancy J. Vickers (eds.), *The Discourse of Sexual Difference in Early Modern Europe* (Chicago: University of Chicago Press, 1986). My reading of this tale has benefited greatly from Nancy K. Miller's *Subject to Change: Reading Feminist Writing* (New York: Columbia University Press, 1988).

5 *De Re Uxoria* translated in *The Earthly Republic: Italian Humanists on Government and Society*, Benjamin Kohl *et al.* (eds.), (Philadelphia: University of Pennsylvania Press, 1978), p. 205.

6 The concept of love in *l'Heptaméron* has been studied by Jules Gelernt, *World of Many Loves: l'Heptaméron of Marguerite de Navarre* (Chapel Hill: University of North Carolina Press, 1966), pp. 66–125; Marcel Tetel, *Marguerite de Navarre's Heptaméron: Themes, Language, and Structure* (Durham: Duke University Press, 1973); Nicole Cazauran, *L'Heptaméron de Marguerite de Navarre* (Paris: Société d'Editions d'Enseignement Supérieur, 1976); Edward Benson, "Marriage Ancestral and Conjugal in the *Heptaméron,*" *Journal of Medieval and Renaissance Studies*, 9 (1979), pp. 261–75; and Raymond Lebègue, "La fidélité conjugale dans l'*Heptaméron,*" in *La Nouvelle française à la Renaissance*, Lionello Sozzi with a commentary by V. L. Saulnier (Geneva and Paris: Editions Slatkine, 1981), pp. 379–95. It is generally accepted that the tenth *nouvelle* can be regarded as a model for the central critical debate on the nature of love in Marguerite de Navarre's text.

7 Marguerite de Navarre, *L'Heptaméron*, M. François (ed.) (Paris: Garnier, 1964). All references will be indicated in the body of the text.

8 On the strategic use of the verbal expression "se delibera" in the story, see Tetel, "Une reévaluation de la dixième nouvelle de l'*Heptaméron,*" *Neuphilologische Mitteilungen*, 72 (1971), p. 566. Edmond Huguet confirms that this word suggests "artifice" and "machination" in *Dictionnaire de la langue française du seizième siècle*, vol. II (Paris, Champion, 1932), p. 760. In *Themes, Language, and Structure*, Tetel studies the amorous confrontations in the tale and its relationship to the verb *guerroyer* as evidence of love as a "testing ground" (pp. 29–30).

9 See Colette H. Winn, "La loi du non-parler dans l'*Heptaméron* de Marguerite de Navarre," *Romance Quarterly,* 33 (1986), pp. 157–68.

10 Lucien Febvre, *Autour de l'Heptaméron* (Paris: Gallimard, 1944). Also see Pierre Jourda, "*L'Heptaméron* et la société du xvɪᴇ siècle," *La Vie intellectuelle,* 14 (1932), pp. 478–97.

11 Tetel, 1973, p. 135.

12 On the *topos* of disfiguration, see Raymond Lebègue, "La femme qui mutile son visaige," in *Académie des inscriptions et belles lettres. Comptes Rendus des séances* (1959), pp. 176–84. Lebègue traces the roots of this *topos* back to three traditions: modern history, folklore, and classical antiquity. The references to the latter are, by and large, the most convincing. In drawing upon the research of Pierre Villey, Lebègue cites the Roman Valerius Maximus who, in the fourth book of his *Facta et dicta memorabilia,* celebrates a young man named Spurina who disfigures himself in the name of chastity. Lebègue points out that Marguerite's father had a copy of this text in his library.

13 Jacques Derrida, *Eperons: les styles de Nietzsche* (Chicago: University of Chicago Press, 1979), p. 96. More recently, John D. Bernard takes a different perspective in his reading of this tale: "Floride's story is not really one of passion either – or not her passion anyway – but of passivity." "Sexual Oppression and Social Justice in Marguerite de Navarre's *Heptaméron,*" *Journal of Medieval and Renaissance Studies,* 19 (1989), pp. 251–281.

4 Pedagogical graffiti and the rhetoric of conceit

1 Some of the more literal interpretations of Montaigne and pedagogy can be found in Paul Porteau, *Montaigne et la vie pédagogique de son temps* (Paris: Droz, 1935); Donald Frame, *Montaigne: A Biography* (New York: Harcourt, Brace and World, 1965); Roger Trinquet, *La Jeunesse de Montaigne* (Paris: Nizet, 1972), pp. 161–560; Frederick Rider, *The Dialectic of Self-hood in Montaigne* (Stanford: Stanford University Press, 1973). On teaching as a literary genre, see "The Pedagogical Imperative," Barbara Johnson (ed.), *Yale French Studies,* 63 (1982).

2 Michel de Montaigne in Maurice Rat (ed.), *Œuvres complètes* (Paris: Bibliothèque de la Pléiade, 1962), p. 147. All subsequent references are from this edition and are indicated in the body of the text.

3 "The essayist is a perpetual student and the student is a perpetual essayist." Richard Regosin, *The Matter of My Book: Montaigne's 'Essais' as the Book of the Self* (Berkeley: University of California Press, 1977), p. 80. On the rapports between teaching, rhetoric, and

psychoanalysis, see Shoshana Felman, "Psychoanalysis and Education: Teaching Terminable and Interminable," *Yale French Studies,* 63 (1982), pp. 21–44.

4 Randle Cotgrave in *A Dictionarie of the French and English Tongues* (London, 1611) defines *conception* as "a conceit; also, sence, apprehension, judgment, understanding; also the conception or conceiving, of a woman with child."

5 "The literary text may be more aptly compared to a [conscious] fantasy to the extent that the fantasy features both primary and secondary processes closely intermingled, the latter reshaping the former by endowing them with a great many attributes pertaining to secondarity." André Green, "The Unbinding Process," trans. Lionel Duisit, *New Literary History,* 12 (1980), pp. 17, 29.

6 "L'œuvre d'art est une inscription originaire mais qui est toujours un substitut symbolique. On peut dire que pour Freud toute représentation est substitutive d'une absence originaire de sens: on est toujours renvoyé de substitut en substitut sans que soit jamais atteint un signifié originaire, seulement fantasmé par le désir." Sarah Kofman, *L'Enfance de l'Art* (Paris: Payot, 1970).

7 Ovid, *Tristia,* trans. A. L. Wheeler (Cambridge: Harvard University Press [Loeb Classical Library], 1965).

8 "... et m'enfante tant de chimères et monstres fantasques les uns sur les autres, sans ordre et sans propos, que pour en contempler à mon aise l'ineptie et l'estrangeté, j'ay commancé de les mettre en rolle, esperant avec le temps luy en faire honte à luy mesmes" p. 34). See Mary B. McKinley, "Horace: A Dialogue about Monsters," in *Words in a Corner* (Lexington: French Forum, 1981), pp. 37–61.

9 Jacques Lacan, *Le Séminaire, Livre XX: Encore* (Paris: Seuil, 1975), p. 110. This lacanian perspective in no way precludes the importance of Socratic *docta ignorantia* in the *Essais.*

10 Ernst Robert Curtius, *European Literature and the Latin Middle Ages,* trans. Willard Trask (Princeton: Princeton University Press, 1953), pp. 476–7.

11 On the symbolic function of Latin, see Jean Starobinski, *Montaigne en mouvement* (Paris: Gallimard, 1982), pp. 144–8, and more recently Mitchell Greenberg, "Montaigne at the Crossroads: Textual Conundrums in the *Essais,*" *Stanford French Review* (1982), pp. 22–7.

12 See D. W. Winnicott, *Playing and Reality* (New York: Basic Books, 1971).

13 "The Articulation of the Ego in the English Renaissance," in *Psychiatry and the Humanities,* vol. IV (New Haven: Yale University Press, 1980), p. 294. See also Rudolph E. Siegel, *Galen's System of*

Physiology and Medicine (Basel: Karger, 1973). Thinking is equated with bodily functions throughout this essay in examples such as "Ceux qui ont le corps gresle, le groississent d'embourrures: ceux qui ont la matiere exile, l'enflent de paroles" (p. 156).

14 "Dans le mot 'savoir', Montaigne a dû comprendre *sapere*, 'avoir de la saveur, du goût'. Savoir quelque chose, c'est proprement le goûter, d'où cette recurrence de métaphores alimentaires." Floyd Gray, *La Balance de Montaigne* (Paris: Nizet, 1982), p. 116. On the binary structure of digestive metaphors see Gray, *Le Style de Montaigne* (Paris: Nizet, 1958), pp. 210–14.

15 Terence Cave, *The Cornucopian Text: Problems of Writing in the French Renaissance* (Oxford: Clarendon Press, 1979), pp. 36–9.

16 On the images of education and their relationship to rhetorical tradition, see Gilbert Mayer, "Les images dans Montaigne d'après le chapitre de l'institution des enfans," in *Mélanges de philologie et d'histoire littéraire offerts à Edmond Huguet* (Paris: Droz, 1940), and Carol Clark, *The Web of Metaphor: Studies in the Imagery of Montaigne's Essais* (Lexington, Ky.: French Forum, 1978), pp. 53–63.

17 "Mourning and Melancholia," in James Strachey (ed.), *Standard Edition of the Complete Psychological Works of Sigmund Freud* (New York: Hogarth Press, 1964), vol XIV, p. 249.

18 Jacques Derrida, "Signature Evénement Contexte," in *Marges de la philosophie* (Paris: Editions de Minuit, 1972). François Rigolot has discussed the importance of La Boétie's loss in the writing of the *Essais* in "Montaigne's Purloined Letters," *Yale French Studies,* 64 (1983), pp. 143–66.

19 Karl Abraham, "A Short Study of the Development of the Libido, Viewed in the Light of Mental Disorders" (1924), in *The Selected Papers of Karl Abraham* (London: Hogarth Press, 1927). On desire and mourning see also the pertinent remarks of Jacques Lacan, "Desire and the Interpretation of Desire in Hamlet," *Yale French Studies,* 55–6 (1977), pp. 24–39.

20 Richard Regosin, "Source and Resources: the 'Pretexts' of Originality in Montaigne's *Essais,*" in *Substance,* 21 (1978), p. 106.

21 *Standard Edition of the Complete Psychological Works of Sigmund Freud,* vol. XIV, p. 249.

22 Both Freud and Abraham refer to a secondary form of narcissism derived from the subject's relationship to the loved object.

23 See my essay, "My Body, My Text" in this volume.

24 Jacques Lacan, "The Subject and the Other: Alienation," *The Four Fundamental Concepts of Psychoanalysis,* trans. Alan Sheridan (New York: Norton, 1978), p. 43.

25 "Et quand il [the ideal student] commencera de se sentir, luy presen-

tant Bradamant ou Angelique pour maistresse à jouïr, et d'une beauté naïve, active, genereuse, non hommasse mais virile, au prix, d'une beauté molle, affettée, delicate, artificielle; l'une travestie en garçon, coiffée d'un morrion luysant, l'autre vestue en garce, coiffée d'un attiffet emperlé" (p. 161).

26 John Lapp has pointed out the philosophical tradition in which the paradoxical pleasures of virtue are adhered to: For the Epicureans, pleasure actually *is* virtue: "cette brave et genereuse volupté Epicurienne qui fait estat de nourrir mollement en son giron et y faire follatrer la vertu, luy donnant pour ses jouets la honte, les fievres, la pauvreté, la mort et les geénes" (p. 402). "A Prose Poem: Montaigne's 'Mother Virtue'," in *O Un Amy! Essays on Montaigne in Honor of Donald M. Frame* (Lexington, Ky.: French Forum, 1977), p. 177. On the imagery of virtue and its relationship to philosophy, see Gray, "Montaigne and the Memorabilia," *Studies in Philology,* 58 (1961), pp. 130–9, and Hugo Friedrich, *Montaigne,* trans. Robert Rovini (Paris: Gallimard, 1968), p. 318.

27 Cotgrave in *A Dictionarie of the French and English Tongues* defines *vertu* as "vertue, goodness, honestie, sinceritie, integritie, worth, perfection, desert, merit; also valor, prowesse, manhood; also force, power, might."

28 Natalie Zemon Davis has discussed the cultural components of gender identity in sixteenth-century France in "Women on Top," in *Society and Culture in Early Modern France,* (Stanford: Stanford University Press, 1975), pp. 124–51.

29 Lapp, p. 183.

5 Montaigne's family romance

1 "Family Romances" (1909), in James Strachey (ed.), *The Standard Edition of the Complete Psychological Works of Sigmund Freud,* vol. IX (London: Hogarth Press, 1953–73), pp. 236–41. Freud suggests that the child's oedipal desires are inextricably linked to early narrative activity.

2 *Ibid.,* p. 236.

3 See the remarks of Gérard Defaux on Erasmus and Montaigne in "Rhétorique et représentation dans les Essais: de la peinture de l'autre à la peinture du moi," *Bulletin de la Société des Amis de Montaigne,* 7 (1985), p. 43.

4 Jacques Lacan, "The Mirror Stage as Formative of the Function of

the I," in *Ecrits*, trans. A. Sheridan (New York: Norton, 1977), pp. 1–7.

5 According to Freud, in certain cases of neurotic inhibition, "writing, which entails making a liquid flow out of a tube onto a white piece of paper, assumes the significance of copulation." *Standard Edition*, vol. xx, p. 90.

6 Charlton T. Lewis and Charles Short, *Andrews' Latin Dictionary* (Oxford: Oxford University Press, 1962 [first edition 1879]).

7 See the interpretations of Michel Butor, *Essai sur les essais* (Paris: Gallimard, 1968); Anthony Wilden, "Par divers moyens on arrive à pareille fin: A Reading of Montaigne," *Modern Language Notes*, 83 (1968), pp. 577–97; François Rigolot, "Montaigne's Purloined Letters," *Yale French Studies*, 64 (1983), pp. 145–66.

8 Lawrence D. Kritzman, "Amitié d'écriture," in *Destruction/Découverte: le fonctionnement de la rhétorique dans les "Essais" de Montaigne* (Lexington: French Forum, 1980), pp. 70–7.

9 On melancholy in the Renaissance see Raymond Klibansky, Erwin Panofsky, and Fritz Saxl, *Saturn and Melancholy: Studies in the History of Natural Philosophy, Religion, and Art* (New York: Basic Books Publishers, 1964); Jean Starobinski, *Histoire du traitement de la mélancolie des origines à 1900* (Basel: J. R. Geigy, 1960); Albert-Marie Schmidt, *La Poésie scientifique en France au xvie siècle* (Lausanne: Editions Rencontre, 1970 [first edition 1938]); Claude-Gilbert Dubois, *Le Maniérisme* (Paris: Presses Universitaires de France, 1979), pp. 200–3; Gisèle Mathieu-Castellani, "Narcisse ou la mélancolie: lecture d'un sonnet de Du Perron," *Littérature*, 37 (1980), pp. 25–36; Michael A. Screech, *Montaigne and Melancholy. The Wisdom of the Essays* (Selinsgrove: Susquehanna University Press, 1984); Julia Kristeva, *Soleil noir. Dépression et mélancolie* (Paris: Gallimard, 1987).

10 "Mourning and Melancholia," *Standard Edition of the Complete Psychological Works of Sigmund Freud*, vol. xiv, p. 249.

11 "Selon la conviction habituellement partagée à son époque, il établit une relation étroite entre solitude et mélancolie (l'on cherche la solitude parce qu'on est mélancolique; l'on devient mélancolique parce que l'on mène une existence solitaire)." Jean Starobinski, *Montaigne en mouvement* (Paris: Gallimard, 1982), p. 37.

12 See Karl Abraham, "A Short Study of the Development of the Libido, Viewed in Light of Mental Disorders," (1924), in *The Selected Papers of Karl Abraham* (London: Hogarth Press, 1927), and Jacques Lacan, "Desire and Interpretation of Desire in Hamlet," *Yale French Studies*, 64 (1983), pp. 143–66.

13 "Mourning and Melancholia," p. 249.

14 Randle Cotgrave in *A Dictionarie of the French and English Tongues* (London, 1611) defines *chagrin* as "anxiety, vexation or anguish of the mind" and *resveries* as "delire, folie, obsession."

15 "Everyman loves his own handiwork better than he would be loved by it if it came alive; and this happens perhaps most of all with poets; for they have an excessive love for their poems, doting on them as if they were their children." *Nicomachian Ethics* in Richard McKeon (ed.), *Introduction to Aristotle* (New York: Modern Library, 1947), p. 507.

16 Starobinski, p. 259.

17 Natalie Zemon Davis, "A Renaissance text to the historian's eye: the gifts of Montaigne," *Journal of Medieval and Renaissance Studies* 15 (1985), pp. 47–56. Also see François Rigolot's critique of Davis in "Mutation de l'Histoire: 'l'accointance des Muses' " in *Les Métamorphoses de Montaigne* (Paris: Presses Universitaires de France, 1988), pp. 15–34.

18 "D'un bout à l'autre cet essai pose le problème du lieu de son énonciation: Montaigne l'écrit-il en tant que père?" Françoise Charpentier, "L'Absente des *Essais*: quelques questions autour de l'Essai ii-8, 'de l'Affection des pères aux enfans'," *Bulletin de la société des amis de Montaigne,* 17–18 (1984), p. 10.

19 "Bien que le chapitre soit adressé à une mère, la remarque n'est pas déplacée, en raison du rôle de Mme d'Estissac: en s'archarnant à assurer à son fils la possession de l'héritage que lui disputaient ses demi-sœurs, elle s'acquittait précisément de la fonction que Montaigne assigne au père." André Tournon, *Montaigne. La Glose et l'Essai* (Lyon: Presses Universitaires de Lyon, 1983), p. 358, note 9. See Roger Trinquet, "En marge des Essais: la vraie figure de Mme d'Estissac," *Bibliothèque d'Humanisme et Renaissance* (1956), pp. 23–36.

20 "Arguments against wet-nursing were articulated by moralists and physicians of the Renaissance who followed Aulus Gellius's translation of Favorinus of Arles in *Noctes Atticae,* Book xii." George D. Sussman, *Selling Mother's Milk* (Urbana: University of Illinois Press, 1982), p. 3.

21 "It is the truth of what desire has been in its history that the subject cries out in his symptom." Lacan, "The Agency of the Letter in the Unconscious," in *Ecrits*, p. 167.

22 Melanie Klein, "Love, Guilt, Reparation [1937], reprinted in *Love, Guilt, and Reparation and Other Works, 1921–1945* (New York: Doubleday, 1977), pp. 306–43. On the representation of the body and aesthetics see "Infantile Anxiety-Situations Reflected in a Work of Art and in the Creative Impulse," in R. E. Money-Kyrle (ed.),

The Writings of Melanie Klein, International Psycho-analytical Library (London: Hogarth Press and Institute of Psycho-analysis, 1975), vol. I, pp. 210–18.

23 "Love, Guilt, and Reparation," p. 334.

24 Claude-Gilbert Dubois, *L'Imaginaire de la Renaissance* (Paris: Presses Universitaires de France, 1985), pp. 26–8. Dubois discusses the Pygmalion complex as an effect of mimetic desire. On the relationship between sublimation and idealization, see Guy Rosoloto, *Essais sur le symbolique* (Paris: Collections Tel, 1964), pp. 170–80.

25 In "The Function of Pygmalion in the *Metamorphoses* of Ovid," *Transactions and Proceedings of the American Philological Association,* 93 (1962), p. 13, Douglas F. Bauer claims that Ovid suggested the "figurative equation between the sculpture of Pygmalion and the art of the poet." See also Richard Regosin, *The Matter of My Book: Montaigne's 'Essais' as the Book of Self* (Berkeley: University of California Press, 1977), p. 156 and Mary B. McKinley, *Words in a Corner: Studies in Montaigne's Latin Quotations* (Lexington: French Forum, 1981), p. 23.

26 "Narcisse et Pygmalion, c'est par conséquent tout un, la perversion du bâtiment dans la confusion du père et de l'enfant, du sujet et du reflet, du nom et du renom." Antoine Compagnon, *Nous Michel de Montaigne* (Paris: Seuil, 1980), p. 217.

27 "L'écrivain est quelqu'un qui joue avec le corps de sa mère . . . pour le glorifier, l'embellir, ou pour le dépecer, le porter à la limite de ce qui, du corps, peut être reconnu." Roland Barthes, *Le Plaisir du texte* (Paris: Seuil, 1973), p. 60.

28 For a somewhat different reading see Terence Cave, "Problems of Reading in the *Essais,*" in I. D. McFarlane and Ian Maclean (eds.), *Montaigne. Essays in Memory of Richard Sayce* (Oxford: Oxford University Press, 1982), p. 152: "Montaigne is both a Pygmalion, bringing to life the dead texts with which he works, and an Actaeon, overtaken by an alien form and fragmented by the very materials he was supposed to control."

29 Davis, p. 55.

30 "If we look at the attitude of fond parents towards their children, we cannot but perceive it as a revival and reproduction of their own long-since abandoned narcissism." Freud, *General Psychological Theory,* trans. Cecil Baines (New York: Collier, 1963), p. 71.

6 Architecture of the utopian body: the *blasons* of Marot and Ronsard

1 On the Renaissance *blason* see Robert Pike, "The *Blasons* in French

Literature of the 16th Century," *Romanic Review*, 27 (1936), pp. 223–47; D. B. Wilson, *Descriptive Poetry in France from Blason to Baroque* (Manchester: Manchester University Press, 1967); John Freccero, "The Fig Tee and the Laurel: Petrarch's Poetics," *Diacritics*, 5 (1975), pp. 34–40; Annette and Edward Tomarken, "The Rise of the Sixteenth-Century *blason*," *Symposium*, 29 (1975), pp. 139–63; Alison Saunders, *The Sixteenth-Century Blason Poétique* (Bern: Peter Lang, 1981). On the body, see Susan Rubin Suleiman (ed), *The Female Body in Western Culture: Contemporary Perspectives* (Cambridge: Harvard University Press, 1986).

2 Françoise Charpentier, "Ordre et triomphe du corps," in Louise Labé, *Œuvres poétiques* (Paris: Gallimard, Collection Poésie), pp. 12–16.

3 A.-M. Schmidt describes the anatomical *blason* in the following way: "un charme . . . une litanie . . . une kyrielle . . . une incantation . . . une suite d'apostrophes savamment variées et volontairement monotones." *Poètes du* xvi*e siècle* (Paris: Editions de la Pléiade, 1964), p. 293.

4 Jacques Lacan, *Ecrits* (Paris: Seuil, 1966), p. 301. Nancy Vickers suggests the following: "The enterprise is fundamentally narcissistic as the dehumanization and reification of the woman creates a self-defined impossible relationship in human terms." "The Poetic and Philosophical Contexts to Descriptions of the Female Body in the Renaissance" (Yale University dissertation, 1976), p. 24. See also *Le Corps et ses fictions,* collected essays ed. Claude Reichler (Paris: Minuit, 1983).

5 Roland Barthes, *Le Plaisir du texte* (Paris: Seuil, 1973), p. 60. See Shirley Nelson Garner, Claire Kahane and Madelon Sprengnether (eds.), *The Mother Tongue* (Ithaca: Cornell University Press, 1985).

6 V. L. Saulnier, *Maurice Scève* (Paris: Klincksieck, 1948), vol. I, p. 77.

7 Guillaume Coquillart, *Sensuyvent les droitz nouveaulx: avec le debat des dames et des armes* (Paris: J. Trepperel, 1532), np, 4, BN Res. Ye 1266.

8 I borrow the concept of the "good" and "bad" object from Melanie Klein in "The Importance of Symbol Formation in the Development of the Ego," and "Early Stages of the Oedipus Conflict," in R. E. Money-Kyrle (ed.), *The Writings of Melanie Klein,* vol. I, International Psycho-analytical Library (London: Hogarth Press and the Institute of Psycho-analysis, 1975).

9 The ideal of female beauty and its relationship to the *topos* of the beautiful breast is already found in the description of *Dame Oyseuse*:

n'avoit jusqu'en Jerusalem

fame qui plus bel col portast;
polis ert et soés au tast.
Sa gorge estoit autresi blanche
come la nois desus la branche
quant il a freschement niegé.

Le Roman de la Rose, ed. F. Lecoy (Paris: Classiques français du moyen âge, 1965), vol. I, p. 18.

10 Clément Marot, *Œuvres,* ed. C. A. Mayer (London: Athlone Press, 1970), vol. V, p. 156. All references will be from this edition.

11

Et s'a un col si acesmé
Qui est de gorge si formé
Plus blanc qu'argent seurestamé.
Gras et rondet,
Droite gorge de barbelet;
Il est si biaus, il est si net,
Il boçoie sus le colet.

Nouveaux Recueil de contes, dits, fabliaux et autres pièces inédites des XIIIème, *et* XVème *siècles,* éd. A. Jubinal (Paris: 1839–42), vol. II, p. 179.

12 According to Marot, the *contreblason* was written in order to valorize the poetic talent of the *blasonneur.*

Et est le Painctre indigne de louange,
Qui ne sçait paindre aussie Diable qu'Ange
Apres la course il fault tirer la Barre,
Apres Bemol fault chanter en Becarre.

Marot, *A ceulx qui apres l'epigramme du beau tétin en feirent d'aultres, Œuvres,* vol. I, p. 215.

13 On the poetics of abjection, see Julia Kristeva, *Pouvoir de l'horreur* (Paris: Seuil, 1980).

14 Rémy Belleau, *Ecologues Sacrées* VII in Charles Marty-Laveaux (ed.), *Œuvres poétiques,* vol. II (Paris: Lemerre, 1878), pp. 319–20.

15 Pierre de Ronsard, *Les Amours,* ed. Henri and Catherine Weber (Paris: Garnier, 1963), p. 16. All references will be to this edition.

16 On the myth of the Medusa, see John Freccero, "Medusa: The Letter and the Spirit," *Yearbook of Italian Studies* (1972), pp. 1–18; Hélène Cixous, "The Laugh of the Medusa," trans. Keith Cohen and Paula Cohen in Elaine Marks and Isabelle de Courtivron (eds.), *New French Feminisms* (Amherst: University of Massachusetts Press, 1980); Gisèle Mathieu-Castellani, *Mythes de l'éros baroque* (Paris: Presses Universitaires de France, 1981), pp. 185–222; Nancy

J. Vickers, "The Heraldry in Lucrece's Face," *Poetics Today*, 6 (1985), pp. 180–3.

17 "Ce n'est plus le corps du monstre menaçant qui se trouve pétrifié; c'est le corps d'Andromède menacée qui se raidit en statue." François Rigolot, "Rhétorique de la métamorphose chez Ronsard," in *Textes et Intertextes. Etudes sur le* xvie *siècle pour Alfred Glauser* (Paris: Nizet, 1979), p. 156.

18 "Elle [la femme] *est* le poème travaillé, fermé, sculpté . . . Le sujet, devenu sculptural, donne au sonnet une densité qui l'apparente d'avance à l'œuvre d'art." Alfred Glauser, *Le Poème–Symbole* (Paris: Nizet, 1967), p. 60. As anatomical part, the thighs are compared to a work of Phidias in the portrait of Olympia, Ariosto, *Orlando Furioso* (Bari: Laterza, 1928), xi, p. 69.

7 Fictions of the body and the gender of the text in Ronsard's 1552 *Amours*

1 Michel de Certeau, "Des outils pour écrire le corps," *Traverses*, 14–15 (1979), p. 12. On the poetics of the body, see John Freccero, "The Fig Tree and the Laurel: Petrarch's Poetics," *Diacritics*, 5 (1975), pp. 34–40; Elizabeth Cropper, "On Beautiful Women, Parmigianino, Petrarchismo and the Vernacular Style," *Art Bulletin*, 58 (1976), pp. 374–94; Nancy J. Vickers, "Diana Described: Scattered Woman and Scattered Rhyme," *Critical Inquiry*, 8 (1981), pp. 265–79; *Le Corps et ses fictions*, collected essays ed. Claude Reichler (Paris: Minuit, 1983); *La Folie et le Corps*, collected essays ed. Jean Céard with Pierre Naudin and Michel Simonin (Paris: Presses de l'Ecole Normale Supérieure, 1985).

2 See Sigmund Freud, *L'interprétation des rêves* (Paris: Presses Universitaires de France, 1967). On the concept of the fragment, see Lawrence D. Kritzman (ed.), *Fragments: Incompletion and Discontinuity* (New York: New York Literary Forum, 1981).

3 "Toute entrée dans le monde des signes implique un assujettissement aux fictions de la représentation institutionnelle, à commencer par celle du langage, qui ne peut pas nommer sans classifier et différer." Ivan Almeida, "Un Corps devenu récit," *Le corps et ses fictions* (Paris: Minuit, 1983), p. 11.

4 See Melanie Klein, *Love, Guilt, and Reparation and Other Works 1921–1945* (New York: Dell Publishing, 1977).

5 Pierre de Ronsard, *Les Amours*, ed. Henry and Catherine Weber (Paris: Garnier, 1963), p. 131. All references are to this edition. On the rhetoric of the *blason*, see Robert Pike, "The *Blasons* in French Literature of the 16th Century," *Romanic Review*, 27 (1936), pp.

223–46; V. L. Saulnier, "Les *blasons* anatomiques," in *Maurice Scève* (Paris: Klincksieck, 1948), vol. I, pp. 72–87; D. B. Wilson, *Descriptive Poetry in France from Blason to Baroque* (Manchester: Manchester University Press, 1967); Françoise Charpentier, "L'ordre et triomphe du corps," in Louise Labé, *Œuvres complètes* (Paris: Gallimard-Poésie, 1983), pp. 12–16.

6   Li occhi sereni e le stellanti ciglia
            La bella bocca angelica, di perle
            Piena e di rose et di dolci parole,
            Che fanno altrui tremar di meraviglia:
            E la fronte et le chiome, ch'a vederle,
            Di state a mezzo dì, vincono il sole.   (CC, 9–14)

Petrarch, *Canzoniere,* ed. Piero Cudini (Milan: Garzanti, 1974). "Malice du langage: une fois rassemblé, pour *se dire,* le corps total doit retourner à la poussière des mots, à l'égrenage des détails, à l'inventaire monotone des parties, à l'émiettement: le langage défait le corps, le renvoie au fétiche. Ce retour est codé sous le nom de *blason.*" Roland Barthes, *S/Z* (Paris: Seuil, 1970), p. 120.

7 "Aimable hirondelle, qui reviens visiter chaque année nos climats, c'est après avoir fait ton nid en été que tu disparais à l'approche de l'hiver, ou vers le Nil ou vers Memphis, tandis que l'Amour en toute saison a construit son nid dans mon cœur. Déjà, dans cette couvée de jeunes Amours, l'un, le Désir commence à essayer ses ailes, l'autre est encore dans sa coquille, un autre est à demi eclos, et toute cette jeune famille réclame à grands cris sa pâture. Les grands élèvent les petits, qui, à leur tour, en font naître d'autres. Quel remède y apporter? Je ne saurais chasser une telle nichée d'Amours." *Odes d'Anarcréon avec* LIV *Compositions par Girodet* trans. Amb. Firmin Didot (Paris: Didot Frères, 1864), pp. 62–3.

8 "Il [Ronsard] donne à la création littéraire la réalité des enfantements. L'œuvre est une procréation." Alfred Glauser, *Le Poème–Symbole* (Paris: Nizet, 1967), p. 46.

9 Roland Barthes, *Fragments d'un discours amoureux* (Paris: Seuil, 1977), p. 20.

10 Randle Cotgrave, *A Dictionarie of the French and English Tongues* (London: 1611; reprinted Columbia, S.C.: University of South Carolina Press, 1950), n. pag.

11 Consult André Chastel, "L'œuf de Ronsard," in *Mélanges Henri Chamard* (Paris: Nizet, 1951), pp. 109–11.

12 On the images of movement, see I. D. McFarlane, "Aspects of Ronsard's Poetic Vision," in Terence Cave (ed), *Ronsard the Poet* (London: Methuen, 1973), pp. 30–3.

13 "Le dernier tercet, malgré le parallélisme apparent, est très différ-

ent, tout entier mouvement, élévation, élargissement. L'image pré-
cise cède la place à des mots plus abstraits d'une résonance plus
ample, qui préparent l'envol du dernier vers." Henri Weber, *La
création poétique au* xvɪe *siècle en France* (Paris: Nizet, 1955), p.
287.

14 See Ludovico Ariosto, *Orlando Furioso* (Bari: Laterza, 1928): "Due
poem acerbe, et pur d'ivorio fatte,/Vengon e van come onda al
primo margo" (vɪɪ, p. 14).

15 The *topos* of the beautiful breast has been studied by Michael
Riffaterre, *Semiotics of Poetry* (Bloomington: Indiana University
Press, 1978), pp. 82–6.

16 The desire to be metamorphosized into a flea was a *topos* cultivated
by the neo-Latin poets of the sixteenth century. On this subject, see
the pertinent remarks of Rosalie L. Colie, *Paradoxica Epidemica*
(Princeton: Princeton University Press, 1966), pp. 107–8.

17 On the *topos* of metamorphosis, consult A. Bartlett Giamatti, "Proteus Unbound: Some versions of the Sea God in the Renaissance,"
in Peter Demetz, Thomas Greene, and Lowry Nelson, Jr. (eds.),
The Disciplines of Criticism (New Haven: Yale University Press,
1968), pp. 437–75, and François Rigolot, "Rhétorique: Métamorphose et Métaphore," in *Le Texte de la Renaissance* (Geneva: Droz,
1982), pp. 187–98.

18 André Gendre, *Ronsard: Pòete de la Conquête Amoureuse* (Neuchâtel: Editions de la Baconnière, 1970), p. 470.

19 My perspective is somewhat different from Thomas Greene's who
declares that this poem "can be read with equal propriety as a
displaced poetic manifesto, the dream of a text that would overcome
the distance to the signified by a mastery which was also a surrender
to liquidity." *The Light in Troy. Imitation and Discovery in Renaissance Poetry* (New Haven: Yale University Press, 1982), p. 210. On
the relationship between the self/object, see André Green, *Narcissime de vie, narcissime de mort* (Paris: Minuit, 1983).

20 The pleasure principle is in service of the death instinct. On this
subject see Sigmund Freud, "Au-delà du principe de plaisir," in
Essais de psychanalyse (Paris: Payot, 1951), pp. 5–75, and Peter
Brooks, "Freud's Masterplot: Questions of Narrative," *Yale French
Studies,* 55–6 (1977), pp. 280–300.

21 "N'est-il pas vrai que le narcissique, tel quel, est précisément quelqu'un incapable d'amour?" Julia Kristeva, *Histoires d'amour* (Paris:
Denoël, 1983), p. 38.

22 Petrarch, *Canzoniere,* cxcvɪ and Ludovico Ariosto, *Lirica,* sonnet
23 (Bari: Laterza, 1924). "Le recours aux mythologies figurées
permet à l'imagination de se représenter l'indéfinissable ambiguïté

d'une coiffure émouvante ... Sur la mode des visages 'gentiment adonisés d'un beau bonnet,' voir Brantôme, Lalanne, ix, p. 313. Les statues antiques représentaient Adonis coiffé du bonnet phrygien. Ronsard fait allusion à une scène du Livre x des *Métamorphoses*: Venus négligeant sa toilette, prend le costume de chasse pour suivre son ami (v, 532–6); la mode était aux déguisements où un personnage emprunte les vêtements d'un autre sexe." Guy Demerson, *La mythologie classique dans l'œuvre lyrique de la Pléïade* (Geneva: Droz, 1972), p. 199.

23 *Dictionaire des mythologies et des religions des sociétés traditionnelles et du monde antique,* ed. Yves Bonnefoy (Paris: Flammarion, 1981), p. 2.

24 "Mieux aimé que Gygès lui qui mêlé à un chœur de jeunes filles, serait merveilleux pour tromper des hôtes au flair subtil, voilant toute différence sous ses cheveux épars et son visage ambigu." Horace, *Odes et Epodes,* vol. i, trans. and ed. F. Villeneuve (Paris: Belles Lettres, 1927), p. 63.

25 "Le moi est la métonymie du désir." Jacques Lacan, *Ecrits* (Paris: Seuil, 1966), p. 640.

26 Consult Pierre Grimal, *Dictionnaire de la Mythologie grecque et romaine* (Paris: Presses Universitaires de France, 1963).

27 Barthes, *Fragments d'un discours amoureux,* p. 85.

8 My body, my text: Montaigne and the rhetoric of self-portraiture

1 On the *topos* of the text as body, see Michel Jeanneret, "Rabelais et Montaigne: l'écriture comme parole," in *The French Renaissance Mind: Studies Presented to W. G. Moore,* ed. Barbara Bowen, *L'Esprit Créateur,* 16 (1976), pp. 78–94; and Richard Regosin, *The Matter of My Book: Montaigne's 'Essais' as the Book of the Self* (Berkeley: University of California Press, 1977), pp. 198–224.

2 This problem is discussed in Bowen, "Montaigne's Anti-Phaedrus: 'Sur des vers de Virgile'," *Journal of Medieval and Renaissance Studies,* 5 (1975), pp. 107–21.

3 Michel de Montaigne, *Œuvres complètes,* ed. Maurice Rat (Paris: Bibliothèque de la Pléïade, 1962), p. 825. All subsequent references are from this edition and are indicated in the body of the text. Several studies discuss the interrelationship between writing and sexuality: Marcel Tetel, "Montaigne et Le Tasse: Imagination poétique et espace imaginaire," *Cahiers de l'Association Internationale des Etudes Françaises,* 33 (1981), pp. 81–98; Robert D. Cottrell, in *Sexuality/Textuality: A Study of the Fabric of Montaigne's Essais* (Columbus, Ohio: Ohio State University Press, 1981), examines the

use of two key metaphors, *accouplage* and *contexture,* which may be taken to designate sexuality and textuality in relation to the creative progress; and Jean Starobinski's very elegant essay "Dire l'amour: Remarques sur l'érotique de Montaigne," *Nouvelle Revue de Psychanalyse,* 23 (1981), pp. 299–323.

4 Erica Harth, "Sur des vers de Virgile: Antinomy and Totality in Montaigne," *French Forum,* 2 (1977), p. 5. "Montaigne relie sexualité et imaginaire. *Sur des vers de Virgile* se consacre à la poésie autant qu'à l'érotisme." Géralde Nakam, "Eros et les Muses dans 'Sur les vers de Virgile'," in *Etudes seiziémistes offertes à M. le Professeur V. L. Saulnier par plusieurs de ses anciens doctorants,* Travaux d'Humanisme et Renaissance, 177 (Geneva: Droz, 1980), p. 401.

5 The perfect unity that Montaigne idealized in "De l'amitié" (I, 28) is no longer possible: "Car cette parfaicte amitié, dequoy je parle, est indivisible: chacun se donne si entier à son amy, qu'il ne luy reste rien à departir ailleurs . . . Depuis le jour que je le [La Boétie] perdy . . . je ne fay que trainer languissant; et les plaisirs mesmes qui s'offrent à moy, au lieu de me consoler, me redoublent le regret de sa perte. Nous estions à moitié de tout; il me semble que je luy desrobe sa part" (pp. 190, 192). On this problem, see Barry Weller, "The Rhetoric of Friendship in Montaigne's *Essais,*" *New Literary History,* 9 (1978), pp. 503–23.

6 Peter Brooks, "Freud's Masterplot: Questions of Narrative," in Shoshana Felman (ed.), *Literature and Psychoanalysis, Yale French Studies,* 55–6 (1977), pp. 289, 296. Brooks borrows his terminology from Sigmund Freud, *Beyond the Pleasure Principle* (1920), in James Strachey (ed.), *Standard Edition of the Complete Psychological Works of Sigmund Freud* (London: Hogarth Press, 1955). J. Hillis Miller in "Ariadne's Thread: Repetition and the Narrative Line," *Critical Inquiry,* 3 (1976), pp. 69–70, regards narrative as a "retracing of a journey already made."

7 "The power to signify is located in the past, just as true sexual potency is located in youth . . . Montaigne refers to the value of his topic as a way of sustaining mentally – or rather textually – the pleasures of his youth." Terence Cave, *The Cornucopian Text: Problems of Writing in the French Renaissance* (Oxford: Clarendon Press, 1979), p. 294.

8 Floyd Gray, *Le Style de Montaigne* (Paris: Nizet, 1958), pp. 155–8, and Albert Thibaudet in Gray (ed.), *Montaigne* (Paris: Gallimard, 1963), pp. 507–14.

9 Richard L. Regosin, "Figures of the Self: Montaigne's Rhetoric of Portraiture," *L'Esprit Créateur,* 20 (1980), p. 68.

10   Dixerat, et niveis hinc atque hinc diva lacertis
        Cunctantem amplexu molli fovet. Ille repente
        Accepit solitam flammam, notusque medullas
        Intravit calor, et labefacta per ossa cucurrit.
        Non secus atque olim tonitru cum rupta corusco
        Ignea rima micans percurrit limine nimbos . . .
        . . . Ea verba locutus,
        Optatos dedit amplexus, placidumque petivit
        Conjugis infusus gremio per membra soporem.   (p. 826)

11 See John C. Lapp, "Montaigne's 'Négligence' and Some Lines from Virgil," *Romanic Review*, 61 (1970), pp. 167–81.

12 Cave, *The Cornucopian Text*, pp. 285–7.

13 Ce que Virgile dict de Venus et de Vulcan, Lucrece l'avoit dict plus sortablement d'une jouissance desrobée d'elle et de mars:

                      belli fera moenera Mavors
        Armipotens regit, in gremium qui saepe tuum se
        Rejicit, aeterno devictus vulnere amoris:
        Atque ita suspiciens tereti cervice reposta
        Pascit amore avidos inhians in te, Dea, visus,
        Eque tuo pendet resupini spiritus ore:
        Hunc tu, diva, tuo recubantem corpore sancto
        Circumfusa super, suavis ex ore loquelas
        Funde. . . .   (p. 850)

14 Jean Laplanche in *Vie et mort en psychanalyse* (Paris: Flammarion, 1970), pp. 30–7, equates sexual excitement with psychic movement which ostensibly becomes a vehicle for the "transformation" of reality.

15 See *Destruction/Découverte: Le fonctionnement de la rhétorique dans les 'Essais' de Montaigne* (Lexington, Ky.: French Forum, 1980), pp. 102–5; 107.

16 According to Bowen (1975), Montaigne obliquely refutes Platonic and Plutarchian notions of love. The essayist decries those who completely repress their libidinal instincts. "(b) Chacun fuit à le [man] voir naistre, chacun suit à le voir mourir. (c) Pour le destruire, on cherche spacieux en pleine lumiere; pour le construire, on se muse dans un creux tenebreux et contraint" (p. 856).

17 "Deviance is the very condition for life to be narratable: the state of normality is devoid of interest, energy, and the possibility for narration." Peter Brooks, "Repetition, Repression and Return: *Great Expectations* and the Study of Plot," *New Literary History*, 11 (1980), p. 523.

18 See Felman, "Turning the Screw of Interpretation," *Yale French Studies*, 55–6 (1977).

19 Jacques Lacan, in *Ecrits* (Paris: Seuil, 1966), claims that the potential loss of the phallus would eliminate the fantasy-producing process, since the male organ is the object from which desire is constituted.

20 Lacan, p. 630.

21 I borrow this term from Brooks (1977).

9 Maurice Scève: the rhetoric of dream and the language of love

1 Maurice Scève, *Délie*, I. D. McFarlane (ed.), (Cambridge: Cambridge University Press, 1966). All references will be to this edition.

2 "Le thème explicite qui forme *l'obsessio* de Délie c'est celui *d'absence,* de séparation, de non-présence." Pascal Quignard, *La Parole de la Délie* (Paris: Mercure de France, 1974), p. 77. The notion of text as buried self-history has been studied by Gregory de Rocher, "The Curing Text: Maurice Scève's Délie as the *Délie,*" *Romanic Review* 78 (1987), pp. 10–24.

3 See Speron Speroni, *I dialoghi* (Vinegia, 1542) and Terence Cave, "Scève's Délie: Correcting Petrarch's Errors," in Jerry Nash (ed.), *Pre-Pléïade Poetry* (Lexington: French Forum, 1985), pp. 112–24.

4 This phenomenon of linguistic incompetency is a psychological relation to the lover's premonitions of rejections (and to the artist's apprehensions of inferiority). He constantly imagines his own inadequacy, anticipates the failure of his 'juste requeste' and, in that process, effectively obstructs the realization of communication before the fact." Kenneth E. Cool, Scève's Agony of Expression and Petrarchan Discourse," *Stanford French Review* (1979), p. 199.

5 Quignard, p. 55.

6 On the question of silence in Scève's *Délie,* see V. L. Saulnier, "Aspects de Maurice Scève: la voix et le silence dans Délie," in *L'Humanisme lyonnais au XVIe siècle* (Grenoble: Presses Universitaires de Grenoble, 1974).

7 Angus Fletcher, *Allegory. The Theory of a Symbolic Mode* (Ithaca: Cornell University Press, 1964), p. 37.

8 "L. Hebreu, in *Philosophie d'Amour traduicte d'Italien en Françoys, par le Seigneur du Parc Champenois* (Lyon, 1551) has at the end of the work an Appendix in the form of a *Dictionaire pour exposition des plus difficiles mots.* This interesting commentary on the word *delicat* is to be found there: 'Délicatesses: douilletteries et accoquineries à quelques voluptés superflues, et non dignes d'un homme robuste et ferme.'" Dorothy Coleman, *Maurice Scève, Poet of Love. Tradition and Originality* (Cambridge: Cambridge University Press, 1975), p. 169, n. 1.

9 "The *royal maintien,* the distance and coldness of the goddess-Délie as she appears in normal everyday life, gives way to a *doux & privé entretien* (Cotgrave gives "familiar" among other words for *privé* and this is precisely what is needed in the context) in the dream world of night. The poet has the illusion of possessing Délie but the encounter is condemned to remain an imaginary one." Coleman, p. 126.

10 *Ibid.*

11 Robert E. Bell, *Dictionary of Classical Mythology* (Santa Barbara: ABC Clio, 1982), pp. 23, 133, 225.

12 "Elle [memory] menace cependant de manquer à ce rôle lorsque le fantôme du passé se présente comme une réalité actuelle sous l'influence trompeuse de l'imagination. Le désir se réveille, grandit, l'image s'impose, cherchant à emporter tout l'être dans un élan qui risque de s'achever comme le mouvement présenté au dizain CXXIII, dans l'abîme des 'oblieuses rives'." Hans Staub, *Le curieux Désir. Scève et Peletier du Mans, poètes de la connaissance* (Geneva: Droz, 1957), pp. 57–8.

13 I. D. McFarlane (ed.), *Délie,* p. 413.

14 *Ibid.*

15 Françoise Charpentier refers to Délie as "cette figure féminine archaïque, mère phallique, signe de perte et de la mort," in "En moi tu luis la nuit obscure," *Europe,* 691–2 (1986), p. 91.

16 On emblems and the relationship between text and image, see Coleman, *An Illustrated Love Canzoniere: The Délie of Maurice Scève* (Geneva and Paris: Editions Slatkine, 1981); Paul Ardouin, *La Délie de Maurice Scève et ses cinquante emblèmes ou les noces secrètes de la poésie et du signe* (Paris: Nizet, 1982); Marcel Tetel, *Lectures Scèviennes* (Paris: Slatkine, 1983).

17 In D.1, Scève's text refers to Délie as the "Constituée Idole de ma vie." "*Constitio,* an order, institution, decree, sentence, constitution, ordinance, act, statute." Randle Cotgrave, *A Dictionarie of the French and English Tongues* (London, 1611).

18 See Deborah Lesko Baker, *Narcissus and the Lover. Mythic Recovery and Reinvention in Scève's Délie* (Saratoga, Calif.: Stanford French and Italian Studies, 1986).

19 "Opem sine corpore amat, corpus putat esse, quod umbra est." Ovid, *Metamorphoses,* trans. and ed. Frank Justin Miller (Cambridge: Harvard University Press [Loeb Classical Library], 1951), vol. I, p. 417.

20 Julia Kristeva, *Polylogues* (Paris: Seuil, 1977), p. 204. On the question of the phallic woman, see Jane Gallop, *The Daughter's Seduction. Feminism and Psychoanalysis* (Ithaca: Cornell University Press, 1982); Mary Jacobus, "Judith, Holofernes, and the Phallic

Woman," in *Reading Woman* (New York: Columbia University Press, 1986), pp. 110–36.

10 Sexuality and the political unconscious in Rabelais' *Quart Livre*: three case studies

1 The prologue to the incomplete *Quart Livre* (1548) and the letter dedicating the complete book to Chastillon tells of the precariousness of Rabelais' position and the heartsickness that his detractors motivated in him. "Mais la calumnie de certains Canibales, misantropes, agelastes, avoit tant contre moy esté atroce et desrasionnée qu'elle avoit vaincu ma patience, et plus n'estois deliberé en escrire un iota" (Odet, p. 6). Rabelais also evokes the possibility of his own execution in this letter. Jean Plattard in *François Rabelais* (Paris: Boivin, 1932), pp. 277–9, 285–7, 301, convincingly demonstrates that Rabelais was attacked by Gabriel de Puy-Herbault, Charles de Sainte-Marthe, Pierre Galland as well as by his supporters Jean Calvin and André Tiraqueau.
2 For a discussion of the therapeutic function of laughter in the context of the Hippocratic novel, see Mikhail Bakhtin, *Rabelais and his World,* trans. Hélène Iswolsky (Cambridge, Mass.: MIT Press, 1968), pp. 360–1.
3 François Rabelais, *Œuvres complètes* (Paris: Garnier, 1962), vol. II, ed. Pierre Jourda, p. 12. All subsequent references will be from this edition and shall be indicated in the body of the text.
4 "The speaker's attitude towards himself is more open and vulnerable . . . the rhetoric of the *Quart Livre* aims less at didactic edification . . . and more at justifying the author's role as artist and privileged manipulator of the audience's sensibilities." William J. Kennedy, *Rhetorical Norms in Renaissance Literature* (New Haven: Yale University Press, 1978), pp. 121–2.
5 Jacques Lacan, *Ecrits* (Paris: Seuil, 1966), p. 111.
6 Rabelais adopts this expression from André Tiraqueau's treatise commenting on an axiom of customary law: *Le Mort saisist le vif.*
7 Michael Screech in *Rabelais* (Ithaca: Cornell University Press, 1979) views this notion as an extension of the syncretism of Greek (the golden mean of Aristotle's *Nicomachean Ethics*) and Christian ethics. "*Mediocritas* for Rabelais was but another form of the Christian virtue of humility," p. 329.
8 Terence Cave in *The Cornucopian Text. Problems of Writing in the*

French Renaissance (Oxford: Oxford University Press, 1979), pp. 194–205, touches upon certain aspects of the sexual metaphor in the prologue to the *Quart Livre*.

9 For a discussion of the Androgyna myth, see G. Mallary Masters, *Rabelaisian Dialectic and the Platonic–Hermetic Tradition* (Albany: State University of New York Press, 1969), pp. 19–22.

10 The role and function of memory and invention in Renaissance writing have been studied by Michel Beaujour in "*Les Essais*: une mémoire intratextuelle," in Floyd Gray and Marcel Tetel (eds.), *Textes et Intertextes. Etudes sur le* xvie *siècle pour Alfred Glauser* (Paris: Nizet, 1979), pp. 29–46, and myself in "La Mémoire en papier," in *Destruction/Découverte: le fonctionnement de la rhétorique dans les 'Essais' de Montagne* (Lexington: French Forum Monographs, 1980).

11 "Writing always includes the moment of dispossession in favor of the arbitrary power play of the signifier and from the point of view of the subject, this can only be experienced as a dismemberment, a beheading or a castration." Paul de Man, "The Purloined Ribbon," in *Glyph* i, ed. Weber and Sussman (Baltimore: Johns Hopkins University Press, 1977), p. 43.

12 See Sigmund Freud, "Analysis of Phobia in a Five-Year Old Boy" (1909) and *Inhibitions, Symptoms, and Anxiety* in J. Strachey (ed.), *Standard Edition of the Complete Psychological Works of Sigmund Freud,* vol. xx (London: Hogarth, 1959), p. 126.

13 Since the time of Catullus (Poem lxiii) castration has provided a major thematic axis on which to hinge reflections on creativity and desire. The most striking example of the castration *topos* in Renaissance French literature is Bonaventure des Periers' *Cymbalum mundi* (1537) where a priest permits himself to be castrated at the request of his housekeeper.

14 The second song that Rabelais inscribes in the prologue invokes the centrifugal movement of desire, the imperative to replace emptiness by the plenitude of satisfaction:

> S'il est ainsi que coingnée sans manche
> Ne sert de rien, ne houstil sans poingnée,
> Affin que l'un dedans l'autre s'emmanche,
> Prens que soys manche, et tu seras coingnée.   (p. 23)

Rabelais' principal strategy – the telos of his libidinal energy – as it appears in this melody, is to plot the immobilization of desire, a displacement in search of cathexis, and ultimately inertia.

15 Several chapters in the *Quart Livre* are devoted to Rabelais' critique of the exorbitant powers of the Decretals. (xlviii–liv).

16 *L'année des couilles molles* signifies *sans virilité.* L. Sainéan, *La*

Langue de Rabelais (Paris: Boccard, 1922). See also *Gargantua,* XXXII. Jupiter, himself a figure of castration, is also limited by the constraints of authority and "fate." We are in fact told that the reason he is obliged to return the hatchet to Couillatris is because "cela est escript es destins."

17 Il [Rabelis] joue le jeu de la médiocrité. Il la parce qu'il ne la vit pas ... La médiocrité est animée au point de devenir son contraire." Alfred Glauser, *Rabelais créateur* (Paris: Nizet, 1966), p. 39.

18 "Rabelais feared that their fate [Clément Marot and Etienne Dolet] would be his own, and his anxiety and despair surge close to the surface of the *Quart Livre*." Alice Fiola Berry, " 'Les Mithologies Pantagruelicques': Introduction to a study of Rabelais's *Quart Livre*," *PMLA,* 92 (1977), p. 471.

19 The most complete literary history on the subject is Michael Screech, *Rabelais* (Ithaca: Cornell University Press, 1979). I borrow the term "comedy of cruelty" from Screech (p. 335).

20 Joel Fineman, "The Structure of Allegorical Desire," in Stephen J. Greenblatt (ed.), *Allegory and Representation* (Baltimore: Johns Hopkins University Press, 1981), p. 26. Some of the more modern notions of allegory have been theorized in Paul de Man, *Allegories of Reading* (New Haven: Yale University Press, 1979); Maureen Quilligan, *The Language of Allegory: Defining the Genre* (Ithaca: Cornell University Press, 1981); Stephen Melville, "Notes on the Re-emergence of Allegory," *October,* 19 (1981), pp. 55–92.

21 The term "symbolic unconscious" comes from Fredric Jameson, *The Political Unconscious* (Ithaca: Cornell University Press, 1981). See also Jean Bellemin-Noël, *Vers l'inconscient du texte* (Paris: Presses Universitaires de France, 1979) and *Essias de Textanalyse* (Lille: Presses Universitaries de Lille, 1988).

22 On the notion of logotherapy, see Alice Fiola Berry, "The Mix, the Mask and Medical Farce: A Study of the Prologues to Rabelais's *Quart Livre*," *Romanic Review,* 71 (1981), pp. 10–27.

23 "L'ordre philosophique et épistémologique du *logos* comme anti-dote, comme force *inscrite dans l'économie générale et a-logique du pharmakon* ... est présentée à Socrate comme un poison mais elle se transforme, par l'effet du *logos* socratique et la démonstration philo-sophique du *Phédon,* en moyen de délivrance, possibilité du salut et vertu cathartique." Jacques Derrida, *La Dissémination* (Paris: Seuil, 1972), pp. 142, 145.

24 See Sigmund Freud, *Jokes and Their Relationship to the Unconscious,* trans. and ed. James Stracey (New York: Norton, 1963).

25 Gilles Deleuze, *Différence et répétition* (Paris: Presses Universitaries de France, 1972), pp. 54–5.

26 "In the real world, it was not the wretched Chicanous who deserved the bashings and the beatings; it was the prior who sent them off with their provocative summonses against the Seigneur de Basché ... This 'fat prior,' Jacques Le Roy, was plaguing with summonses the real Seigneur de Basché, a loyal servant of the crown who fought against Pope Julius II in Italy." Screech, p. 340. "Cette racaille est particulièrement esclave du clergé. Chiquanous est volontiers 'serviteur de moinerie, appariteur de la mitre abbatiale.' On nous présente en ces termes le débat typique où il trouve son emploi: 'quand un moine, prestre, usurieur ou advocat' veut du mal à un gentilhomme. D'où un aspect particulier de satire anticléricale." V.-L. Saulnier, *Rabelais dans son enquête* (Paris: Société d'Editions d'enseignement supérieur, 1982), p. 66.

27 Mikhail Bakhtin has studied the notion of carnival in the rabelaisian world as an attempt to challenge the hierarchy of the existing social order in *Rabelais and His World,* trans. Hélène Iswolsky (Cambridge, Mass.: MIT Press, 1968). "The carnival form can evolve so that it can act both to reinforce order and to suggest alternatives to the existing order," Natalie Zemon Davis, "The Reasons of Misrule," in *Society and Culture in Early Modern France* (Stanford: Stanford University Press, 1975), p. 123. For a more complete analysis of carnival within the context of the *Quart Livre,* see Marcel Tetel, "Carnival and Beyond," *L'Esprit créateur,* 21 (1981), pp. 88–104.

28 René Girard has discussed the concept of agonistic encounters and scapegoating in the origins of culture in *La Violence et le sacré* (Paris: Grasset, 1972).

29 Jacques Lacan, "L'Instance de la lettre dans l'inconscient ou la raison depuis Freud," in *Ecrits* (Paris: Seuil, 1966), p. 518.

30 Terence Cave, *The Cornucopian Text: Problems of Writing in the French Renaissance* (Oxford: Oxford University Press, 1979), pp. 198–9.

31 "*L'or de Tholose,* duquel parle Cic., *lib.* 3, *de Nat. deorum*; A. Gellius, *lib.* 3; Justi; *lib.* 22: Strabo, *lib.* 4, porta malheur à ceulx qui l'emporterent, sçavoir est Q. Cepio, consu, Romain, et toute son armée, qui tous, comme sacrileges, perirent malheureusement ... *Le cheval Sejan,* de Cn. Seius, lequel porta malheur à tous ceulx qui le possederent. Lisez A. Gellius, *lib., cap.* 9" (p. 253).

32 The psychoanalytical dimensions of the inner dynamics of narrative texts have been studied by Peter Brooks, *Reading for the Plot: Design and Intention in Narrative* (New York: Knopf, 1984), p. 104.

33 "A sadist is always at the same time a masochist, although the active or the passive aspect of the perversion may be the more strongly

developed in him and may represent his predominant sexual anxiety." Freud, *The Standard Edition of the Complete Psychological Works of Sigmund Freud,* ed. James Strachey (London: Hogarth Press, 1966), VII, p. 159. The "pleasurable unpleasurable" tension of sexual excitement is discussed by Leo Bersani, "Sexuality and Aesthetics," *October,* 28 (1984), pp. 27–42. "Not only is sexuality characterized by the simultaneous production of pleasurable and unpleasurable tension; perhaps even more bizarre is the fact that the pleasurable unpleasurable tension of sexual stimulation seeks not to be released, but to be increased" (p. 30).

34 On the use of the metaphor "to beat the drum," see Raymond C. La Charité, "The Drum and the Owl: Functional Symbolism in Panurge's Quest," *Symposium,* 28 (1974), pp. 154–65.

35 On sublimation, see Jean Laplanche, *Problématiques* III: *la sublimation* (Paris: Presses Universitaires de France, 1980).

36 "The absence of clearly established footlights is characteristic of all popular festive forms . . . It was customary to permit the devils [in the *diableries*] to run loose around the streets wearing their costumes; sometimes they were free to do so for several days before the performance . . . The actors, disguised as devils, felt that they were somehow out of bondage." Bakhtin, pp. 265–6.

37 See Lacan, "Fonction et champ de la parole et du langage en psychanalyse," in *Ecrits* (Paris: Seuil, 1966), pp. 111–208.

38 On the notion of the "ex-cathedra infallibility" of the Vatican, see Michael Screech, *Rabelais* (Ithaca: Cornell University Press, 1979), pp. 404–5.

39 On the relation of this episode to the Gallican crisis, see Lucien Febvre, *Le Problème de l'Incroyance au* XVIe *siècle; La Religion de Rabelais* (Paris: Albin Michel, 1942); Screech, *L'Evangélisme de Rabelais* (Geneva: Droz, 1959); Robert Marichal, "*Quart Livre*: Commentaires," *Etudes Rabelaisiennes,* 55 (1964), pp. 100–146.

40 "Decretals are sharply distinguished from *decrees* (papal ordinances enacted with the advice of the cardinalate) and *canons* (ecclesiastical laws enacted by ecumenical councils or synods)," Screech (1979), p. 405.

41 The concept of "optomanie" has been coined by François Rigolot, *Les Langages de Rabelais* (Geneva: Droz, 1972), p. 110.

42 Screech (1979), p. 409.

43 Michel Jeanneret discusses the notion of nominalism and its Cratylic implications in "Les Paroles Dégelées," *Littérature* (1975), p. 16.

44 "L'organisation du langage demeure isomorphe à celle de la société . . . l'identification du signifiant et du signifié entretient l'illusion d'une parole sacrale qui ne saurait, bien entendu, mentir – et cette

parole, c'est celle même dont use le régime pour assurer sa propre fondation. La nature sert ici et là à farder en nécessaire un arbitraire qui se dérobe à la conscience et que la coutume représente comme 'allant de soi'," Jean Paris, *Rabelais au futur* (Paris: Seuil, 1970), pp. 172–3.

45 See Terence Cave, *The Cornucopian Text: Problems of Writing in the French Renaissance* (Oxford: Oxford University Press, 1979).

46 "The devotees of fetishes ... extol the advantages they offer for erotic gratification," "Fetishism," in James Strachey (ed.), *The Collected Papers of Sigmund Freud* (London: Hogarth Press, 1950), p. 198.

47 "Tous les textes de loi ou de règlement n'ont pas droit à notre révérence. En matìre religieuse, la seule vérité est dans les 'saincts bibles' ... or les fameuses Décrétales en sont tout le contraire: decisions d'hommes, et non parole révélée," V. L. Saulnier, *Rabelais dans son enquête* (Paris: Société d'Editions d'enseignement supérieur, 1982), vol. II, p. 106.

48 In the Renaissance, the saffron-yellow color was displayed by those associated with fraudulent bankruptcy. It is interesting to note that at the end of the *Quart Livre,* Panurge's fear forces him to excrete waste in the color of "sapphran d'Hibernie" (p. 248).

49 "In its implications the distortion of a text resembles a murder: the difficulty is not in perpetrating the deed, but in getting rid of its traces ... In many instances of textual distortion, we may nevertheless count upon finding what has been suppressed and disavowed, hidden away somewhere else, though changed and torn from its context," Freud, Strachey (ed.), *Standard Edition* (London: Hogarth Press, 1966), vol. XXIII, p. 43.

50 On the "generation of meaning through resonance," see J. Hillis Miller, "Williams' *Spring and All* and the Progress of Poetry," *Daedalus* 99 (1970), and Joel Fineman who suggests that "the movement of allegory, like the dreamwork, enacts a wish that determines its progress – and, of course, the dream-vision is a characteristic framing and opening device of allegory," "The Structure of Allegorical Desire," in Stephen J. Greeblatt (ed.), *Allegory and Representation*, p. 26.

BIBLIOGRAPHY OF WORKS CITED

Abraham, Karl, "A Short Study of the Development of the Libido, Viewed in Light of Mental Disorders" (1924), in *The Selected Papers of Karl Abraham* (London: Hogarth Press, 1927).

Agrippa, Henri Corneille, *Declaration de la Noblesse et Preexcelence du sexe feminin,* trans. Martin Le Pin (Lyon: François Juste, 1537).

Almeida, Ivàn, "Un Corps devenu récit," in Claude Reichler (ed.) *Le corps et ses fictions* (Paris: Minuit, 1983), pp. 7–18.

Antonioli, Roland, *Rabelais et la Médecine,* [*Etudes Rabelaisiennes,* vol. XII] (Geneva: Droz, 1976).

Ardouin, Paul, *Maurice Scève, Pernette du Guillet, Louise Labé. L'Amour à Lyon au temps de la Renaissance* (Paris: Nizet, 1981).

La Délie de Maurice Scève et ses cinquante emblèmes ou les noces secrètes (Paris: Nizet, 1982).

Ariosto, Ludovico, *Lirica* (Bari: Laterza, 1924).

Orlando Furioso (Bari: Laterza, 1928).

Baker, Deborah Lesko, *Narcissus and the Lover. Mythic Recovery and Reinvention in Scève's "Délie"* (Saratoga, Calif.: Stanford French and Italian Studies, 1986).

Bakhtin, Mikhail, *Rabelais and His World,* trans. Hélène Iswolsky (Cambridge, Mass.: MIT Press, 1968).

Barthes, Roland, *S/Z* (Paris: Seuil, 1970).

Le Plaisir du Texte (Paris: Seuil, 1973).

Fragments d'un discours amoureux (Paris: Seuil, 1977).

Bauer, Douglas F., "The Function of Pygmalion in the *Metamorphoses* of Ovid," *Transactions and Proceedings of the American Philological Association* 93 (1962).

Beaujour, Michel, "Les *Essais*: une mémoire intratextuelle," in Floyd Gray and Marcel Tetel (eds.), *Textes et Intertextes. Etudes sur le* XVIe *siècle pour Alfred Glauser* (Paris: Nizet, 1979), pp. 29–46.

Bell, Robert D., *Dictionary of Classical Mythology* (Santa Barbara: ABC Clio, 1982).

Belleau, Rémy, *Œuvres complètes,* ed. Charles Marty-Laveaux (Paris: Lemerre, 1878).

Bibliography of works cited

Bellemin-Noël, Jean, *Vers l'inconscient du texte* (Paris: Presses Universitaires de France, 1979).

Essais de Textanalyse (Lille: Presses Universitaires de Lille, 1988).

Benjamin, Jessica, *The Bonds of Love: Psychoanalysis, Feminism, and the Problem of Domination* (New York: Pantheon, 1988).

Benson, Edward, "Marriage Ancestral and Conjugal in the *Heptaméron*," *Journal of Medieval and Renaissance Studies*, 9 (1979), pp. 261–75.

"'Jamais vostre femme ne sera ribaulde, si la prenez issue de gens de bien': Love and War in the *Tiers Livre*," *Etudes Rabelaisiennes* 15 (1980), pp. 55–76.

Berger, John, *Ways of Seeing* (London and New York: Penguin, 1973).

Bernard, John D., "Sexual Oppression and Social Justice in Marguerite de Navarre's *Heptaméron*," *Journal of Medieval and Renaissance Studies*, 19 (1989), pp. 251–81.

Berry, Alice Fiola, "Les Mithologies Pantagruelicques: Introduction to a study of Rabelais's *Quart Livre*," *PMLA*, 92 (1977), pp. 471–80.

"The Mix, the Mask and Medical Farce: A Study of the Prologues to Rabelais's *Quart Livre*," *Romanic Review*, 71 (1980), pp. 10–27.

Bersani, Leo, "Sexuality and Aesthetics," *October*, 28 (1984), pp. 27–42.

Billon, François de, *Le Fort inexpugnable de l'honneur du sexe feminin* (Paris: 1555).

Bowen, Barbara, "Montaigne's Anti-Phaedrus: 'Sur des vers de Virgile'," *Journal of Medieval and Renaissance Studies*, 5 (1975), pp. 107–21.

Brooks, Peter, "Freud's Masterplot: Questions of Narrative," *Yale French Studies*, 55–6 (1977), pp. 280–300.

"Repetition, Repression and Return: *Great Expectations* and the Study of Plot," *New Literary History*, 11 (1980), pp. 503–26.

Reading for Plot: Design and Invention in Narrative (New York: Knopf, 1984).

Butor, Michel, *Essais sur les essais* (Paris: Gallimard, 1968).

Cave, Terence, *The Cornucopian Text: Problems of Writing in the French Renaissance* (Oxford: Oxford University Press, 1979).

"Problems of Reading in the *Essais*," in I. D. McFarlane and Ian Maclean (eds.), *Montaigne. Essays in Memory of Richard Sayce* (Oxford: Oxford University Press, 1982), pp. 133–66.

Scève's *Délie*: Correcting Petrarch's Errors," in Jerry Nash (ed.), *Pre-Pléïade Poetry* (Lexington: French Forum, 1985), pp. 112–24.

Cazauran, Nicole, *L'Heptaméron de Marguerite de Navarre* (Paris: Société d'Editions d'Enseignement Supérieur, 1976).

Bibliography of works cited

Céard, Jean, with Naudin, Pierre, and de Simonin, Michel, *La Folie et le Corps* (Paris: Presses de l'Ecole Normale Supérieure, 1985).

Certeau, Michel de, "Des outils pour écrire le corps," *Traverses*, 14–15 (1979).

Charpentier, Françoise, "Notes pour le *Tiers Livre* de Rabelais," *Revue belge de philologie et d'histoire,* 54 (1976), pp. 780–96.

"L'ordre du corps," in Labé, Louise, *Œuvres complètes* (Paris: Gallimard-Poésie, 1982), pp. 12–16.

"L'Absente des *Essais*: quelques questions autour de l'Essai II–8, 'de l'Affection des peres aux enfans'," *Bulletin de la société des amis de Montaigne,* 17–18 (1984).

"En moi tu luis la nuit obscure," *Europe,* 691–2 (1986), pp. 83–94.

Chastel, André, "L'œuf de Ronsard," in *Mélanges Henri Chamard* (Paris: Nizet, 1951)

Cixous, Hélène, *La Jeune née* (in collaboration with Catherine Clément) (Paris: Union Générale d'Editions, 10/18, 1975).

La Venue à l'écriture (in collaboration with Annie Leclerc and Madeleine Gagnon) (Paris: Union Générale d'Editions, 10/18, 1977).

"The Laugh of the Medusa," trans. Keith Cohen and Paula Cohen in Elaine Marks and Isabelle de Courtivron (eds.), *New French Feminisms* (Amherst: University of Massachussetts Press, 1980), pp. 245–64.

Clark, Carol, *The Web of Metaphor: Studies in the Imagery of Montaigne's Essais* (Lexington: French Forum, 1978).

Coleman, Dorothy, *Maurice Scève Poet of Love Tradition and Originality* (Cambridge: Cambridge University Press, 1975).

An Illustrated Love Canzoniere: The Délie of Maurice Scève (Geneva–Paris: Editions Slatkine, 1981).

Colie, Rosalie L., *Paradoxica Epidemica* (Princeton: Princeton University Press, 1966).

Compagnon, Antoine, *Nous Michel de Montaigne* (Paris: Seuil, 1980).

Cool, Kenneth E., "Scève's Agony of Expression and Petrarchan Discourse," *Stanford French Review* (1979), pp. 193–210.

Coquillart, Guillaume, *Sensuyvent les droitz nouveaulx: avec le débat des dames et des armes* (Paris: J. Trepperel, 1532).

Cotgrave, Randle, *A Dictionarie of the French and English Tongues* [London, 1611] (Columbia, S. C.: University of South Carolina Press, 1950).

Cottrell, Robert D., "Pernette du Guillet's *Rymes*: An Adventure in Ideal Love," *Bibliothèque d'Humanisme et Renaissance,* 31 (1969), pp. 553–71.

Sexuality/Textuality: A Study of the Fabric of Montaigne's "Essais" (Columbus: Ohio State University Press, 1981).

Bibliography of works cited

Cropper, Elizabeth, "On Beautiful Women, Parmigianino, Petrarchismo and the Vernacular Style," *Art Bulletin,* 58 (1976), pp. 374–94.

Curtius, Ernst Robert, *European Literature and the Latin Middle Ages,* trans. Willard Trask (Princeton: Princeton University Press, 1953).

Damiens, Suzanne, *Amour et intellect chez Léon l'Hebreu* (Toulouse: Privat, 1971).

Davis, Natalie Zemon, "The Reasons of Misrule," in *Society and Culture in Early Modern France* (Stanford: Stanford University Press, 1975).

"Women on Top," in *Society and Culture in Early Modern France* (Stanford: Stanford University Press, 1975), pp. 124–51.

"A Renaissance text to the historian's eye: the gifts of Montaigne," *Journal of Medieval and Renaissance Studies,* 15 (1985), pp. 47–56.

Defaux, Gérard, "Rhétorique et représentation dans les *Essais:* de la peinture de l'autre à la peinture du moi," *Bulletin de la société des amis de Montaigne,* 7 (1985), pp. 21–48.

Deleuze, Gilles, *Différence et répétition* (Paris: Presses Universitaires de France, 1972).

de Man, Paul, "The Purloined Ribbon," Weber and Sussman (eds.), *Glyph* I (Baltimore: Johns Hopkins University Press, 1977).

Allegories of Reading (New Haven: Yale University Press, 1979).

Demerson, Guy, *La mythologie classique dans l'œuvre lyrique de la Pléïade* (Geneva: Droz, 1972).

de Rocher, Gregory, "The Curing Text: Maurice Scève's *Délie* as the *Délie,*" *Romanic Review,* 78 (1987), pp. 10–24.

Derrida, Jacques, *La Dissémination* (Paris: Seuil, 1972).

"Signature Événement Contexte," in *Marges de la philosophie* (Paris: Minuit, 1972), pp. 367–93.

Eperons: les styles de Nietzsche (Chicago: University of Chicago Press, 1979).

Dictionnaire des mythologies et des religions des sociétés traditionnelles et du monde antique, ed. Yves Bonnefoy (Paris: Flammarion, 1981).

Donaldson-Evans, Lance K., "The Taming of the Muse: The Female Poetic Voice in Pernette du Guillet's *Rymes,*" in Jerry Nash (ed.), *Pre-Pléïade Poetry* (Lexington: French Forum, 1985), pp. 84–96.

Dubois, Claude-Gilbert, *Le Maniérisme* (Paris: Presses Universitaires de France, 1979).

L'Imaginaire de la Renaissance (Paris: Presses Universitaires de France, 1985).

Febvre, Lucien, *Le Problème de l'incroyance au* XVIe *siècle: La Religion de Rabelais* (Paris: Albin Michel, 1942).

Autour de l'Heptaméron (Paris: Gallimard, 1944).

248

Bibliography of works cited

Felman, Shoshana, "Psychoanalysis and Education: Teaching Terminable and Interminable," *Yale French Studies,* 63 (1982), pp. 21–44.

Ferguson, Margaret W., Quilligan, Maureen, and Vickers, Nancy J., *The Discourse of Sexual Difference in Early Modern Europe* (Chicago: University of Chicago Press, 1986).

Fineman, Joel, "The Structure of Allegorical Desire," in Stephen J. Greenblatt (ed.), *Allegory and Representation* (Baltimore: The Johns Hopkins University Press, 1981), pp. 26–60.

Fletcher, Angus, *Allegory: The Theory of A Symbolic Mode* (Ithaca: Cornell University Press, 1964).

Frame, Donald M., *Montaigne: A Biography* (New York: Harcourt, Brace and World, 1965).

Freccero, John, "Medusa: the Letter and the Spirit," *Yearbook of Italian Studies* (1972), pp. 1–18.

"The Fig Tree and the Laurel: Petrarch's Poetics," *Diacritics,* 5 (1975), pp. 34–40.

Freud, Sigmund, *General Psychological Theory,* trans. Cecil Baines (New York: Collier, 1963).

Jokes and Their Relationship to the Unconscious, trans. and ed. James Strachey (New York: Norton, 1963).

James Strachey (ed.), *Standard Edition of the Complete Psychological Works of Sigmund Freud* (London: Hogarth Press and the Institute of Psychoanalysis, 1966), 24 vols.

Friedrich, Hugo, *Montaigne,* trans. Robert Rovini (Paris: Gallimard, 1968).

Gallop, Jane, *The Daughter's Seduction. Feminism and Psychoanalysis* (Ithaca: Cornell University Press, 1982).

Garner, Shirley Nelson, Kahane, Claire, and Sprengnether, Madelon (eds.), *The Mother Tongue* (Ithaca: Cornell University Press, 1985).

Gelernt, Jules, *World of Many Loves: l'Heptaméron of Marguerite de Navarre* (Chapel Hill: University of North Carolina Press, 1966).

Gendre, André, *Ronsard: Poète de la Conquête Amoureuse* (Neuchâtel: Editions de la Baconnière, 1970).

Giamatti, A. Bartlett, "Proteus Unbound: Some Version of the Sea God in the Renaissance," in Peter Demetz, Thomas Greene, and Lowry Nelson, Jr. (eds.), *The Disciplines of Criticism* (New Haven: Yale University Press, 1968), pp. 437–75.

Girard, René, *La Violence et le sacré* (Paris: Grasset, 1972).

Glauser, Alfred, *Rabelais créateur* (Paris: Nizet, 1966).

Le Poème–Symbole (Paris: Nizet, 1967).

Grandeur et suprematie des femmes, feminist manifesto, trans. Alexis Bertrand, *Archives de l'anthropologie criminelle, de médecine*

Bibliography of works cited

légale et de psychologie normale et pathologique, vol. xxv (Paris: 1910).

Gray, Floyd F., *Le Style de Montaigne* (Paris: Nizet, 1958).

"Montaigne and the Memorabilia," *Studies in Philology*, 59 (1961), pp. 130–9.

La Balance de Montaigne (Paris: Nizet, 1982).

Green, André, "The Unbinding Process," trans. Lionel Duisit, *New Literary History*, 12 (1980), pp. 11–39.

Narcissisme de vie, narcissisme de mort (Paris: Minuit, 1983).

Greenberg, Mitchell, "Montaigne at the Crossroads: Textual Conundrums in the 'Essais'," *Stanford French Review* (1982), pp. 21–34.

Greene, Thomas, *The Light in Troy. Imitation and Discovery in Renaissance Poetry* (New Haven: Yale University Press, 1982).

Grimal, Pierre, *Dictionnaire de la mythologie grecque et romaine* (Paris: Presses Universitaires de France, 1963).

Guillet, Pernette du, *Rymes*, annotated ed. Victor E. Graham (Geneva: Droz, 1968).

Harth, Erica, "Sur des vers de Virgile: Antinomy and Totality in Montaigne," *French Forum*, 2 (1977), pp. 3–21.

Hebreu, Léon, *Dialogues d'Amour*, trans. Pontus de Tyard and ed. T. Anthony Perry (Chapel Hill: University of North Carolina Press, 1974).

Horace, *Odes et Epodes*, trans. and ed. F. Villeneuve (Paris: Belles Lettres, 1927).

Huguet, Edmond, *Dictionnaire de la langue française du seizième siècle* (Paris: Librairie Arienne Edouard Champion, 1925–67), 7 vols.

Irigaray, Luce, *Ce sexe qui n'en est pas un* (Paris: Minuit, 1977).

Jacobus, Mary, "Judith, Holofernes, and the Phallic Woman," in *Reading Woman* (New York: Columbia University Press, 1986), pp. 110–36.

Jameson, Fredric, *The Political Unconscious* (Ithaca: Cornell University Press, 1981).

Jeanneret, Michel, "Les Paroles dégélées," *Littérature* (1975), pp. 14–30.

"Rabelais et Montaigne: l'écriture comme parole," *L'Esprit créateur*, 16 (1976), pp. 78–94.

Johnson, Barbara, ed., "The Pedagogical Imperative," *Yale French Studies*, 63 (1982).

Jondorf, Gillian, "Petrarchan Variations in Pernette du Guillet and Louise Labé," *Modern Language Notes*, 71 (1976), pp. 766–78.

Jones, Ann Rosalind, "Assimilation with a Difference: Renaissance Women Poets and Litarary Influence," *Yale French Studies*, 62 (1981), pp. 135–53.

Bibliography of works cited

Jourda, Pierre, "*L'Heptaméron* et la société du XVIe siècle," *La vie intellectuelle,* 14 (1932), pp. 478–97.

Kelly, Joan, "Did Women Have a Renaissance?" in *Women, History and Theory* (Chicago: University of Chicago Press, 1984).

Kennedy, William J., *Rhetorical Norms in Renaissance Literature* (New Haven: Yale University Press, 1978).

Kerrigan, William, "The Articulation of the Ego in the English Renaissance," in *Psychiatry and the Humanities:* IV (New Haven: Yale University Press, 1980), pp. 261–308.

Klein, Melanie, *Love, Guilt, and Reparation and Other Works 1921–1945* (New York: Dell Publishing, 1977).

The Writings of Melanie Klein, ed. R. E. Money-Kryle (London: Hogarth Press and Institute of Psychoanalysis, 1975).

Klibansky, Raymond, Panofsky, Erwin, and Saxl, Fritz, *Saturn and Melancholy: Studies in the History of Natural Philosophy, Religion, and Art* (New York: Basic Books, 1964).

Kofman, Sarah, *L'Enfance de l'art* (Paris: Payot, 1970).

L'Enigme de la femme (Paris: Galilée, 1981).

Kohl, Benjamin, ed., *The Early Republic: Italian Humanists on Government and Society* (Philadelphia: University of Pennsylvania Press, 1978).

Kristeva, Julia, *Polylogue* (Paris: Seuil, 1977).

Pouvoirs de l'horreur (Paris: Seuil, 1980).

Histoires d'amour (Paris: Denoël, 1983).

Soleil Noir. Dépression et Mélancolie (Paris: Gallimard, 1987).

Kritzman, Lawrence D., *Destruction/Découverte: le fonctionnement de la rhétorique dans les 'Essais' de Montaigne* (Lexington: French Forum, 1980).

Fragments: Incompletion and Discontinuity (New York: New York Literary Forum, 1981).

"Le Roman de la Pierre ou Montaigne et l'archéologie du moi," in Claude Blum (ed.), *Montaigne et l'accomplissement des Essais, Bulletin de la société des amis de Montaigne* (Paris: Aux Amateurs des Livres 1989), pp. 119–128.

Lacan, Jacques, *Ecrits* (Paris: Seuil, 1966).

Le Séminaire, XI: *Les Quatre concepts fondamentaux de la psychanalyse* (Paris: Seuil, 1973).

Le Séminaire, XX: *Encore* (Paris: Seuil, 1975).

"Desire and the Interpretation of Desire in Hamlet," *Yale French Studies,* 55–6 (1977), pp. 11–52.

La Charité, Raymond C., "The Drum and the Owl: Functional Symbolism in Panurge's Quest," *Symposium,* 28 (1974), pp. 154–65.

251

Bibliography of works cited

Laplanche, Jean, *Vie et mort en psychanalyse* (Paris: Flammarion, 1970).

Problématiques II: *Castration–Symbolisations* (Paris: Presses Universitaires de France, 1980).

Problématiques III: *la sublimation* (Paris: Presses Universitaires de France, 1980).

Lapp, John, "Montaigne's 'Negligence' and Some Lines from Virgil," *Romanic Review*, 61 (1970), pp. 167–81.

"A Prose Poem: Montaigne's Mother Virtue," in *O Un Amy! Essays on Montaigne in Honor of Donald M. Frame* (Lexington: French Forum 1977), pp. 172–89.

Lazard, Madeleine, *Images de la femme à la Renaissance* (Paris: Presses Universitaires de France, 1985).

Lebègue, Raymond, "La femme qui mutile son visage," in *Académie des inscriptions et belles lettres. Comptes Rendus des séances* (1959), pp. 176–84.

"La fidélité conjugale dans l'*Heptaméron*," in *La nouvelle française à la renaissance,* ed. Lionello Sozzi and V. L. Saulnier (Geneva–Paris: Editions Slatkine, 1981), pp. 379–95.

Lewis, Charlton T. and Short, Charles, *Andrews' Latin Dictionary* (Oxford: Oxford University Press, 1962 [first edition 1879]).

Lorris, Guillaume de, *Le Roman de la Rose,* ed. F. Lecoy (Paris: Classiques français du moyen âge, 1965).

MacLean, Ian, *The Renaissance Notion of Woman* (Cambridge: Cambridge University Press, 1980).

Marçonville, Jean de, *De l'heur et malheur du mariage* (Paris: 1564).

Marichal, Robert, "Quart Livre: Commentaires," *Etudes Rabelaisiennes,* 5 (1965), pp. 100–46.

Marks, Elaine, ed., *New French Feminisms* (Amherst: University of Massachusetts Press, 1980).

Marot, Clément, *Œuvres,* ed. C. A. Mayer (London, Athlone Press, 1958).

Master, G. Mallary, *Rabelaisian Dialectic and the Platonic–Hermetic Tradition* (Albany: State University Press, 1969).

Mathieu-Castellani, Gisèle, "Narcisse ou la mélancolie: lecture d'un sonnet de Du Perron," *Littérature,* 37 (1980), pp. 25–36.

Mythes de l'éros baroque (Paris: Presses Universitaires de France, 1981).

"La parole chétive: les *Rymes* de Pernette du Guillet," *Littérature,* 73 (1989), pp. 47–60.

Mayer, Gilbert, "Les Images dans Montaigne et d'après le chapitre 'de l'institution des enfans'," in *Mélanges de philologie et d'histoire littéraire offerts à Edmond Huguet* (Paris: Droz, 1940), pp. 110–18.

Bibliography of works cited

McFarlane, I. D., "Aspects of Ronsard's Poetic Vision," in Terence Cave (ed.), *Ronsard the Poet* (London: Methuen, 1973), pp. 13–78.

McKeon, Richard, ed., *Nicomachian Ethics* in *Introduction to Aristotle* (New York: Modern Library, 1947).

McKinley, Mary B., "Horace: A Dialogue about Monsters," in *Words in a Corner* (Lexington: French Forum, 1981), pp. 37–61.

Meisel, Perry, ed., *Freud: Twentieth-Century Views* (Englewood Cliffs, N.J.: Prentice Hall, 1981).

Melville, Stephen, "Notes on the Reemergence of Allegory," *October,* 19 (1981), pp. 55–92.

Ménager, Daniel, *Rabelais* (Paris: Bordas, 1989).

Miller, J. Hillis, "Williams' *Spring and All* and the Progress of Poetry," *Daedalus,* 99 (1970).

"Ariadne's Thread: Repetition and the Narrative Line," *Critical Inquiry,* 3 (1976), pp. 57–78.

Miller, Nancy K., ed., *The Poetics of Gender* (New York: Columbia University Press, 1986).

Subject to Change: Reading Feminist Writing (New York: Columbia University Press, 1988).

Montaigne, Michel de, *Œuvres complètes,* ed. Maurice Rat (Paris: Bibliothèque de la Pléiade, 1962).

Nakam, Géralde, "Eros et les Muses dans 'Sur des vers de Virgile'," in *Etudes seiziémistes offertes à M. le Professeur V. L. Saulnier par plusieurs de ses anciens doctorants,* Travaux d'Humanisme et Renaissance, 177 (Geneva: Droz, 1980), pp. 395–403.

Navarre, Marguerite de, *L'Heptaméron,* ed. M. François (Paris: Garnier, 1964).

Nouveau recueil de contes, dits fabliaux et autres pièces inédites des xiiième, xivème, et xvème siècles, ed. A. Jubinal (Paris: 1839–42).

Odes d'Anacréon avec liv *Compositions par Girodet,* trans. Amb. Firmin Didot (Paris: Didot Frères, 1864).

Ovid, *Metamorphoses,* ed. and trans. Frank Justin Miller (Cambridge, Mass.: Harvard University Press [Loeb Classical Library], 1951).

Tristia, trans. A. L. Wheeler (Cambridge, Mass.: Harvard University Press [Loeb Classical Library], 1965).

Paré, Ambrose, *Opera Omnia* (Paris: 1585).

Paris, Jean, *Rabelais au futur* (Paris: Seuil, 1970).

Perry, T. A., "Pernette du Guillet's Poetry of Love and Desire," *Bibliothèque d'Humanisme et Renaissance* 35 (1973), pp. 259–73.

"Dialogue and Doctrine in Leone Ebreo's *Dialoghi d'amore,*" *PMLA,* 89 (1974).

Petrarch, Francesco, *Canzoniere,* ed. Piero Cudini (Milan: Garzanti, 1974).

Bibliography of works cited

Pike, Robert, "The *Blasons* in French Literature of the 16th Century," *Romanic Review,* 27 (1936), pp. 223–46.

Plattard, Jean, *François Rabelais* (Paris: Boivin, 1932).

Poètes du xvie *siècle,* ed. A. M. Schmidt (Paris: Bibliothèque de la Pléïade, 1964).

Poteau, Paul, *Montaigne et la vie pédagogique de son temps* (Paris: Droz, 1935).

Quignard, Pascal, *La Parole de la Délie* (Paris: Mercure de France, 1974).

Quilligan, Maureen, *The Language of Allegory: Defining the Genre* (Ithaca: Cornell University Press, 1981).

Rabelais, François, *Œuvres complètes,* ed. Pierre Jourda (Paris: Garnier, 1962).

Regosin, Richard, *The Matter of My Book: Montaigne's "Essais" as the Book of the Self* (Berkeley: University of California Press, 1977).

"Source and Resources: the 'Pretexts' of Originality in Montaigne's *Essais," Substance,* 21 (1978), pp. 103–15.

"Figures of the Self: Montaigne's Rhetoric of Portraiture," *L'Esprit créateur,* 20 (1980), pp. 66–80.

Reichler, Claude, *Le Corps et ses fictions* (Paris: Minuit, 1983).

Rider, Frederick, *The Dialectic of Selfhood in Montaigne* (Stanford: Stanford University Press, 1973).

Riffaterre, Michael, *The Semiotics of Poetry* (Bloomington: Indiana University Press, 1978).

"The Intertextual Unconscious," *Critical Inquiry,* 13 (1987), pp. 371–85.

Rigolot, François, *Les Langages de Rabelais* (Geneva: Droz, 1972).

"Rhétorique de la métamorphose chez Ronsard," in *Textes et Intertextes. Etudes sur le* xvie *siècle pour Alfred Glauser* (Paris: Nizet, 1979).

Le Texte de la Renaissance (Geneva: Droz, 1982).

"Montaigne's Purloined Letters," *Yale French Studies,* 64 (1983), pp. 143–66.

"Mutation de l'Histoire: 'l'accointance des Muses'," in *Les Métamorphoses de Montaigne* (Paris: Presses Universitaries de France, 1988), pp. 15–34.

Ronsard, Pierre de, *Les Amours,* ed. Henri and Catherine Weber (Paris: Garnier, 1983).

Rosoloto, Guy, *Essais sur le symbolique* (Paris: Collections Tel, 1964).

Sainéan, L., *La Langue de Rabelais* (Paris: Boccard, 1922), 2 vols.

Saulnier, V. L., "Etudes sur Pernette du Guillet et ses *Rymes," Bibliothèque d'Humanisme et Renaissance,* 4 (1944), pp. 7–119.

Maurice Scève (Paris: Klincksieck, 1948), 2 vols.

Bibliography of works cited

"Aspects de Maurice Scève: la voix et le silence dans *Délie*," in *L'Humanisme lyonnais au xvie siècle* (Grenoble: Presses Universitaires de Grenoble, 1974).

Rabelais dans son enquête (Paris: Société d'Editions d'enseignement supérieur, 1982).

Saunders, Alison, *The Sixteenth-Century Blason Poétique* (Bern: Peter Lang, 1981).

Scève, Maurice, *Délie*, ed. Ian D. McFarlane (Cambridge: Cambridge University Press, 1966).

Schmidt, Albert, *La Poésie scientifique en France au xvie siècle* (Lausanne: Editions Recontre, 1970 [first edition 1938]).

Schor, Naomi, "Dreaming Dissymmetry: Barthes, Foncault and Sexual Difference" in Alice Jardine and Paul Smith (eds.), *Men and Feminism* (New York: Methuen, 1987), pp. 98–110.

Screech, Michael, *The Rabelaisian Marriage. Aspects of Rabelais's Religion, Ethics & Comic Philosophy* (London: Edward Arnold, 1958).

L'Evangélisme de Rabelais (Geneva: Droz, 1959).

Rabelais (Ithaca: Cornell University Press, 1979).

Montaigne and Melancholy. The Wisdom of the Essays (Selingsgrove: Susquehanna University Press, 1984).

Showalter, Elaine (ed.), *Speaking of Gender* (New York: Routledge, 1989).

Siegel, Rudolph, *Galen's System of Physiology and Medicine* (Basel: Karger, 1973).

Speroni, Speron, *I dialoghi* (Vinegia, 1542).

Spivak, Gayatri, "French Feminisms in an International Frame," *Yale French Studies,* 62 (1981), pp. 154–84.

Starobinski, Jean, *Histoire du traitement de la mélancolie des origines à 1900* (Basel: J. R. Geigy, 1960).

"Dire l'amour: Remarques sur l'érotique de Montaigne," "Dire": *Nouvelle Revue de Psychanalyse,* 23 (1981), pp. 299–323.

Montaigne en mouvement (Paris: Gallimard, 1982).

Staub, Hans, *Le Curieux Désir. Scève et Peletier du Mans, poètes de la connaissance* (Geneva: Droz, 1967).

Suleiman, Susan Rubin, ed., *The Female Body in Western Culture: Contemporary Perspectives* (Cambridge, Mass.: Harvard University Press, 1986).

Sussman, George D., *Selling Mother's Milk* (Urbana: University of Illinois Press, 1982).

Tetel, Marcel, "Une réevaluation de la dixième nouvelle de *l'Heptameron,*" *Neuphilologische Mitteilungen,* 72 (1971), pp. 565–9.

Marguerite de Navarre's Heptameron: Themes, Language, Structure (Durham: Duke University Press, 1973).

Bibliography of works cited

"Carnival and Beyond," *L'Esprit créateur,* 21 (1981), pp. 88–104.

"Montaigne et le Tasse: Imagination poétique et espace imaginaire," *Cahiers de l'Association Internationale des Etudes Françaises,* 33 (1981), pp. 81–98.

Lectures Scèviennes (Paris: Slatkine, 1983).

"Le Luth et la lyre de l'école lyonnaise," in Antonio Possenti and Giulia Mastrangelo (eds.), *Il Rinascimento a Lione* (Rome: Edizioni dell'atteneo, 1988), pp. 951–62.

Thibaudet, Albert, *Montaigne,* ed. Floyd Gray (Paris: Gallimard, 1963).

Tomarken, Annette and Edward, "The Rise and Fall of the Sixteenth-Century *Blason," Symposium,* 29 (1975), pp. 139–63.

Tournon, André, *Montaigne. La Glose et l'Essai* (Lyon: Presses Universitaires de Lyon, 1983).

Trinquet, Roger, "En Marge des *Essais*: la vraie figure de Mme d'Estissac," *Bibliothèque d'Humanisme et Renaissance* (1956), pp. 23–36.

La Jeunesse de Montaigne (Paris: Nizet, 1972).

Vickers, Nancy J., "The Poetic and Philosophical Contexts to Descriptions of the Female Body in the Renaissance," (Yale University Dissertation, 1976).

"Diana Described: Scattered Woman and Scattered Rhyme," *Critical Inquiry,* 8 (1981), pp. 265–79.

"The Heraldry in Lucrece's Face," *Poetics Today,* 6 (1985), pp. 171–84.

Weber, Henri, *La Création poétique au XVIe siècle en France* (Paris: Nizet, 1955).

Weller, Barry, "The Rhetoric of Friendship in Montaigne's *Essais," New Literary History,* 9 (1978), pp. 503–23.

Wilden, Anthony, "Par divers moyens on arrive à pareille fin: A Reading of Montaigne," *MLN,* 83 (1968), pp. 577–97.

Wilson, D. B., *Descriptive Poetry in France from blason to baroque* (Manchester: Manchester University Press, 1967).

Win, Colette H., "La loi du non-parler dans l'*Heptaméron* de Marguerite de Navarre," *Romance Quarterly,* 33 (1986), pp. 157–68.

"Le chant de la nouvelle née," *Poétique,* 78 (1989), pp. 207–17.

Winnicott, D. W., *Playing and Reality* (New York: Basic Books, 1971).

INDEX OF NAMES

SUBJECT INDEX

Cambridge Studies in French

General editor: MALCOM BOWIE

Also in the series